ROAR LIKE A WOMAN

ROAR LIKE A WOMAN

How Feminists
Think Women Suck
and Men Rock

NATALIE RITCHIE

SYDNEY, AUSTRALIA

Published by Natalie Ritchie (Sydney, Australia)
roarlikeawoman.com

Cover and Design: Sandy Cull, gogoGingko
Typeset by J&M Typesetting
10 9 8 7 6 5 4 3 2 1
National Library of Australia Cataloguing-in-Publication data is available

ISBN: 978-0-6480038-0-9 (paperback)

ISBN: 978-0-6480038-1-6 (e-book)

To my grandmothers,
Elsie Kruger
and
Joyce Lee

CONTENTS

The women and men I quote or describe in these pages are real, but their names, and in some cases their occupation or the sex of their children, have been changed to preserve their privacy. I have not been following my fellow parents around with a notebook and voice recorder all my years as a mother, so I may not have quoted them word-perfectly. However, their words as related are true to the spirit of what they said.

This book makes occasional reference to God. Take those references literally, only to the extent that you want to. Swap in 'the Universe' or whatever higher power you care to recognize, as you like.

N.R.

"And What Do You Do?"

"And what do you do?"

My inquisitor was a feminist marketing director for an eight-figure non-profit outfit working to improve the lives of Third World children. She and I were at an evening cocktail gathering of company directors and senior managers from the businesses which sponsored her charity, partners from the law firms which provided bona fide services to her organization, high-profile media, and politicians. Waiters moved through the crowd as we overlooked the city lights far below us from our uptown premises on the thirty-first floor. 'Achievement' and 'power' hung in the air.

"I am a mother," I replied.

Her eyes widened. She frowned. Then she shook her head with swift little side-to-sides. She looked at me in disbelief, then alarm. Had she just heard me offer up motherhood as a real occupation, without any evidence of a man-identical career as a backstop to shore up my acceptability? On seeing I was serious, she turned to jelly, and nearly wobbled off her feet.

"A *mother*?" I could see her thinking. "Is she for real? Mothers give birth to and shape the lives of children; what a waste of time! A mother is a woman! Women are not legitimate human beings.

Everyone knows that! Everyone knows that, to be legitimate, a woman must secure a paid job in the workplace alongside men. Only men, and women who do what men do, live in the truth. What kind of freak could be so out of touch as to not know what an *embarrassment* she is to herself?"

She leaned toward me. Her cold smile pretended to be amused, as if I had misunderstood her question, and couldn't possibly have meant to reply as I did. Speaking with condescension and disapproval, as if I were little more than a child myself, she said:

"Yes, but what do you *do?*"

Did this exchange take place? No. I made it up. But it might have happened, mightn't it? It reads like a real event because it takes place in many gatherings, in many sectors, in many cities and countries in the developed world. Chances are, if you have ever been a stay-at-home mother any time in the last 40 years, that some variant of this scene has happened to you. Probably more than once.

Every mother knows 'what I do' as a mother, because they do it too. Yet the denial of motherhood's workload and value in this scene above is embedded in our culture. Knowledge of what mothers do is hidden to all except other mothers. In those first 48 hours or so after her first child's birth, a mother enters a new and vastly changed reality that will last for the next 20 years. It will be a world of suffering and unremitting effort and sacrifice and hyper-responsibility. There'll be lots of good things, too, like joy, hilarity and horizonless love.

Feminism, and society at large, will almost entirely ignore her new circumstances. As if that weren't bad enough, her status will switch from valid (career-woman) to non-valid (stay-at-home mother). Almost from that very moment, feminism will hound her to go back to work.

If and when she tries to do that, she will re-enter a working world utterly unmade for mothers. Workplace timetables are designed for the childless, and will not budge to suit her. The tax system will treat her as a man, though her financial life-path is dramatically different to his. She cannot leave the office three hours early to take her six-year-old to the dentist, because the workplace says that paid work is 'serious' and that safeguarding her children's teeth is not. She cannot have her children come by the office after school, because an invisible sign outside the workplace door says "Only Women Without Kids and Mothers Who Act Like Women Without Kids May Work Here; No Mothers Who Actually Act Like Mothers by Having Kids in Their Presence Allowed." Her employer may free up floor-space for shower cubicles so workers can cycle to work, but will refuse her request for a play-lounge where toddlers and teens can hang out after school in their mother's company while she works. Not that she would dare make that request.

This is not how a feminist world was supposed to look.

You would think that, with the advent of the feminist era, motherhood would take pride of place as the world's most respected job. You would assume that workplace spaces and timetables would transmogrify into mother-friendly shapes. You would think that women's massive contribution as home-makers would step forward out of the shadows of living room recesses into the light of public acclaim. You could expect that our institutions, our workplaces, our financial products, our civic architecture, our social customs, our weekly schedules would transform into a marvelous new woman-esque pattern that wrapped itself around her domestic reality as housewife and mother (and parceled out that immense domestic reality more equally to men). You might expect to celebrate the onset of an age in which women's feminine strengths—not just our intellect which is equal to a man's, but our connectedness, our undying engagement with emotional truth, our limitless capacity for hard work 24/7 x 365, our embodiment of peace and love—could glory in the same recognition our society awards to the qualities of men, who taken as a sex possess none of these strengths, at least not in the same quality and quantity.

But it was not to be. Instead of bringing women's supreme contribution as mothers and housewives out into the public gaze, feminism ridiculed and suppressed it. Instead of advocating for feminized working hours to accommodate home-makers and mothers, feminists resoundingly reinforced the existing masculine schedule. Instead of calling for a feminized social infrastructure, be it a woman-only taxi service, breastfeeding rooms at the mall, or customs like a 'go to the head of the queue' policy for mothers grappling with toddlers at the airport check-in desk, feminism focused almost solely on bulldozing women into careers alongside men. That gigantic issue, child care, was never a serious item on their agenda.

In fact, feminism morphed into the very opposite of what it set out to be. Instead of rejecting the oppression of women, feminists rejected women themselves. They laid waste to womanhood's powers, and handed women nothing but men's powers in their place. Feminism became masculinism.

BORN IN 1966, I HAVE fully—all too fully—lived the feminist life. Until my children were born in 2003 and 2004, I worked full-time as a media relations consultant in the tourism industry, and jetted around the world as a freelance travel writer, always for free, much of the time in first class. Measured by the feminist yardstick, it was a glamorous and 'successful' life. Behind the 'empowered' facade, however, I was unhappy. I was over-worked. Like just about every woman, I already had a job as a home-maker, to which feminism turned a blind eye. I was charged with cooking meals for two nightly. Paid work displaced the time I needed to plan, shop for, and cook dinner. I was cooking too late in the evening, when I was over-hungry and past a comfortable eating time, and when I needed to attend to personal affairs like migrating data from my old laptop to the new one, or researching a new cell phone contract, or hand-washing the sweaters to put them away for summer. That pushed those tasks on to Saturdays, when I needed to do the errands and grocery shopping and laundry for two, which typically required several days in any case. That squashed more of the errands and grocery shopping and laundry on to Sundays, when I badly needed a rest-day. That pushed the rest-day into midweek, when I went without a rest-day because I was working five days. I lived in a state of permanent frustration at the great feminist denial that housework is just that—work.

At work, my frustration continued. In the office, feminism required me to make like a man. I was supposed to act as if I were as free of domestic constraints as a man is, as if it were as easy for me to leap behind a desk at 9 a.m. and stay there all day as it was for him. Work that women typically perform like cooking, shopping, cleaning, laundry, errands and personal administration was deemed to exist in another dimension that no one in the workplace needed to acknowledge.

Something I found more subtly disempowering was that I was expected to be as motivated and energized by my work as a man is, despite the fact that, as a woman, I already had a motivation to attend to my sizeable unpaid workload in the house. Feminism pretended I had no desire to see to my home-running and personal affairs at all, beyond whatever desire a man might have to do those things. His priorities and motivations were considered to be the only ones a woman could have and feel.

Yet not only did I have a motivation to run my home, I also had a woman's outward-reaching impulses to care for family and friends and community. Those caring impulses translate into work. Not paid work, and not work that is always strictly necessary, but work that is nonetheless enriching, both to me and to the people on the receiving end of that care. In these supposedly pro-woman days, however, that work counts for zilch. Only the kind of work men do, the paid kind, bestows legitimacy on women in feminists' eyes.

What Is a 'Feminist'?

What does this book mean by a 'feminist' and 'feminism'?

It does not set out to criticize the classically liberal political stance of Betty Friedan, author of *The Feminine Mystique* in 1963, who set us women on our way to shaking off our circumscribed place in the world, or Germaine Greer, whose *The Female Eunuch* in 1970 flung open the doors to a world of action and intellect for women.

In this book, the word 'feminist' means that stereotypical career-woman with a lurking air of disapproval of anything that smacks of femininity. She wears a severe expression, and is super-conscious of appearing 'business-like'. She describes women as being 'in charge' of their lives and 'strong', and her definition of 'strong' is a woman who thinks, walks and talks indistinguishably from the way a man thinks, walks and talks. She uses the word 'advance' to describe every occasion on which a woman comes closer to being like a man. She wears a suit like he does, and keeps her mothering and domestic workload out of public view, like he does. She makes a show of finding men offensive, while flattering them with imitation at every turn.

I know what you're going to say. "That femo-Nazi is, like, from the *'80s!*" you might cry. "That was a previous geological age!" You will probably protest that my feminist caricature is hardly a complex picture of a feminist. You may say, "But I'm a feminist, and I'm no career-or-die tragic! Feminism moved on from that long ago. Feminism is way more subtle and sophisticated than that these days!"

I don't believe that the portrait of a feminist above is nearly as out-of-date as it sounds. It is indeed an image from the neo-conservative 1980s, but that is when feminism shriveled from an outward-looking, celebratory movement to a juggernaut of self-actualization-as-women-by-emulation-of-men. It's been the same ever since. The shoulder-pads may be gone in body, but in spirit, they're still perched on the shoulders of feminists today. The mindset of that stereotypical career-woman is alive and well, and her generation is at the most senior level in the femocracy, politics, academia, law and corporations. Others of her ilk are already retired or have passed away, but their refusal to forge a woman-shaped world has left an impossible legacy for today's women.

Chances are you identify as a 'feminist'. Many of us do. It is not my intention to talk down all us women who call ourselves feminists, and who love our jobs, or who simply want to work for extra income, or who have to work, and who also run homes, and who very likely have kids, or have had kids, or are planning to have them. That's a lot of women.

This book's target is those feminists who sneer at housewifery and motherhood, who disavow their female sensibilities and priorities, who trumpet that their sensibilities and priorities are identical to those of men, who hold career dear over every other kind of human endeavor, and who insist that a career means exactly the same thing to a woman as it does to a man. And that's a lot of women, too. In fact, there is at least a little of that feminist woman in just about all of us. I did my fair share of sneering and jeering at motherhood and home-making, and made more than my fair share of burnt offerings to the Career-god, in my twenties and thirties, like most other women inculcated into the feminist cause.

When it uses the word 'feminist', this book means the feminist leadership, not those of us who follow. It aims to hold to account those women who exhort women to seek their womanhood through living out men's experience. In taking a stand against feminism, this book is not out to insult, demean or criticize the much greater numbers of women who get pulled along in feminism's wake. There is really no alternative to the feminist life for most women today, in any case, so we are just about all 'feminists' in practice, even though a lot of us reject the label, and many of us are crushed, or at least frustrated, by feminism's failure to handle women's reality.

Nor do these pages deal with the many strands and sects of academic feminism. They're theory. It is mainstream feminism that's up for discussion here, because that is the kind that leaves an imprint on real women's flesh.

Let's not engage in a turf war about the definition of the word 'feminist'. It is anti-woman attitudes and actions that are under the spotlight in this book, irrespective of the word we use to describe those responsible for them. Because the women who engage in those anti-woman attitudes and actions call themselves 'feminists', that's what this book calls them, too.

Men Are Not the Benchmark

The feminist world-view says motherhood and housework and caring for the wider community (work largely performed by women) does not count, paid work (traditionally men's work) does, that 'successful' women must have a job and, more ambiguously, that 'successful' women are those who do the job like a man. Almost every woman today probably knows that this is starkly at odds with reality, especially if she is a mother, but even most mothers are seduced by that over-riding feminist ideology to some degree. Most of us are trying to piece career into our lives after a fashion of our choosing (without much success, in the case of the majority of my friends and fellow moms). What this grappling for 'work-life balance' fails to recognize, however, is that in our decision to work at all, most of us are still in thrall to the same crude kernel of an idea that drives the most fanatical feminist: the belief that without a job like a man, we are failures as women.

To plant a seed of unworthiness in a woman who did not work, and then inform her that she could reinstate her worth if she took a paid job, and to present this re-legitimization as a terrific gift of empowerment and opportunity, was an act of great hostility to women on the part of feminism. Our need to re-secure our self-worth through a career is a blight on many women's lives, and an insult to every woman.

It's an insult even if she loves working. Most working women I know today are crippled by over-work, either because no woman-friendly jobs present themselves, or because they buy the feminist spiel that says women who fit a man-shaped world are superior to women who can't or won't.

Other women I know are at-home mothers who feel like failures thanks to feminist derision, or who remain staunchly proud mothers, but must get by without the pompom-shaking that feminism lavishes on career-women. Feminism's savage sneering at stay-at-homes has abated somewhat since the '80s and '90s, but the full-time mother is still accorded scant tolerance.

Of course, a woman who has never had a job, and never plans to, is not just low-status in feminism's hierarchy. She is virtually *sub-human*.

After more than 50 years of feminism if we start counting from 1963, both work and motherhood should be realms of opportunity, power and legitimacy for mothers. It is entirely thanks to feminism that they are not.

Female Presidents? Equal pay? Broken glass ceilings? These things all sound so good, don't they? And they *are* good, in themselves. If you set out to make women more like men, you can't fail but do a lot of good, because men had it so good. No one could argue that feminism hasn't done good things for women. The feminism of the 1960s and '70s is arguably the greatest single social achievement in human history, outside of democracy itself.

Bewitched by our equal pay packets and glass shards, however, what we don't see is that from the 1980s onwards, these good things have been almost all results of a concerted process of masculinization, not feminization. Those feminists who applaud as you toil alongside men in the workplace are those same women who scorn your toil as a mother outside it. Those feminists who won you your glitzy LinkedIn profile are those same women who turned your parallel job description of 'housewife' (for we are almost all housewives) into an insult. Those feminists who crow over how they fought for your right to earn an income are those same women who permit your husband to legally abandon you as a mother of a newborn, leaving you with no income at all. Those feminists who campaigned for equal pay also campaigned for equal hours, demanding you work a man's full-time day despite your pre-existing job as a mother and/or home-maker.

Obviously, none of this is to say that women shouldn't have smashed-up glass ceilings. It is to say that women should be able to work below and above the ceiling on women's terms. It is also to say that many women do not care for the power they can wield from the corner office, or not only about that, and some women do not care about a career at all. Feminists care about the corner office because men care about the corner office. If men jumped off cliffs, feminists would jump too.

I WROTE THIS BOOK AT the kitchen table. It is a homespun book by an ordinary mother. To write a scholarly book would require a full-time career as an historian. This is not that book. I have a post-grad degree in history, but not in the history of feminism, and I don't need a degree in feminism to write about being a woman. We none of us need a college degree in womanhood. My only qualifications for writing this book are that I am a woman, and a woman who grew up in the 1970s, a time when women stood tall, with or without a career.

You won't find many statistics in these pages. Feminism too often deploys them in a conscious attempt to rinse the woman right out of the picture by reducing her to a sexless number, denying her uniquely womanly circumstances, and thereby treating her like a man. One set of statistics I do employ, however, are those that feminism never hawks around—my own calculations of how much women work as mothers and home-makers.

It is not 'equality' we are aiming for when we seek to make women over in men's image; it is masculinization. It is past time for women everywhere in the Western world to find the strength to be true women, not *ersatz* men. We must forge a world that is shaped around women's needs equally as much as it is currently shaped around the needs (and indulgences) of men. In a world that empowers women, a woman gets her due, equally as much as a man gets his due. That is the kind of equality women need.

1

Heroes and Zeroes

*How Feminism Writes Men Up
and Writes Women Down*

A COUNSELOR ONCE TOLD ME that "measurement is the male paradigm." That is a handy way to look at a man's paid work. His work is easy to measure. He clocks in at a set time. He works at a place clearly designated as a place for work, be it an office, a truck or a building site. He works continuously until a set time at the end of the day, and takes a clear-cut hour or half-hour for lunch. While the demarcations of the work day are fuzzier than they used to be, as today's workers show up early, sandwich through at their desk, and go home late, or work remotely, what they do is nonetheless identifiable as 'work'. Men's work is clearly separated from the rest of their lives by time slots, location, and its qualitative nature as activity that they wouldn't do were they not getting paid.

Women's work in the home is much less measurable. It is not always clearly identifiable as work, and it is not separated from the rest of women's lives. In the pages below, we're going to take that masculine tool of measurement, and put a dispassionate figure on the immense output of women outside the workplace.

Women are loathe to put a value on their work in the home. There has probably never been a time when their work as mothers and home-makers was not grossly minimized, trivialized, ignored, ridiculed or outright denied. Even though many of us are mothers ourselves, and virtually all women are home-makers, we women are all conditioned to believe that the paid work traditionally done by men carries more credit points than the unpaid work traditionally done by us.

In the bad ol' days before feminism, men claimed the right to interpret women's experience. She did 'not work', men said. Her days were spent in leisure. She was 'kept' by her husband. The undemanding tenor of her days was a privileged state 'provided' to her by him. She floated about the house in a haze of insignificant occupations too trivial for him to need to know about.

Protected in this weightless state, men rationalized, she had no reason not to be ever-ready to wait on him, be it cooking his breakfast at 5:20 a.m. after she'd paced the floor with a newborn all night, picking out his tie, or rummaging up a midnight snack when he brought work-mates home after a night on the town while she stayed in with the rampaging toddler and the screaming baby.

Apart from the mild feat of housekeeping and being present while the children brought themselves up, her contribution in his eyes was zero. Motherhood carried no credit towards 'work'. Motherhood in his eyes was nothing but a sweet, workless joy. He considered his contribution to the 'work' done in the household to be 100 percent.

Paid work in the economy used to be one of the major justifications for a man's superior status to his wife. There are two obvious reasons for that. Firstly, it brought in income. Women's unpaid work could not compete on that score. Secondly, paid work is unquestionably work. No one can deny that when a man (or woman) is at paid work, they are working.

The nature of women's work, more problematically, did not shout loud and clear that it was as much *work* as the work done in a paid job. Women's work doesn't have clear start and stop times. It's in the background. It takes place in the private world of home that a man equates with being 'off duty'. This very vagueness as to just what constitutes a woman's day was a major obstacle to women's work getting the recognition it deserves.

But then along came feminism, and dissing women's contribution in the home got a whole lot easier. In one of the most amazing displays of hostility to women in history, feminists turned on their own kind. Far from putting paid to men's contemptible claim that it is men who do most of the work in society, feminists set about agreeing with them. They made no effort to spell out the vast, byzantine, thudding reality of women's workload. Instead, to women's already under-appreciated work in the home, they dished out a broth of denial and excoriating disdain.

Mothers, said feminists, do nothing. They just kaffee-klatsch and paint their nails all day. To 'stay at home' became a derogatory synonym for 'not working'. No longer was it accepted that women had stuff to get done around the house, however inferior their housework might be to men's paid work, and that they needed to at least be present with the children, even if it didn't take mothers any actual effort to raise them. Women's urgent need for a re-ordered society that relieved them of the full brunt of housework and child care was paid scant heed by feminism. In fact, feminists ground all recognition for women's unpaid work under their pump-clad heels. The work a woman did as a mother and housewife was unworthy, menial, shameful, said feminists. The much more nebulous but critical work she did as a carer for her extended family, for neighbors and community members, for her nation's citizens; as society's heart and soul and force for good; as the marvelous being who lives and laughs and spreads the light, was barred from mention. (Chapter 6 looks more deeply into this fundamental contribution by women as society's 'soul'.)

As the same time as it denigrated women's roles, feminism lionized men's role in the paid workforce. His career was the source of his power and glory and status, so if she takes on a job like a man, feminists reasoned, a woman can share in his power and glory and status.

From there, feminists made a long leap to deciding that a career was not only the best source of power, glory and status for every woman, but the only source. Men were an inherently self-actualized sex who needed little changing, save for some window-dressing to pretty up their sexist language and to tone down their aggression. Theirs was the only legitimate gender.

No longer did a man need to pull the wool over his wife's eyes, tricking her into believing that his job was more important than hers. Feminists did it for him, passionately concurring with him that his arena of business and state was far more important than a woman's arena of community, family, home and the collective human soul. Fueled by their awe of men, feminists embarked on a wholesale strategy of sending women out into the workforce on the very same terms as a man with a 24/7 wife at home to do all his domestic work for him. She had to work the same 40 hours per week, 48 to 50 weeks per year, same personal and organizational working styles, and same conditions: no kids in the workplace, stay at your desk all day, no domestic or personal tasks to be done at work, no school vacations free. And she had to do the world's busiest job, motherhood, at the very same time, while being prevented from doing it. To be *like* a man was the only way to be *as good as* him.

And that was feminism's big mistake. In its drive to give women the same power and glory and status as men, feminism transferred its support from women-who-do-whatever-women-do to women-who-make-like-men. It was a purblind strategy that has ultimately served to elevate the masculine—men's sensibilities and priorities, men's working styles and workplace conditions and timetable, men's paid activity, men's relationship with their careers—into a position of unassailable superiority. And with that tricky jumping of the tracks, feminism ceased to be woman's champion, and became man's champion instead. In its bid to bust the patriarchy, it became the patriarchy.

Key to feminism's plan to glorify women-who-make-like-men was the tactic of ridiculing women-who-make-like-women. Instead of staking out a valid status for women alongside (and in some ways, above) men, feminism gutted womanhood of any worth whatsoever, except to the extent that women could replicate men's behaviors. Anything a woman does, feels or is that is not something a man also does, feels or is—running homes, mothering, caring for others, making time for beauty in her life, the sheer power of delighting in loving and being as only a woman can do—was walled out of society's recognition and accommodation. To be different to a man— that is, to be a woman—was to be a failure.

"A woman is just a man without a job," was feminists' loud and clear message. "Once she has a job too, the missing piece of her worth will fall into place. Then she'll be as good as him!"

To feminists, a man was a hero. It was *women* who were the zero.

Getting the Measure of Motherhood

When a woman is asked "And what do you do?", she is always expected to answer with a paid occupation. Only her career-based work—that is to say, her man-identical work—is considered to carry any weight. Her 'woman's work' outside the workplace is not con- sidered to count.

But it does count. And in table 1 on p. 18, we're going to count it.

In this table, I tabulate the work of a non-working woman with a baby and a toddler, against the work a father is likely to do in our society. The woman in this table is me (although my children are older now). The figures in the mother's columns are accurate, because I know exactly how much work I do as a mother. The only modification I have made is to use my first baby, Robbie (born 2003), as the model for the second baby, rather than my actual second baby, Lachlan (it's a Scottish name, pronounced 'Lochlen', born 2004). That is because Lachie was an unusually easy baby, so to use him as the model would make motherhood look easier than it really is for the average mother. Admittedly, Robbie was an unusually difficult baby who cried every waking minute. Nevertheless, I am going to use the difficult baby as the model, rather than the easy one, to show just how much work mothering can entail.

The man in table 1 is imaginary. He is an amalgam, based on the current crop of dads (a few of whom do more than the man in this table), my observations of my friends' husbands (some of whom do considerably less than the man in this table), my former husband, my observations of men at large, and my own father. My father was a tireless Rotarian who devoted much of his time outside work to helping others but, like most men of his generation, did pretty much zip in the home.

What qualifies me to measure mothers' work? Am I a statistician? No. An economist? No. A mathematician? No. I am a mother. No one but a mother is in a position to know a mother's workload. Anyone who says I did not work the kind of hours presented in this table when my children were young can come work them for me.

What She Does vs. What He Does

So overleaf in table 1 is 'what I do' as a mother and housewife. As you can see in the final section of this table, I perform the equivalent of almost seven 40-hour weeks every week to a father's fewer than two. I work a total of 275 hours per week to his 72 hours—almost four times as hard as him. It was not uncommon in the pre-feminist era, and it is not unheard of for men today, to claim that their paid work comprises 100 percent of the work in a household, but that's not what table 1 shows. What table 1 shows is that a woman with two young children does 79 percent of all the combined paid and unpaid work in a household. He pulls 21 percent—and he only does that much if he puts in two 11-and-a-half-hour days of unpaid work on weekends and an hour or two each weekday. In other words, the majority of the work performed by a family with young children is not done within the economy. It is done in the home.

This table derives from my personal experience as a mother of my two particular sons. It won't match your experience exactly. No

TABLE 1

A Mother:Father Ratio of Weekly Working Hours

(for an at-home mother and a full-time working father
caring for one six-week-old baby and one 18-month-old toddler)

TASKS	MOTHER Daily Hours (Mon-Fri)	MOTHER Daily Hours (Weekends)	FATHER Daily Hours (Mon-Fri)	FATHER Daily Hours (Weekends)
Baby *Hold crying baby every minute to stop the crying. Care for baby. Breastfeed around the clock.*	13 hrs, 25 mins	12 hrs, 25 mins	0 (zero)	1 hr
Toddler *Entertain, supervise, feed and care for toddler.*	10 hrs, 15 mins	5 hrs, 45 mins	1 hr, 30 mins	6 hrs
The 'Extra Pair of Hands' *Assist mother on and off throughout the day.*	6 hrs, 15 mins	3 hrs, 30 mins	15 mins	3 hrs
Housekeeping *Meal preparation, cleaning, shopping, laundry, errands and general household chores, administration and maintenance.*	14 hrs, 20 mins	5 hrs	0 (zero)	1 hr, 30 mins
Paid work	0 (zero)	0 (zero)	8 hrs	0 (zero)
SUB-TOTAL: Daily Hours	44 hrs, 15 mins	26 hrs, 40 mins	9 hrs, 45 mins	11 hrs, 30 mins
TOTAL: *Weekly Hours (rounded to nearest hour)*	**Mother (Weekdays + Weekends) 275 hrs**		**Father (Weekdays + Weekends) 72 hrs**	
RATIO Mother:Father	3.8 : 1			
As a fraction **As a percentage**	4/5ths (just under) 79%		1/5th (just over) 21%	
No. of 40-Hour-Week Equivalents	6.8		1.8	
TOTAL Household Weekly Hours	**Unpaid Hours Only: 307 hrs** **Paid and Unpaid Hours: 347 hrs**			

one mother, father, child is the same. It is not my intention to put one woman's experience forward as the definitive experience. You may not do as much (or as little!) as 79 percent. As you can see from the table, one of the greatest components of my load was the need to hold a baby all day, and entertain a toddler all day. Your baby may have been an 'easy' baby (not that any baby is easy, but some are a lot easier than others) who happy-babbled in his crib while you browned the mince for dinner. Your toddler may play alone, leaving you to get on with your day. You may have only one child, not two. All those things will reduce your side of the ratio.

And, as explored in more detail below, your husband may do more than the man in this table. He may get up at 3 a.m. to the fretting 18-month-old while you sleep on; and he may do the late-night emergency room shift when a pen-knife closes on your eight-year-old's finger. That will ratchet up his side of the ratio.

Some kids have special needs like a dairy-free diet or ADHD or a disability that demands many extra hours of attention from one or both parents. That can send the total hours worked by both parents soaring. Some families have three, four or more kids, which pumps up the workload dramatically. If the father in this table were to do nothing in the home (as too many men still do today), that would leave the whole 307 unpaid hours with her. Of course, if you are a single parent, the whole 100 percent of paid and unpaid load may fall on your shoulders.

Therefore, when this table puts my own personal experience forward, it's not meant to be a universal calculation of how much more all women do than all men. I expect that most women will agree with the spirit of the calculations I have made, however, even though their own circumstances may differ substantially from the letter of them. Don't get hung up on the math. The aim is to show that, anyway we slice it, motherhood is far, far more than the equivalent of one 40-hour paid job.

What Fathers Do

You might protest that a man today does a good deal more than the 21 percent of the combined paid and unpaid household work I arrive at in table 1. I have deliberately kept the man's contribution in the table sparser than it might be in some homes, in order to reflect the historical lack of involvement in domestic duties by most men. My father's generation in the 1960s and 1970s was expected to take the trash out, manage the household finances (which were usually simple), effect repairs to the house, and maybe mow the lawn. Maybe men brushed kids' teeth at night, or took the kids to the park on occasion, or bathed the four-year-old, but this kind of help was not outright demanded of them, and plenty of dads in my own father's day did not do these things.

Obviously, many men today contribute more than the imaginary man in this table. For starters, many men in the workforce work considerably more than the standard eight hours. A 10-hour working day, or even longer, is commonplace now. Today's dads are typically much more involved than in times past. If a man has a home-office, he may take Tuesday afternoons off to drop his daughter to ballet class, then take his toddler son to the park for the class's duration, then collect the daughter and take both kids home. Men ferry the kids about to weekend karate class and tennis fixtures. They put disinfectant on the four-year-old's stubbed toe, and help the nine-year-old with her homework graphs. They maybe clear the table. They may even cook some meals.

Nonetheless, when a man is home, he is not likely to bring a full 50 percent application to all the unpaid work in his household. Sure, most dads help out around the house more than they did in their own dad's generation. But 'helping' is not the same as pulling a full 50 percent of the primary weight of child care and running a home every minute that he is home. His contribution tends to be of a secondary nature. He functions more often as an assistant, not as a fully committed co-carer. He doesn't 'own' the responsibility the way a woman does.

Come the weekend, he will probably not prepare meals three times a day plus a mid-morning and mid-afternoon and bed-time snack for the kids, and handle the intermittent requests for a drink or a different snack or more snacks. He is unlikely to be the one sorting the laundry into coloreds, warms, colds and hand-washes, checking pockets for tissues and stray rocks, tying drawstrings and opening buttons in preparation for the load, putting the hosiery in a lingerie bag to stop it tying up the washing in knots, checking every garment for stains and applying a general-purpose stain remover and waiting five minutes for it to sink in, soaking all the whites in a bleach bucket, hand-washing the five woolen sweaters (warm water), palazzo pants (cold water) and silk tops (tepid water) that can't go in the machine, stuffing the washing machine seven times throughout Saturday, drying the loads, folding and ironing the clean stuff, noticing the chocolate ice-cream stain on the two-year-old's T-shirt that didn't come out in the wash and re-applying a harder-working stain remover to that stain and waiting 60 seconds like the manufacturer says and hand-rubbing it under running warm water and repeating the process when it doesn't quite come out the first time.

More likely his wife will do all that, and he will just slip the clean clothes on to the two-year-old. He is not thinking at 8:40 p.m. Wednesday night about what to buy as a gift for the six-year-old's classmate's birthday party, he is not texting an RSVP to the party, he is not diarizing a note that the party guests should bring socks to the party's indoor play-center venue. Come party day, he will not wrap the gift that his partner bought, nor write the card. He may or may not take his son to the party and sit out the duration of the fun with the other parents. On weekends, he probably does not bust the amorphous mess all over the house, or take everything out of the refrigerator and rinse off all the shelves. He may make a 10-minute duck down the street for Turkish bread for that special once-a-month Sunday lunch, but he will probably not head to the supermarket for that routine 90-minute once-a-week grocery shop.

On weekday mornings, many men seem to feel their home responsibilities fall away altogether. He shaves and dresses and breakfasts and gets ready for the day, largely unburdened by child care and housework. He may make a broad-brush engagement with the kids with occasional orders to stop food-fighting shouted from the bathroom as he's shaving, but he will probably leave to his wife the up-close response to their pleas for tied shoelaces, and for toys they want to take to school but which the school rules forbid, and for a strand of shells to go with the mermaid skirt the four-year-old wants to wear to day care. He might engage with the kids over the breakfast table, but might not fix their breakfast. He may clear his breakfast dishes, but possibly not those of the kids. He probably does not dress them, or think about what they need to take today (library book? swimming bag? something red-white-and-blue to wear to the French class's walk to the French café three blocks from school for *pain au chocolat* this morning? plus a raincoat as he checked the weather forecast specially for the outing and it looks like rain? clarinet plus musical composition notes for their weekly lesson? a signed permission slip for next week's excursion to the wetlands education center?). He probably does not comb the house for the geography project the seven-year-old thinks she did last night but isn't sure she did and can't remember where she left it, or plait his daughter's hair. He walks calmly out the door, having stretched himself maybe some, but maybe not much, and maybe not at all.

His wife, by contrast, will be hurling herself into a whirlwind of activity around him, grappling with the load of as many as five people at once in a two-child household with a baby and toddler: one who cares for the baby, one who cares for the toddler, one who serves as an extra pair of hands to the first two carers, one who acts as housekeeper preparing breakfast and lunches and clearing up, and one who gets ready for work and travels to her paid job, if she has one. (Table 2 in chapter 2 delineates her five-person-load day in detail.) Her partner does not appear to notice. If we add his routine of dressing/feeding/preparing himself for work as a sixth person-load, then he should do three person-loads and so should she. Yet in most households, this doesn't happen.

If she were to challenge him to contribute half of the six person-loads of the morning's work, he would offer his paid work as an excuse. "I can't. I have to go to work," he would say. Society considers this an acceptable reason for him, but not her, to evade doing his share until it's time to leave for work.

In the evenings, the same principle applies. He comes home from work and feels entitled to attend to his own affairs first, to undress and shower, to check e-mails, maybe even to do some simple task in the garden or online to help him unwind. His partner has no such luxury. Her shower may be a couple of hours later while he is relaxing, or it may be done with children shrieking for her attention outside the bathroom door. She will have no e-mail time. 'Unwinding' is something a mother of preschoolers must likely put on hold for years.

Some men forego their unwinding time rather than face the pressure to pull their weight. My friend and mother-of-three, Camilla, is married to a high-powered accountant. Men have historically presented themselves as the household's hard workers while they dismiss mothering as a breeze. Yet oddly, he stayed longer at work when the kids were preschoolers.

"It just seems suspicious he stayed at work until 9 p.m. every night when the children were little, and now they are older he is home by 6:30 p.m. or 7 p.m.," she observed with subdued annoyance. As many mothers would probably agree, the 'witching hour' of dinner-time and baths and bedtime routines for little children can be a real 'horror hour', as Camilla called it. If work is so tough and mothering so cruisy, why didn't Camilla's husband come home?

It's not just 'witching hour' that men escape. Many men do not do anything like as much as the 11-and-a-half hours that table 1 allots to a father on weekends, or even the 90 minutes or so that the table allots to him on a weekday. And the table makes no allowance for vacations. A man gets two to four weeks' vacation from his paid job. A woman gets none from her unpaid job. Not a single day. On important holidays like Christmas Day, she works harder than ever. Her workload during his vacation time lightens only to the extent that he is willing to take on some of her load.

The man in table 1 is doing only 72 hours, or 21 percent, of the combined paid and unpaid work in this household. If the woman were to do no more than match his 72 hours, instead of the 275 hours that I calculate she actually does, that leaves 203 hours to split between them. The woman in table 1 is doing 100 percent of those 203 hours, when she should only be doing 50 percent of them. To argue that a man's contribution is 'equal' to hers is to fly in the face of the math.

What Mothers Do

Chapter 2 looks in depth at child care, so for now, let's just give ourselves a quick bird's-eye view of a mother's load as tabulated in table 1.

My first child, Robbie, is the model for the baby in this table. Robbie cried every single moment he was awake. If I held him, he calmed straight away, but only if I stood up. If I sat down to hold him, he cried. He did not sleep at all during the day, which meant standing up and holding him all day to head off the crying. That is why I have allotted more than 13 hours to the care of the baby in the table.

If a baby is a big challenge, many parents say that a toddler is a bigger one. For just about every mother, caring for a toddler is a wipe-out. Setting up a dolls' picnic, or making a dinosaur costume out of cardboard boxes, while the child clings to her legs and moans; hoisting the toddler up and down stairs, into the car-seat, into the stroller; watching them in public every second, and restraining them from running into the traffic while grappling with a stroller and shopping bags; cleaning up the cookie-baking or finger-painting mess; navigating the hair-tearing frustrations of toilet-training; catering to the ceaseless need to engage with the toddler every single moment of the day, is truly epic.

What the 'Extra Pair of Hands' Does

A mother who is holding or entertaining a baby or toddler all day needs an extra pair of hands. What does an extra pair of hands do? Everything.

She tends to the administration associated with a baby. She makes doctor's appointments. She draws up a list of prospective day care centers and visits them. She looks up articles on reflux or strange rashes, and holds baby while Mommy reads up on them.

She packs for outings. A diaper bag will contain not just diapers and wipes and plastic bags for the used diapers, but two changes of clothes and a hat and sunscreen and anti-itch gel for insect bites and formula and baby food and maybe a sweater and maybe also a coat and gloves and scarf for both baby and mother, and a bottle of water and a flask of tea and snacks for Mommy, and a sandwich for Mommy to eat in the car on the way home because she is voraciously hungry when breastfeeding, and there won't be time to eat lunch when she gets home for she will have to hurl herself into baby- and toddler-care then.

A lot of the time of an extra pair of hands is spent fetching things: a pacifier, a toy robot from a shelf the toddler can't reach, a last-minute run back to the house to retrieve the forgotten referral notice from the doctor to the pediatrician while Mommy straps the kids in the car in a frenzied rush to make the appointment on time.

She deals with the many 'unexpecteds' that are part and parcel of parenting. As just one example, when Robbie was only a few weeks old, I sat down with him on my newly made bed. His tummy emptied spectacularly into his diaper, and the contents cascaded out the sides, all over me and onto the freshly fitted white sheets and the mattress protector. He was dirty; I was dirty; the bed was dirty.

There was nowhere to put a dirty baby except the hard timber floor, which made the floor dirtier and left him squalling. Fetching clean-up gear myself without spreading the mess was all but impossible, creating more mess. Robbie needed a bath, which meant I needed to get all his bath things prepared while I was still dirty. I needed a shower. The sheets and protector needed stripping, the soiled bedding and all our clothes needed to be rinsed and bleached and washed and dried, and the bed needed re-fitting.

Had there been no mattress protector on the bed, the mattress would have been ruined. That would have required an outing for a new mattress in what were pre-online shopping days, a nightmare with an ever-crying baby who needed breastfeeding every two to three hours, and whose feeds took fifty minutes a time. I would have had to shift the soiled old mattress off the bed, and store it goodness knows where, and make arrangements to dispose of it; I would have had to make up the sofa-bed until the new mattress arrived, which would mean heavy work shifting the sofas and the toys spread all over the living room floor; when the new mattress came, the sofa-bed would then have to be stripped and folded away, and new bedding put on the new mattress, and the other sofas and toys put back in place.

An extra pair of hands could have engineered a lot of that. Had the floor been carpet instead of timber, I would have had to fetch soapy water and disinfectant and clean up the worst of the mess. Then I would have had to call in a steam-cleaning professional. I would have needed to be awake to see off the old mattress, and to take delivery of the new one, and to bring in the steam-cleaner. Those three visits from the cleaner and mattress delivery guys and the guy who carts the old mattress away might overlap with the baby or toddler's nap-time, and so wake the children, generating a further 36 hours of fretful behavior from the napless kids on three different occasions. If she sleeps when the children sleep, as so many mothers desperately need to do, a mother would need to be awake for any afternoon carpet-cleaning or mattress delivery appointments. For a mother who has been up to care for children at night, every night for months or even years, a sleepless afternoon is an intolerable prospect.

Not only is it work inside the house a mother must do alone. Without an extra pair of hands, a mother must run errands with a crying baby who needs feeding and a fractious toddler who needs food, milk, second-by-second supervision and engagement, and visits to the bathroom at very inconvenient moments; and then she must manage the disaster when the toddler doesn't make it to the bathroom in time. An extra pair of hands can run these errands for a mother, or stay home with the children while mother goes out. There will be late-night trips to the pharmacy for anti-histamine, or day-time trips to pick up a bigger size of bottle teats. Baby will need new clothes, or a new car-seat as he grows. It's hard to believe, but mother herself might actually need stuff, too, like new reading glasses, or flat comfy shoes for getting around with children, or a raincoat for trips in the rain with the stroller. Until she does these things, she struggles to focus on print on the toddler's anti-biotics bottle that she can't see through sleep-deprived eyes, staggers with weakness in too-high heels on outings with a baby and toddler on the back of no sleep for hundreds of nights past, and pushes a stroller and holds an umbrella at the same time. None of these things are workable.

Given that table 1 allots a whole day straight to holding a crying baby, the extra pair of hands would also relieve the mother of some of those hours to allow the mom to complete the basics—to dress, eat, shower and most importantly, sleep a good three hours or more in the afternoon to make up for her wakeful night-time nursing duties.

Fathers and those without children might say that a mother doesn't need an extra pair of hands. They might say that a mother should just put the baby down, and ignore the toddler clinging to her legs, and let both cry while she gets on with the housework. That is what I might have said before I had children. But that is to suggest that enduring a crying baby and shaking a toddler from your legs, while performing all the associated tasks of caring for those children and running a home, are humanly manageable tasks. They are not.

If you think they are, look at it this way. No one would expect a man to put up with even a smidgen of baby-crying at his work-place, let alone unrelenting roaring for eight hours a day, five days a week. No one would expect a man at work to tolerate a toddler whining and clinging to his legs and begging to be entertained for even 12 seconds, let alone the 12-plus hours a toddler is awake. A man needs to be free of encumbrances to get on with his job, we say. Yet we are contemptuous of a mother's need for the much smaller measure of freedom provided by the extra pair of hands, even though, by table 1's calculations, she is doing 44 daily hours to his eight in the workplace.

I've allotted six-and-a-half hours to the 'extra pair of hands' in table 1. Whether you feel that's an over- or under-calculation, the main aim is to identify that the work done by that pair of hands exists.

What the Home-maker Does

In addition to the work contributed by the extra pair of hands that few mothers are lucky enough to have, a mother must also run a house. If caring for a baby is work for one, and caring for a toddler is work for a second person, making the extra pair of hands in a two-child household a 'third pair of hands', then keeping house is work for a 'fourth pair of hands'.

Not only are there as many as three daily meals to prepare and clean up after, plus separate toddler-friendly meals, plus snacks, and routine weekly chores like cleaning, laundry and grocery shopping, housework is also many one-off chores, and errands, and personal administration like auto-club renewals and tax returns and live-chatting with your Cloud account provider about how your changed password hasn't translated across all devices, and occasions to plan like christenings and camping trips and having family come visit. It is a lot of 'stuff with no name' like throwing out dead flowers and rinsing out the vase, or trawling the stores for new shelves for the kids' toys and assembling them, or sorting through the kids' artwork gallery and scanning the masterpieces into a digital book to send to the grandparents.

In my own personal household with two kids, housework can take up over 80 hours every week—more than twice a man's standard 40-hour week. That's not caring for the kids directly. That's just the meals, cleaning, groceries, errands and household admin including the planning of festivities and social life (the kids', mostly, not mine; a mother scarcely has a social life). You might say, "Oh, you don't spend that many hours on the house." Well, no, and yes. I do that work simultaneously with caring for the children, or I cram the tasks into a much shorter time than they require, or I reach madly for ingenious ways to double up on tasks, or I crimp on the quality of the work as I fly through the week grabbing bites at household chores as I go, or I leave the work undone and then wear the negative consequences. The point is that there is 80+ hours of housework to do, whether it gets done by mushing a sole woman across a multi-person workload, or gets done poorly, or doesn't get done at all. Chapter 3 takes a more forensic look at housework.

Playground Is Work, and Work Is Play

A man does a 40- or 50-hour per week paid job, or 100 to 125 percent of a 40-hour week, to a mother's 275 hours, or almost 700 percent of a 40-hour week, based on table 1. Some men may work at full steam all day, while others don't pull their full 100 percent. Plenty of industrious men may work at perhaps 125 percent capacity as they face a range of complex demands that clamor for their attention at once. At their very busiest, say at times of crisis or seasonal pressures, or if they run their own business where they are all things to all people, some men may work at, say, 150 percent capacity. Of course, if a man works at heavy manual labor or in extreme conditions like severe heat or cold, his work deserves extra credit.

But manual labor or desk-job, a man is usually never required to do more than one man can handle. Most working days last only eight to 10 hours, rarely more than 12. The mother in table 1 works 44-plus hours in a 24-hour period every weekday, or more than a 40-hour week. Even with a lot of help from her husband on a weekend day, she is working almost 27 hours in a 24-hour period. Most men and women in the paid workforce do not work at above 100 per-cent capacity for more than finite stretches of time throughout the day, week, month or year, and certainly not 365 days a year, all day and much of the night, as a mother does. At any given minute on a weekday, a mother is working at around 300 to 400 percent capacity.

Moreover, a man has traditionally done his job with very little additional strain occasioned by housework and child care. Whereas every single task a mother does must be spent holding a crying baby and wrangling a toddler, at work all that is required of a man (or woman) is that he does his job. In fact, his employer says, "We don't want you to do anything else. We have especially made this workplace a distraction-free zone so you are free to get on with the job." There are rarely any kids in the workplace. Kids, expressly or implicitly, are not even *allowed* in the workplace. No one would say to a factory line worker, "Okay, you have to sort out the brown peas from the green ones before they enter the canning machine, and oh, you have to hold and feed and change this crying baby, too."

No such conditions pertain in a mother's workplace in the home. By comparison to her day, the child-free, one-job-to-one-person deal in the eight-hour day of the workplace is lotus-eating land.

A mother's work in dealing with children who incessantly yell, whine, bicker and throw tantrums is more than mere work. It is agonizing and dehumanizing. In her book, *The Crying Baby*, the anthropologist and famed childbirth writer, Sheila Kitzinger, describes the sound of an ever-crying baby as "just about the most disturbing, demanding, shattering noise we can hear." She is right. A crying baby is not just *like* torture. It *is* torture. Whatever love or amazement a mother may feel for her baby, a mother of crying children endures a kind of torment that no one in the paid workforce is ever required to endure. In fact, it is probably illegal to ask an employee to handle torture. I endured it myself about 12 hours a day for eight straight months after the birth of my first son, followed by years of entrenched whining as my baby grew into a toddler and pre-schooler, and I was still enduring it from my children far too often at the ages of nine and 10. The whining has really only eased off since they hit their 'tweens.

It is not the intention of this book to belittle the stresses and strains of any man or woman at paid work. But it is this book's intention to put it in perspective. Paid work is torture-free. Where much of a mother's work is extraordinarily mentally debilitating, repetitive, and calls for constant sacrifice, a job in the paid workforce is often intellectually stimulating, and affords novelty and an opportunity to grow. Not all paid work is positive in these ways, of course, but a lot of jobs are.

If his work is stressful, a man is free to bring every ounce of his mental attention to bear on its challenges. He can delegate down to subordinates or across to equals or upwards to his superior. He can unlock productivity with new technology. He can draw emotional and logistical and problem-solving support from his colleagues, even if he spends much of his working day in isolated conditions. If it comes to the worst, he can quit and find a new job. Besides all that, he is paid.

A mother at home can do none of these things. Far more than 100 percent of her mental, physical and emotional resources are sucked up by the children, which paradoxically drains her of the strength to care for them. She cannot delegate down or across or up. There is no 'killer app' that will untangle the tentacled embrace of child care and housework. She usually cannot share the load in synergistic ways, at least not very often; hardly anybody wants to look after somebody else's baby, and even if she has friends and neighbors with young babies, few synergies present themselves beyond playgroups in the park or the odd babysitting swap. There is no one to help her solve problems at home; books and websites can be useful, and her social media network, favorite blogs, and forums can be very supportive, but she will have to read them while holding the crying baby and stopping the toddler drawing on the walls. There is no one physically present most of the day to give her moral support. She cannot resign. Indeed, she is not considered to be working in the first place. And she is not paid.

Men can no longer claim 'mystery' about their work the way they used to. In pre-feminist days, he assigned his job a gravitas it didn't warrant. His job demanded of him unusual exertions, so his argument went, that his little-headed wife could not be expected to understand, and these exertions entitled him to privileged treatment at home, like never having to cook a chicken tikka tonight, cook roast lamb tomorrow, cook beef noodles the next night or cook every other dinner he is going to eat for the rest of his life, sweep the bathroom floor, take the diaper bucket out, sponge out the cupboard under the sink, or take the kids for hair-cuts.

Virtually no man matches the full domestic and child-rearing load that a woman carries, but almost all women today have matched a man's full-time job in the paid workforce, at least at times in their lives. Women have been on the factory floor, in the legal chamber, on the sales route. We know just what paid work is like. And almost every mother on the planet can report that it is easier to be at work than to take care of the kids. Suggest to a mother that paid work is more challenging or tiring than mothering, and most will stare at you in a blank, disbelieving silence for a second, then burst into gales of self-assured laughter. They leave you in no doubt which job they find harder. And unlike everyone else, when it comes to judging whether mothers or non-mothers work hardest, mothers actually know what they're talking about.

The real battleground for many mothers is the playground; the real playground is at work.

"It's just a *job*!" exclaimed Yvonne, a mom at my kids' elementary school who had just returned to the workforce in accounting. She was describing her new paid position. She buzzed up and down on the spot and rolled her eyes in a bedazzled fashion to indicate how easy she found it. "All you have to do is your *work*!" she continued. "And you get to drink a cup of tea!"

If you won't take a woman's word for it that motherhood is hard work, take a man's. Mitt Romney, 2012 U.S. Presidential candidate, tells in his book, *No Apology: The Case for American Greatness* (St. Martin's Press, 2010) how, when running for Governor of Massachusetts, he spent a day every few weeks in other people's jobs. He was a garbage collector, a cook, a hay-bale stacker, a road-worker, an emergency room volunteer—and a child care worker. He wrote, "I'm often asked which was the hardest job—it's child care, by a mile." I have never heard a feminist engage with that truth.

The Silent Motive: Validation

To have any legitimacy in the brave new woman-denying world of feminism from the early 1980s, a woman had to make like a man. And that meant getting a job. Even with a new baby. The following stories of just two women I know illustrate our lust to pursue our feminine self-worth through the masculine channel of a job.

My friend, Carmel, is an ardent feminist in her early fifties. She put her only son into full-time day care at just six weeks to return to a demanding operations career in the finance industry.

I was aghast when she told me this. The notion of crippling myself with a high-energy 40-hour job and a newborn—it seemed a preposterous undertaking.

"I wanted my own *money*," she hedged over coffee. I knew her husband earned a high income. She did not need money, and wanting her *own* money seemed like a very thin motive indeed for calling such catastrophic destruction down on her own head.

"In any case," I felt like replying, "it's already your money." Feminism agrees with the outrageous male idea that because he earned the money, it is his. That is why feminism loves to trumpet its gift of 'financial independence' to women. However, married women already were financially independent. A wife and husband are a financial unit; 50 percent of the authority over the money (or more accurately, 100 percent 'joint and several' authority over the money) is hers.

Based on the breakdown of labor in table 1, we could argue it's 79 percent Carmel's money, because the woman in table 1 contributes 79 percent of the work in her household. "If your husband wants 50 percent of the say over the money," I felt like telling Carmel, "he needs to pull 50 percent of the weight."

Outside my kids' day care center one morning, graphic designer, Phoebe, had just dropped off the youngest of her four girls. She was jumping up and down with that frantic agitation standard in working mothers today brutalized by their triple, quadruple, quintuple workloads. She was in a rush to get the 45 minutes across town to her office, where she worked three days a week in an agency.

When I expressed concern at how much she was doing, and asked her why she was working so hard with four preschool and elementary school girls to care for, she didn't hesitate. She knew exactly why she was working. She didn't hand me the usual feminist spin: "Because I love it!" Nor did she use that feminist fall-back: "For the money." I knew enough of her personal circumstances to know she didn't need the money in the slightest.

What did she say?

"Validation," she said emphatically, throwing the words over her shoulder as she dove for the car. "I'm doing it for validation."

I doubted very much that Phoebe found her schedule workable. As she drove away, my frustration on her behalf was intense. In this supposed age of women, why should a mother of four young children need to saddle herself with a paid job for validation?

What Carmel and Phoebe were doing is what pretty much all women have been doing since feminism really took hold in the 1980s—working like a man for validation as a woman.

How Feminism Became Man's Best Friend

Feminists assert that paid work is not 'men's work' but equally 'women's work'. Women have an equal right to men to be in the workforce, they say. And they're right. Women do have the right to be neurosurgeons or bus depot supervisors or comedy club managers, just like men.

But so is mothering and running a home and caring for others and resonating with the sheer life-force of humanity 'women's work'. Mothering work accounts for many more weekly hours than a paid job, and those will almost certainly be much more demanding hours. Yet feminism scorns and denies mothers' work. Why? Precisely *because* it is women's work. If it's women's work, says feminism, it sucks, because women suck. That a woman is naturally inferior to a man is an article of faith with feminism.

Feminism cares about career not because it sees career as women's work, but because it sees it as men's work, and therefore as the pathway to self-actualization for women. That is what feminism degenerated into in the 1980s after the first great explosion of positive self-awareness in the 1960s and '70s—a movement devoted to the self-actualization of women through man-identicality. The strong feminists of the 1960s and '70s gave us our right to work; the weak feminists of the 1980s made it an imperative. Women did not just have the *right* to do what men did; women *had* to do what men did to validate their womanhood. To be like a man is the greatest honor she can know, feminists told women. Only when she does what he does can she break through into a place of truth, power and enlightenment.

Moreover, without a man's economic and law-making power, said feminists, women have no power at all, because nothing a woman does, like giving birth to people, or shaping the next generation, or caring for others, or making a beautiful home, or forging a strong community, or radiating her uniquely female moral authority, or being a fount of wise and sensible things knowable only by women, is ever powerful. In other words, women need to emulate men to lift them out of the sucky state of womanhood in which they wallow.

To tell a woman groaning under the equivalent of table 1's 6.8 40-hour weeks as a mother and home-maker and center of a family that she is not good enough, and to then force her to duplicate a man's paid 40-hour week before she is deemed admissible to the ranks of humanity, is patently not a pro-woman philosophy. It is man-worship. What we have been practicing these past 40 years is masculinism.

Even so, to claim that feminism is anti-woman might seem bizarre. After all, feminism has done away with so much harm to women. No more female bank regulators and auto engine designers and chief operating officers stuck at home when they didn't want to be, forced to do nothing but clip recipes and knit baby booties. No more financial 'dependence' on a man. No more stereotyping of women as unfit for a good many activities that men do. No more denying women ownership of property of various kinds, or barring them from certain places or decisions. Feminism's benefits for women are immense and undeniable.

But that doesn't make feminism women's friend. Since the 1980s, feminism has been achieving all these good things by seeking to make women more like men. That makes feminism men's friend, not women's. When it comes to doing good things for women by treating them differently to men, feminism usually runs for the hills.

By camouflaging themselves as women's saviors, feminists buy themselves immunity from prosecution. They are masculinist wolves in pro-woman sheep's clothing who have cleverly aligned themselves with 'women's interests', so that to attack their masculinist agenda is to be seen to attack women. And what woman wants to think herself anti-woman? Anyway, it's called 'feminism', isn't it? Doesn't that mean it's a movement that advocates for women? If it was called 'masculinism', which is what it really is, I bet a lot fewer women would be keen to champion feminism's cause.

Leaving aside those of us who need the income, the only women who should be in the workforce are those who want to be there. And a great many of us do want to be there, of course. We want to work for all kinds of positive reasons, like a sense of purpose, or mental stimulation, or social contact, or the chance to help others, or to make our mark. And many of us financially have to work. However, not all of us financially have to, at least once we're married or in a stable relationship, and not all of us want to. If women were not working for validation en masse today, we would see at least some women choosing to spend their entire exciting, fulfilling lives outside the economy.

Working for validation is a negative motive to work. No woman should ever need to do what a man does, or be like a man in any way, to feel like a powerful, admired and valid member of society.

When I raise this point among my female friends and fellow school moms, many of them instantly—a little too instantly—come back with "Oh, but I have to work." There is 'have to' and 'have to'. Single women, obviously, have to (although that should not be so for single mothers, as chapter 9 explores). Married women whose husbands have a very low income or are unemployed or incapacitated, have to. Mothers saving for a college fund, or funding an elderly parent's retirement home, may have to. Lots of us need or choose to earn money for all kinds of robust reasons like those.

But then there's a negative kind of 'have to'. It's when a woman 'has to' work because every other woman is working. Once a critical mass of women enters the workforce, every other woman is obliged to work, too, or she will be left behind by all the two-income households.

Too often, 'have to' is the beard. It disguises a woman's real motive to work, validation. The majority of my friends and fellow school-moms who say they 'have to' work are married to men who earn multi-six-figure and seven-figure salaries. They live in houses worth $2 million, $3 million and up. I have a friend who lives in a $6 million house, another in an even more expensive house. They send their children to private school at $25,000-$30,000 per child per year, and take frequent holidays abroad.

You may say that their lives are hardly representative of most women. However, their wealth is what makes them such a great testing ground for our true attitudes to ourselves, for these are women with all the choices in the world.

And with those choices, what do they do? Work.

And not just a little work. They cripple themselves with work. They stay up past midnight e-mailing clients, they twist themselves like a giraffe made from balloons to go on overseas business trips, they obliterate their days and nights to write press releases, or source quotes for their new product launch, or book-keep. They shove their domestic duties into unworkable times of the week designed for rest or sleep—ironing name labels on football shorts at 7:27 p.m., designing a poster for the 'donate your old bicycle for African kids' drive as part of their eight-year-old's social justice project at 11:08 p.m., trawling websites for exercise book covers at 1 a.m.—to make way for paid work in the day-time. These women will not do themselves the service of according their unpaid work the prime time it deserves.

Many work for no reason they can identify. Relatively few work for pleasure or purpose. When I ask my fellow school moms and friends why they're working, they rarely say, "Because it's terrific!" More often, they look blank, and stop short in consternation. They face the 'not-working' world in their mind, and quickly recoil from it as a place of shame. Most get a little angry, as if by pointing to the possibility of a non-working womanhood, I have dragged them into some mire, and they scoot back quickly to the safe, clean, 'male' territory of paid work. Wherever the men are is the only permissible place to be under feminism.

The cowardly ones in my circle reply that they financially "have to" work, when they clearly don't. Some spout the feminist line that work is "fulfilling" when I can see that for those particular women, it isn't. The more honest ones simply don't have an answer.

A One-Way Equality

The belief that women 'have to' work has infected men as much as women. When I ran into an old colleague, Ally, and her husband in a café, she was dandling her first-born six-month-old on her knee. I asked them how it was going. Her husband looked stressed and rolled his eyes.

"Trying to get by on one income!" he groaned. He seemed to think himself hard done by, even though he had a high income, and far the easier part of the deal. Why should the reality of having a baby be anything other than one income? His wife was already working far harder as a mother than he ever would as a bread-winner. To listen to him, you would get the impression that he thought she should be working as well as looking after the baby and running the house.

And, of course, that is exactly what he did think. Feminism has now groomed two whole generations of men to expect a second income, and *for nothing in return*. After all, as feminism makes clear to men, their wives have nothing else to do.

If feminists think paid work is 'women's work' as much as it is 'men's work', how come they don't see women's unpaid work as equally 'men's work'? We don't hear feminists calling for Ally's husband to match her share of the domestic and mothering load with anything like the fervor with which they call for Ally to match his paid contribution. If feminism was sincere in its commitment to equality, its calls for men to do more in the home would have been as strident as its calls for women to do less.

Yet on both counts, feminists were silent. Reducing the burden on women and getting men to take on more of the strain of child care and housework should have been an essential co-factor in freeing women up to take on paid work. It should have been one of feminism's first and biggest tasks. But feminism ignored it. The greater share men take in fathering and household duties today has happened more by default than by any express pressuring from feminists. As far as feminism is concerned, he can do as little or much as he likes.

No such luck for women. Defying the evidence, feminism targeted women, not men, as the under-contributors. A mother is the busiest person on earth, yet it is on her head that feminism has heaped a full-time pile of extra work. Feminism can protest that a woman can 'choose' to work part-time, but it has done almost nothing to encourage employers to provide part-time work, and it makes it clear that a woman who works part-time is inferior to one who works full-time. In feminists' eyes, a man doesn't have to take on 100 percent of a woman's workload in the home, or even one percent of it, to be 'equal' to her; but she must match 100 percent of his paid load before she is 'equal' to him.

It is not equality to which feminists have devoted themselves these past five decades. It is *inequality.* Did feminism take steps to make women 'equally' excused from the grueling burden of housework, mothering, caring for others? 'Equal' in the nonchalance enjoyed by men who never frantically service customer accounts from a home office, while searching the help-desk to solve their seven-year-old's computer game glitch, while cutting up the kids' watermelon when they get in from school, while hollering at them three, four, five times to not leave their shoes on the door-mat, while enrolling their 10-year-old in the upcoming school camp by the end-of-day deadline, all at the same time? Equal in time to devote to her own affairs? Equal in time to *rest*? No.

Yet, incredibly, feminism has convinced women that today's cripplingly uneven division of labor leaves them 'equal' and 'liberated'.

How do they get away with it? By packaging their denial of women's unpaid work with our equal *right* to a career, and the status and other benefits that come with a paid job.

"Look how much we do for you!" they cry as they hold out that irresistible career candy. "You have an equal right to this!" What a temptation, huh? It's hard to knock back a deal that came with full entry to the workplace for the first time in history. Access to career is undeniably a fabulous thing in itself. And even if we didn't want to take part in the working world, even if we wanted to be lifelong housewives, most of us totally wanted the *right* to work. We rightly wanted the same rights he had.

What we should not want is the gross inequality we are forced to shoulder to access those rights. Women today carry a workload that is unequal to a truly shocking degree. Never in history has a woman been expected to perform not only her 50 percent of all the work that comes with motherhood and running a home, and much or all of his 50 percent share of that work, but to also match 100 percent of his paid work, before she is considered to be his 'equal'.

One of the most common manifestations of masculinist inequality is the '50/50' tactic, touted in the last few years as 'gender equality' policies. This is the feminist rule that says women should make up 50 percent of the ranks of every field of human endeavor. You know the kind of thing: newspaper headlines that decry the fact that "Only 0.00003% of Fortune 500 CEOs are women!" or magazine articles that note in forbidding tones that "a mere 0.07% of auto sales personnel are women" or press releases that cry "Women lagging men in 279 growth sectors; Government announces urgent taskforce to close the gender gap."

Fifty/fifty sounds so seductively 'equal', doesn't it? Yet it is quite the opposite. Fifty/fifty is just another way of saying 100/100. What 50/50 actually means is that 100 percent of women must do what 100 percent of men do. One hundred men drive racing cars? Then 100 women must burn rubber, or women will not make up 50 percent of the ranks of racing car drivers. One thousand men become deep-sea divers? Then 1000 women must drop to the depths, too, or more men than women will be deep-sea divers. Ten thousand men sit on company boards? Then 10,000 women must be board directors, or else women won't be half of all directors. And to not do what men do, as every good feminist knows, is to fail as a woman.

If women are not shadowing men activity for activity, feminism reasons that the only explanation is that 'obstacles' must be in the way. There must be something 'wrong'. 'Discrimination' must be at work that prevents a woman from reaching her 'full potential', by which feminism always means replication of a man's life. The media is full of plaintive calls by feminists to put these 'wrongs' right, remove these 'obstacles' and 'discrimination' and get women to the only place that matters—the place wherever the men are.

Observation that a woman may be doing different things to men because hers is a gender in its own right with a whole different gamut of priorities and interests and career-choices is swept aside, as if the suggestion were an insult and a mark against her. That a woman's gargantuan workload of motherhood and housework might be getting in the way is hardly ever raised as a possibility. This denial of a woman's contribution is simply jaw-dropping.

I cannot think of a single instance when the 50/50 policy has been applied in women's favor. Have you ever once heard a high-profile feminist loudly claim that men would never be women's equal until they made up 50 percent of the members of quilt-alongs, or bake-sale coordinators, or moms scouring the malls for glow-in-the-dark shoe-laces to put in the loot bags at their six-year-old's birthday party? Has a feminist ever lamented that male board directors would continue to suffer in a distressing state of inferiority until they did 50 percent of their own housework and parenting? Even less likely, have you ever heard a feminist claim that a male board director must do the near-100 percent of housework and parenting in his household, just like a female board director does in her household, before he can finally take his place alongside her as her equal?

The 50/50 rule is sometimes about empowering women, but way too often, it is about *disempowering* women. It is too often the '0/100' rule—women have zero say, and men have 100 percent of the say in what activities humanity pursues. Men get to decide, and women must obey. The 50/50 'gender equality' rule sets out to eradicate women's goals and desires and actions and interests and values, and replace them with those of men.

If women are forced to do the things men do, it follows that there will be no women left over to do the things women do. She can only own a beauty salon, say, or run a ballet school, if he owns a beauty salon or runs a ballet school. Society will be denied beauty salons and ballet schools unless a man feels like operating one. In the 50/50 world, any uniquely female contribution is obliterated.

Why should women fill half of all jobs in the paid world of the economy and politics, unless they want to, when they already work so much harder in the unpaid world of home and family and community? And outside the economy, why should women's interests overlap with men's at all? There is no particular reason why a woman might want to do even one percent of what a man does as a hobby or passion. Absolutely, women should race cars or deep-sea-dive if they want to, but only if they want to. If every woman in the world would rather get a hot rock treatment at the day spa, or go to a henna hand-painting workshop, that should be okay, too.

We women are easy to push around. Feminists can froth at the mouth all they want at that heresy; it is true. Tell us to stay away from the polling booth for millennia before the suffragette movement at the turn of the twentieth century, and we did. Tell us to obey at the altar until the 1970s, and we did. Tell us to stay out of the workforce before the 1980s, no matter how desperately we needed more than a house and kids to satisfy us, and we did.

In the last quarter of the twentieth century, the oppression continued, only this time it was feminists doing the oppressing. Tell us to wipe ourselves out with a full-time career designed for a man with a 24/7 wife at home, no matter how colossally over-worked we were already with house and kids, even with a newborn, and we did. Tell us to look down our noses at our own profound and exhausting contribution as wives and mothers, and we did. Tell us to do the job like a man rather than like a woman, and we did.

One of the reasons we women are so easy to push around is that we are so obliging and adaptable and enduring. Obligingness and adaptability and endurance are not weaknesses. They are three of women's most impressive *strengths*. However, with strengths like those, it is easy for others to take advantage of us. Feminism was supposed to protect women from a patriarchal society that found it all too easy to ride roughshod over them.

Instead, feminism has turned women's obliging nature to its own malevolent ends, and ridden roughshod over women itself. Feminism simply replaced one kind of masculinist oppression, the old kind applied by overbearing men who used their wives as broodmares and domestic servants, with a new kind of masculinist oppression applied by feminist commandants who dissolved women's self-worth outside the workplace, and farmed them out to the economy as CV's on legs, by which means feminism told women they could get their self-worth back.

It has not been difficult for feminism to co-opt two whole generations of women, and now three, into tearing themselves to pieces with over-work, deriding their own contribution as mothers and housewives, defying their own female sensibilities and needs. So under the thumb of feminism's masculinist tenets have many of us been for the past 40 years, that we will steam-roll our children's happiness, the sanctity of our family life, our control over our time, our health, our sleep, our leisure, our passions, our womanly perceptions and responses and pleasures, our very womanhood itself, just to win feminism's approval with a career.

One morning around 2010, I watched a couple heading off to work at my local train station. He was swinging his arms, head high, striding along with enthusiasm. He walked with the cheerful and uncomplicated energy of someone whose world presented him with no obstacles and invited him to thrive. What he wanted to do and what the world demanded of him and praised him for were one and the same—a day's paid work.

By his side walked his wife. She took small meek steps, head down. She did not seem energized by the demands of the day to come, but beaten down. She was dressed in the demeaning default-male business suit that has been standard dress code for working women these past four decades. She would perform the same day of paid work as her husband.

However, where he joyfully answered the embrace of the pattern of the day, the day's pattern seemed to cut across her. It sat at odds with her many domestic and family tasks, her energies, her priorities, her emotions, her perceptions, all her many contributions as a woman that career would prevent her from making that day. She seemed stymied, blocked off, demoralized.

For several years afterwards, I kept returning to that scene in my head. I found the inherent woman-denial in it upsetting. As an editor, I know that there is a word in the English language for just about everything. I searched and searched for the word to pinpoint exactly what it was I found so off-putting about seeing that woman forced to live like a man. 'Lobotomized'? Yes, for her woman-power had been surgically removed by feminism's masculinist insistence that she work like a man, dress like a man, and pretend to a man's relationship with her career; but that was not the word I was looking for. 'Thwarted'? Certainly, for she was prevented from getting to her womanly chores and desires and bringing her emotional woman-power to the world that day, but that was not the word, either. Nor was 'diminished', 'trapped' or 'submissive', although they were all a good fit.

Then one morning at home, I was mulling over how Germaine Greer's *The Female Eunuch* had probably done more good for more human beings than any secular book in history. It calls for women to stop buying into their own disempowerment at the hands of men. And then the word came to me: *'eunuch'*. That woman trotting obediently off to a man-shaped day in the masculinized zone of the workplace looked like a eunuch. "We're still eunuchs," I thought to myself. When we let feminism tell us we suck unless we live like a man, we're buying into our own disempowerment at the hands of feminists. We're castrated. De-womanized. Eunuchs.

It can't go on. It's time for masculinism to stop. A woman is a fabulous, valid being in her own right, *with or without a career*. If every woman is working for validation, and just about all of us are, then no woman is truly free. Our work as mothers is more important, not less important, than a man's paid work, without any disrespect to all the amazing stuff he does at work. Our work as housewives is just as important, not less important, than his paid work. When we do paid work, we have the right to do the job to our own female timetable, to our own female conditions, and in our own female way. We have our own relationship with career that is not the same as his. We are capable of far more than just the paid work men do, for we are the creators of people, the fount of love, and the light of humanity's soul. We have all kinds of feelings and perceptions and knowledges that he does not have. This book is going to explore all a woman does and is and knows both inside and outside her career, all that uniquely womanly wonderfulness.

It's time to take back the woman.

2

Child's Play

A Mother's Working Day

"WELCOME TO THE PARALLEL UNIVERSE," said our friend Luke in those devastating weeks after our first child's birth.

Shell-shocked by new parenthood, we nodded. Luke was dad to a one-year-old, and so a veteran parent from our vantage point. My then-husband and I were astounded by the obliteration of body and mind, aggrieved at the unrelenting pace, dismayed that the nature of parenthood had been kept from us.

"It's a rude shock," said a mom in my baby playgroup. "It's hidden," said my friend Gina, biting down on her anger as her 18-month-old shrieked and wriggled in his parents' arms. "It's a conspiracy," my child-free friend, Annalies, reported a new mother in her circle as saying. In those first months of motherhood, I was open-mouthed in amazement. How in this supposedly pro-woman era could motherhood, the world's most uniquely female experience, stay relegated to a parallel universe?

The answer is that feminism connived to keep it there.

MY FIRST CHILD, ROBBIE, SET up crying on day seven and never stopped. One of my mothercraft manuals said that crying babies often start crying the day after coming home from hospital, and so it was with us. As I said in the last chapter, if I held Robbie, he was happy—but only if I stood up. If I sat down and cuddled him on my lap, he cried. Thankfully, I didn't have to pace to calm him, as so many parents of crying babies do. I just had to stand. Robbie's roaring wrenched me from bed as early as 4:30 a.m. every morning, so that every day I woke skewered on rage.

Every moment he was awake, I had two options. I could stand and hold him, know the heavenly quiet, and know the hellish futility of getting nothing done; or I could put him down, get something done, and steep myself in his screams. The rage of a crying baby or the rage of paralysis were my two choices. I oscillated between them throughout the day. Neither was bearable.

For Robbie, I made a Herculean effort to hold the rage in every single second and present a patient, smiling facade to him. Almost always, I succeeded. Very occasionally, much less than one percent of the time, I let rip, although I tried never to do this in his company. I shrieked. I slammed cupboard doors. I hung on my bedroom door jamb and railed against the incessant agony of listening to him yowl. Expressing the anger like this did nothing to relieve it.

Mostly, I opted for the rage of paralysis. I stood, ablaze in frustration at getting nothing done, as Robbie looked calmly over my shoulder. Standing all day, every day, became a torture of its own. It developed into a sort of physical pain inside my ribs. Leaning against the wall with the baby in my arms provided a limited but intensely welcome balm from the rigor of holding myself upright every minute. Closing my eyes at the same time provided a surprising degree of relief from severe sleepiness. A lot of days, I just leaned there and cried.

Because Robbie was a 'vertical' baby who disliked lying horizontally in my arms, I had to hold him upright, which took my second hand to support his head for the first three to four months. After that, he could support his own head. In theory, that meant

I could hold him with one arm and do something with the other. That should have been liberating, but doing things with one hand is not as easy as it looks. Television advertisements like to show a smiling mother with a baby tucked in one elbow as she sashays in a multi-tasking waltz between sink, kids and a tablet computer on the kitchen bench. Motherhood is a breeze, the ad says, so lightweight that it can double with fixing dinner, which in turn is so lightweight that it can triple with tele-conferencing with the office. These media images convey a sense of ease that very few mothers of young babies actually experience. In truth, few tasks can be performed with one hand. Try undoing a screw-top jar; or opening a sealed packet of crackers; or wringing out a baby sleep-suit soaking in the tub. I spent my day in repeated attempts to bust tasks with one hand, but rarely met with success. I was to learn the hard way over the painful years to come that a deep, existential frustration at never getting anything done would be endemic to my life as a mother.

After the 9 a.m. feed, Robbie sometimes kicked happily at the toy-string slung across his cot. That interlude lasted as long as 40 minutes some days, never longer. It was my one slot of peace in the whole day, for he cried every other moment, and never slept. On a good day, I could eat breakfast, dive into the shower, dress, and spend a whole 20 minutes in the thrill of *getting stuff done*! On a bad day, his happiness lasted only 20 minutes, not long enough to get past breakfast and showering. On worse days, I stepped into the shower in splendid peace, but stepped out of it to his cries. In the shower, I could not hear him cry. Every day I would turn off the water on tenterhooks, listening for that noise. I rejoiced if I heard nothing, tore into savage pieces if he was crying.

If Robbie fell asleep after a feed throughout the day, I tried to put him down. Typically, he woke crying mid-air as I lowered him into the cot. Sometimes, I could make touchdown on the mattress, but then he would wake and howl. On occasion, he would sleep for 20 seconds or so, and I would creep away, reveling in 20 glorious seconds of freedom! Then that wail would set up again, and I was back to rage.

The Job with No Quitting Time

Not many moms hate every minute of motherhood, but then not many moms love every minute of it, either. Just about all mothers are in a giant washing machine of emotions, tumbling around between love and hatred (hatred of the torments, that is, not of their children), delight and despair, thrill and exhaustion, astonishment and dejection, bottomless joy and boundless fury, uncontainable excitement and dehumanizing emptiness. They can experience these contradictory states in the very same breath.

No matter what we feel about motherhood, mothers share many of the same travails and triumphs, although we all have our own individual take on them. Some of us like taking the eight-year-old to Saturday baseball fixtures but loathe getting the family lunches. Others loathe the homework but like the housework. Some have babies who sleep through at six weeks; others are still up at 3 a.m. three years on. Some of us revel in stay-at-home motherhood until the kids leave home; others find it drives us nuts when the baby is two weeks old. We fight some different battles but, love or hate motherhood, we fight the same war.

Whatever our co-ordinates on the motherhood battlefield, feminism blanks us. To the mother who treasures motherhood, feminism gives no praise, visibility or validation. On the contrary, it seeks to deprive her of this most vast and precious of human experiences, and treats motherhood as an irrelevance in her life beside the main and only game, that of working alongside men in a career, and bullies her back to the office.

To the mother who finds motherhood an ordeal, feminism gives no support, visibility or validation, either. Instead of doing all it can to relieve her of some of the burden (most obviously, by offering validation, and getting fathers to take a greater share of the burden), it treats a career alongside men as the antidote, and bullies her back to the office.

What this chapter aims to show is not that motherhood sucks—because for most mothers, it doesn't, at least not totally, and for pretty much all mothers, even those who don't like it, it is the richest human experience there is—but that motherhood is *work*.

Feminism says it's not. When feminism declares a mother can work full-time, it is declaring that motherhood's workload is so minimal that it can be soaked up in the early mornings and evenings and weekends that are the free parts of a man's week. It comes with no credit points of its own, needs no dedicated time allotment of its own, and needs no adjustment to the male workplace timetable.

To show just how much work mothering is, overleaf in table 2 I have tabulated one 24-hour day in my own life as a mother of a crying baby and a typically active toddler. I have used my sons, Robbie and Lachlan, as the models. The only modification I have made is to use Robbie as the model for both the toddler and the second baby, as I did in table 1 in the last chapter. As I said there, that is because Robbie was an unusually difficult baby, and although my second child, Lachie, was a settled baby, I feel it is important to use a difficult baby as the model to show just how tough life with a toddler and baby can be.

This table is based on my own experience. I am not trying to tell you that my experience is your experience. "Don't you hate it the way motherhood is presented as universal?" my friend, Alexis, observed acutely as we sat with our babies one morning. She is right. Every mother has a different experience of motherhood. Nonetheless, it is safe to say that almost all mothers of babies and preschoolers have a day that is some variant of the day outlined in this table. Unless she has eerily compliant children or extensive support, virtually every mother shares much of the chronic overload, the demands, the sacrifices that this table chronicles.

TABLE 2
A Mother's 24-Hour Day

(caring for one six-week-old baby and one 18-month-old toddler)

Time	Column 1 (The baby's carer)	Column 2 (The toddler's carer)	Column 3 (The 'extra pair of hands')	Column 4 (The housekeeper)	Column 5 (The career-woman)
6 a.m.	Woken by baby's cries. Change and breastfeed baby.	Sleep.	Sleep.	Sleep.	Sleep.
6:40 a.m.		Toddler wakes. Change diaper and dress him.			Dress and prepare for work.
6:50 a.m.	Dress. Eat breakfast.	Feed toddler breakfast.	Hold crying baby while Mother 1 dresses, eats breakfast.	Fix breakfast for mother and toddler.	
7:30 a.m.	Stand and hold crying baby.	Entertain toddler. Toilet-training: toddler has an 'accident' on sofa. Undress him, take him to bathroom, sponge him, dry him, change him.	Fetch clean clothes for toddler and rinse out his wet clothing. Strip cover from wet sofa after toddler's 'accident'. Soak cover. Sponge and blot sofa cushion and place in sun to dry.	Clear breakfast dishes and clean table, toddler's high-chair and messy floor underneath. Stack dishwasher, wash up non-dishwasher items. Sort laundry. Bleach kids' food- and mud-stained items. Wash sheets from toddler's wet bed last night. Put in dryer. Start sweeping and mopping floors: kitchen, bathroom, laundry.	Travel to work.
8:40 a.m.	Change baby's diaper. Dress and breastfeed baby.	Brush toddler's teeth and hair, wash his face. Put his shoes on. Toddler rips them off. Put them on again.	Pack outing bag for baby, toddler and mother. Pack bag, toddler's tricycle, ball, picnic rug, stroller and mother's coat in car.	Fix morning snacks for mother and toddler, and formula bottle for toddler.	

52

8:55 a.m.	Entertain toddler.	Take toddler to bathroom and teach him to use the lavatory.	Clean up 'spill' on lavatory floor after toddler misses the bowl.	Continue sweeping and mopping.	Arrive at work.
9:30 a.m.	Strap crying baby into car. Drive to playground while baby cries. Get crying baby into the stroller and into the playground. / Stand and hold crying baby. / Baby wets his clothes just after a diaper change. Change baby's clothes and diaper again.	Put toddler's coat on. Toddler rips off shoes again; put them back on. Take toddler downstairs to car and strap him in. Entertain toddler in car en route to playground to stop him whining. Get toddler out of the car and into the playground. Supervise toddler in playground.	Carry bag, trike, ball, outing bag and other stuff to playground. Fetch cup of tea for Mothers 1 and 2. Hold crying baby, then supervise toddler, while both mothers take turns to drink tea.	Household e-mails and online administration.	Express milk.
10:40 a.m.	Breastfeed baby while sitting uncomfortably on ground because the playground lacks seating.	Feed toddler morning snack. Take toddler to bathroom and change diaper. Supervise toddler in playground.	Fetch mother's feeding wrap and water bottle. Assist in bathroom with toddler.	Put laundry in dryer.	
11:15 a.m.	Pack crying baby back into stroller, take him to the car. Drive home while baby cries. Take crying baby upstairs.	Chase toddler and get him to the car. Entertain toddler in car on way home to stop the whining. Take him upstairs.	Take bags and toys back to car. At home, take all the gear upstairs and unpack it, and clean it if needs be.	Put third laundry load on. / Clean out refrigerator. / Fix lunch for mother and toddler.	
12:05 p.m.	Stand and hold crying baby.	Feed toddler lunch. Take toddler to bathroom and change diaper.		Clear lunch dishes and clean table, toddler's high-chair and messy floor underneath.	Express milk.

TABLE 2 (CONT.)
A Mother's 24-Hour Day
(caring for one six-week-old baby and one 18-month-old toddler)

	Column 1 (The baby's carer)	Column 2 (The toddler's carer)	Column 3 (The 'extra pair of hands')	Column 4 (The housekeeper)	Column 5 (The career-woman)
12:40 p.m.	Eat lunch.	Toddler's sleep-time: Read three stories on the bed, lie down and pat him until he falls asleep, re-settle him as he jumps up five times.	Hold crying baby while Mother 1 eats lunch.	Put more laundry in dryer. Start designing invitations for baby's christening.	
1 p.m.	Stand and hold crying baby.		Make doctor's appointment for toddler.		
1:40 p.m.	Change baby's diaper. Breastfeed baby.		Pack up toddler's toys and generally tidy up. Set out new toys. Baby has a rash. Read up on it online and in baby-care manual.	Visit stores: buy new winter underwear for mother, next-size-up sweater and warm tops for baby, postage stamps, a new-mother-and-baby gift and card for a friend, and birthday gift for toddler's friend.	
2:35 p.m.	Stand and hold crying baby.	Toddler wakes. Take toddler to bathroom and change diaper to underpants. Entertain toddler all afternoon. Feed toddler afternoon snack.	Fix afternoon snack for mother and toddler. Help Mother 2 entertain toddler: fetch broomsticks and blankets to build cubby; fetch and make up and lay out craft supplies. Pack up cubby and craft supplies afterwards, and clean up after craft session.		Express milk.
4:05 p.m.	Change baby's diaper. Breastfeed baby.		Toddler has another toileting 'accident'. Rinse out the soiled clothes and soak them, and clean up the floor.	Wrap both gifts; write cards. Cut tags off new clothing and put it away. Fold and put away laundry.	

Time					
4:50 p.m.	Baby vomits all over mother and self due to reflux. Change baby's clothes and diaper. Take baby to pharmacy for emergency reflux treatment. Buy treatment for rash at the same time.	Continue entertaining toddler.	Hold crying baby while Mother 1 washes reflux vomit from arm, changes clothes. Go downstairs to fetch stroller from garage, erect stroller and its rainshade and pack raincoat for mother, re-stock diaper bag.	Fix dinner. Make muffins while fixing dinner.	Leave work.
5:30 p.m.	Change baby's diaper. Dress baby in pajamas. Breastfeed baby.	Serve toddler dinner.		Turn muffins out to cool.	
6 p.m.		Pack toddler's toys away. Get protesting toddler to help.		Serve dinner.	
6:25 p.m.	Put baby down to sleep. Eat dinner.	Bathe toddler and dress him in pajamas and new diaper.		Clear dishes and clear up kitchen. Clean table, high-chair and messy floor underneath. Stack dishwasher/wash up non-dishwasher items.	
7 p.m.	Shower.	Read bedtime story and put toddler to bed.		Wash and sterilize formula bottles. Ironing.	Arrive home.
7:20 p.m.	Go to bed.				
7:55 p.m.		Toddler re-appears. Put him back to bed.		More household e-mails.	
9:10 p.m.	Go to bed.	Go to bed.		Go to bed.	Go to bed.

TABLE 2 (CONT.)
A Mother's 24-Hour Day
(caring for one six-week-old baby and one 18-month-old toddler)

	Column 1 (The baby's carer)	Column 2 (The toddler's carer)	Column 3 (The 'extra pair of hands')	Column 4 (The housekeeper)	Column 5 (The career-woman)
10:55 p.m.	Woken by baby's crying. Change baby's diaper. Breastfeed baby.				
11:45 p.m.	Put baby back to bed.	Toddler wakes crying with a wet bed. Sponge toddler and dress him in dry clothes. Soothe him back to sleep with a bottle of milk.	Strip bed, make new bed. Fetch dry clothes for toddler, make up a warm bottle of milk.		
12:10 a.m.		Go back to bed.			
2:05 a.m.	Woken by baby's crying. Change baby's diaper. Breastfeed baby.				
3:15 a.m.	Put baby back to bed.				
Sub-Total	13 hrs, 25 mins	11 hrs, 45 mins	6 hrs, 30 mins (est.)	14 hrs, 20 mins	11 hrs, 30 mins
TOTAL Daily Hours (Unpaid)		46 hours			n/a

56

As you can see, I estimate that a mother of two small children does 46 hours *every day*. That is more than the weekly working hours of many men. Her workload diminishes only to the extent that he pitches in. And he only does that if he wants to. For most of the feminist era, he has been excused by feminists from contributing to the parenting workload. It is only in the last five years or so that men are coming under any public pressure at all to put their shoulders to the domestic wheel, and that pressure is very soft indeed.

A Mother's Morning Up Close

A concise summary of a mother's workload like table 2 can make the individual tasks look sanitized. The reality is much murkier, more debilitating, and far, far more detailed. Behind any one procedure laid out in this neat table hides a myriad of mini-procedures. These all compound to drive a mother up into the air from below, crush her from above, and tear her to shreds from the sides all at once.

Let's put a magnifying glass on just one slice of time in her day: the rows in the table from 9:30 a.m. to 1 p.m. when she is taking the kids to the playground. As the table shows, a mother's day across columns 1 to 4 contains the workload of far more than one person. It is a job for three to four people. To understand her day, we must compress all four columns into one person's time and energy, just like a mother does.

Let's start with column 1. This is the column in which a mother is devoted pretty much entirely to caring for her baby. If she has a never-put-down baby who never sleeps, like Robbie, one 12-hour-plus stretch is spent literally holding the baby. It takes up every waking minute, and many of her sleeping ones. Even dressing/eating/showering is beyond her without the aid of the 'extra pair of hands' in column 3, or without leaving the baby to cry, which is torture and so not a viable long-term option, even if she were willing to leave a baby unattended for lengthy periods, which she probably isn't. If she does all the work in column 1, columns 2, 3 and 4 do not get done at all. Obviously, that is unworkable. She must drop some tasks from column 1 and pick up some from columns 2 to 4; or she must do more than one thing at once.

Which tasks should she drop and pick up, or do all at the same time?

Starting at 9:30 a.m., if we look horizontally across the columns, we see that she must leave the crying baby to roar while she chivvies the 18-month-old down the stairs as he protests that he wants to stop to inspect the grub on the leaf by the gate, and he tries to crush and eat the grub and she has to rescue it with one hand (not easy) and restrain him with the other (not easy), and she straps him into the car-seat as he struggles and frets and pulls the car wet-wipes out of their container and throws them on the floor. Then she must hurry back upstairs and carry all the paraphernalia she packed earlier for the outing down to the car while the baby cried and the toddler ran rampant: diaper bags, maybe a tricycle for the bike track and a tip-truck for the sandpit, and a ball, plus coats, gloves and scarf for toddler and herself if it's cold, her own tote-bag and perhaps a picnic blanket, snacks for the toddler, different snacks for her. Then she must go back upstairs and get the baby, who is still roaring. The baby needs a sudden diaper and clothing change; she changes the baby in a great hurry while the toddler starts to cry with anxiety down in the garage.

The mother is not an automaton. Her baby's anxiety at being left upstairs and her toddler's anxiety at being left downstairs generate anxiety in her, too. That anxiety is corrosive and exhausting. Nor is she doing this outing at a leisurely pace. She is forcing herself and the children to move with military determination because she knows she must be at the playground by 10 a.m. to leave in time for lunch and the early afternoon nap. She has little time to waste. Ceaselessly plumbing her own reserves to beat the clock all day hollows a mother out.

The baby howls as she straps him into the car. En route to the park, her baby will howl all the way, and the toddler will gripe and maybe cry and throw things unless she makes sure there is nothing for him to throw. On arrival, she must lug the stroller out of the trunk, erect it, de-load the crying baby from the capsule to the stroller, maybe put the stroller's sun- or rain-shade on, pack all the bags and coats in the stroller and wear the diaper bag as a backpack, strap on her valuables in a belt-bag, wedge the tip-truck into the stroller tray where it doesn't quite fit and it spills sand from yesterday's play session all over the coats and into the snack-bag, unpack the trike, and position them all ready to go for when she gets the toddler out of the car because she cannot let go of the toddler's hand at that point. She must lock the car while holding the toddler's hand, push the heavy stroller with one hand, push the trike with the other hand, lets go of the toddler's hand with strict instructions to the toddler to hold the rein attached to the stroller which she tries to make sound like a game while the toddler races away to chase a bird and she chases after him and pulls him back with a warning not to do that, and he does it again and she has to wangle the stroller out of the way of an oncoming car and retrieve the toddler at the same time, and she enforces the first warning by taking the heavy tip-truck out of the stroller with her one free hand and dragging the upset toddler back to the car with the other and unlocking the trunk and putting the truck back in the car as a deterrent to show she means it as she holds his hand the whole time, and together they all resume their painfully slow progress towards the playground. Every inch of the way, she must watch the toddler like a hawk to be sure he doesn't waft into the path of more cars. The baby is still howling, and the toddler is wailing about the loss of the truck.

At the park, she must either leave the baby to cry in the stroller while she helps the toddler on the play equipment and chases after him as he runs down by the lake and takes him to the bathroom, or she must hold the baby while she does all this. Holding the baby will take at least one hand, two hands when he wriggles or needs his eyes shaded from the sun, and two hands all the time until the baby is three to four months old if the baby will not lie horizon-tally. Supporting the toddler on the play equipment and wresting him back from the lake and helping him in the bathroom is also going to take two hands. Chasing after a runaway toddler is some-where between difficult and impossible when holding a baby. Add the dragging weight of holding a baby for any sustained length of time, especially if the baby cries if you sit down, as mine did, and the morning is looking grim.

Taking a toddler to the bathroom needs both a mother's hands. She must undo that tight button at the top of his trousers, help him undo the zipper, lift him onto the lavatory seat, tear paper off the roll several times with one hand (not easy) while steadying the child on the seat with the other, help the child down off the seat, pull up trousers that resist getting pulled up over hips and waist, tuck the top clothes in, pull up the zip and do that tough button back up, pull the toddler's sleeves back to keep them dry, turn the tap on, hoist a little person up to the basin, help them soap up with one hand while grappling to hold him horizontally in the air with the other hand and supporting him on her bent thigh while she stands on one leg, help him dry his hands, and wash her own hands.

But the whole time, her own hands have been occupied by the baby. To take the toddler to the bathroom, she must put the baby down in the stroller to cry. If the stroller will not fit into the restroom, she must leave the baby in the stroller outside, something that makes a mother extremely anxious. Someone may steal her bags from the stroller; a crow may come down and peck at the baby's eyes; someone may steal the baby. Anyone who tries to talk down a mother's work-load by belittling these concerns as over-protectiveness is dismissing a mother's most primal and exquisitely honed sense of vigilance. That vigilance is one of humanity's greatest capacities in action.

Come breastfeeding time, if her toddler is too young to play unassisted or is a habitual runaway, she must strap the toddler in the stroller for the duration of the feed. Some babies feed for as little as

10 or even five minutes. Robbie fed for as long as 50 minutes. Thirty-five minutes was his average. The shortest feed I could get away with was 20 minutes. Enduring a protesting toddler in a stroller for that long, while trying to entertain him with stickers or a toy that pales in comparison to the playground's pull, while calmly feeding a baby, is not feasible.

The alternative is to feed standing up while helping the toddler on the play gym and chasing after him down by the lake and taking him to the bathroom. Feeding while standing is uncomfortable at best for the great majority of mothers, and feeding while chasing after a toddler is impossible. A breastfeeding mother needs to sit down and back. Her shoulders cramp and hurt too much to hold a heavy baby to her bosom for long. She needs a hand free to drink water to slake the thirst that leaps on her as the baby draws milk.

While taking a toddler and baby to the park might look like a minimum two-person job, it is actually a job for three people, at least some of the time. It needs that extra pair of hands drawn from column 3 as a general aide. Mother 1 tends to the baby, and Mother 2 supervises the toddler. Mother 3, the extra pair of hands, washes the toddler's hands while Mother 2 lifts the toddler up to the bathroom basin with both arms. Mother 3 fixes snacks; takes bags and sporting gear to and from the car; fetches that much-needed cup of tea from the café and holds the baby so that Mother 1 actually gets to drink it; re-fills Mother 1's water bottle at breastfeeding time, and takes the toddler's discarded sweater from the play gym back to the bag while Mother 2 stops the toddler falling out of the play-castle turret; rinses out the bib the baby erped on while Mother 1 holds the baby; or fetches Mother 2's tea and relieves her on toddler supervision while she visits the bathroom herself as Mother 1 changes baby's diaper.

But the morning's work is not over. Let's move across to column 4, devoted to housework. While she is at the park from 9:30 a.m., our mother in column 4 is also at home, searching online for size

2 shorts and T's for the toddler, paying the data bill, searching for a hotel room for her visiting in-laws and calling to make enquiries and book a room, texting an RSVP to her friend's baby shower and making a search online for a shower gift, rinsing the soaking bibs and play-suits in the laundry and putting them in the washing machine, starting to clean out the refrigerator, and getting lunch waiting for herself and her children.

To avoid missing the afternoon nap, Mothers 1, 2 and 3 must race home from the park in time to fix lunch. That means a cumbersome repeat of the procession it took to get the kids out of the car and into the playground in the first place, with the added disincentive for the kids that it's time to go. I used to plan my exit from the park with a ruthless timetable. I left the park by 11:15 a.m. to get home by noon, while the baby cried the entire trip home. I launched myself into the lunch routine and then into the toddler's sleep routine, ideally by no later than 12:30 p.m. This last routine absolutely was not to be delayed beyond 12:50 p.m., or chances were the toddler would not sleep at all. That would mean the agony of no afternoon nap for me, and a further 36 hours of grumpy, unsettled toddler.

So from five minutes past midday to 1 p.m., according to table 2, Mother 1 is supposed to stand and hold a howling baby, and eat lunch. Mother 2 is supposed to get the toddler into the house, take the toddler to the bathroom, maybe bathe him and change him if he got sandy at the playground, speedily feed the toddler (and who ever speedily fed a toddler?), and get him down to sleep, itself a fraught process of book-reading and shoulder-patting that does not always end in the target of sleep. Mother 3 brings all the bags up from the car in two or three trips, and unpacks them and shakes the sand out of them, maybe vacuums the sand out of the car-seat and sponges the spilled milk off the seat and car floor, as well as helping bathe, change and feed the toddler, and also holds the crying baby while Mother 1 eats lunch. Mother 4, the housekeeper, clears away the lunch things and gets on with the laundry.

If we estimate that Mother 3 is occupied for half the time, then the 9:30 a.m. to 1 p.m. slice of a mother's day has been work for three-and-a-half people.

Entertain Us!

One day at eight months of age, when babies sit up and begin to play, Robbie made his way to the sofa where I lay wrecked with exhaustion. I had put him on the floor, a cute little blob among his toys, expecting that now he could sit up, he would play with them. To my vexation, he began to whine. He wanted me to play with him. I was appalled. You mean now he was no longer a cot-bound baby, I had to *entertain* him?

Children today do not play. At least, not by themselves. Robbie and Lachlan would play any game if Mommy played it too. If I left them to their own devices among their toys, they cried and whined and clung to my leg demanding play. Before I had children, I had expected to be available for my children, and to facilitate their play, and to occasionally join in, but not to be a permanent playmate. For a grown adult to spend literally every waking minute entertaining a child was, to me, madness.

To my bewilderment, it seemed most of my fellow parents didn't agree. They expected and accepted that their kids would need their involvement in play every second of the day. The parents I knew were often drained by all this, but not always, and not distressed. Not only did they seem unfazed by their children's demands for entertainment, they seemed to find it amusing. "Oh, it's different now," most parents said to me with a laugh, begging the question and waving away my despairing observation that kids won't play alone.

When I was a kid, I played non-stop. My mother said that apart from teaching me shapes and colors, she never really entertained me. I pottered in the chicken coop. I drew in my coloring books. I rolled my toy cars over roads in the sandpit. I galloped on my rocking horse. I stood on my head in the living room. I played with my dolls among the child-size dining setting and Welsh dresser my grandfather had made. I dug up lizard's eggs in the garden, and rolled down the hill. I rode high on my swing. As I grew older, I set up a show-jumping course with chairs and broomsticks in the backyard, and hurdled around it pretending to be a thoroughbred with glamorous pedigree names I made up. I threw a tennis ball with Ross, the boy next door, and we tore endlessly around the house playing cops and robbers. We climbed the mango tree and chatted about stuff. We gathered macadamia nuts from the tree in his yard, set them in cracks in the concrete and smashed them open with a hammer. As we got older, we walked to the corner store to buy candy. By then the chickens were gone, so we turned the coop into a fabulous cubby complete with flower gardens. We dressed up in fabric scraps from the sewing room of Ross's aunt who lived across the street. We lay on our backs in the grass and spotted dragons in the clouds. The grass made our backs itch, and we knew that that was the price of happiness.

It was not just me who knew how to play. All kids did. Nor was it the fact that as a girl, I might have been readier to throw myself back onto my own resources than a boy. Ross next door, my younger brother, the boys in the street, my male cousins, the boys at school, all entertained themselves, too. To kids, adults were just boring people who kept you safe and fed you and told you what to do sometimes.

I was born in 1966. Fast forward to 2003 and 2004 when my kids were born, and play had all but disappeared. My kids won't go outside in the garden. They won't doodle in their activity books. Those same toy cars of mine, plus many more of theirs, sit in their crate on the shelf. I have never seen them ride their rocking horse, or stand on their head. They only attended teddy tea-parties if I set up the picnic and poured the tea. They have never explored for lizard's eggs, and I have only seen them roll down a hill once. They rarely climb trees. Their father dismantled their timber cubby house due to lack of interest. They have almost never ridden their first, second or third skateboards. Their totem-tennis goes ignored. So does their golf set. One child builds with construction bricks sometimes, the other rarely does. The first in a series of mystery books for children which links to an interactive website is still unopened from several Christmases ago; in fact, I have come to expect that some of their Christmas gifts every year will not leave their shrink-wrap because the boys don't bother to open them. I lure them into a board game Saturday nights with a bowl of candy, but once the candy runs out, so does their interest. Jigsaw puzzles and brainteasers gather dust; so do the magic kit and the science kit. My kids would not even ride their bikes until they were about seven; they do now, but not with much enthusiasm or frequency.

Company was the antidote. My kids would not play alone, but would play with other kids. I joined three mom-and-bub social groups, and I visited with my own network of friends with kids. We gathered at one another's homes, in parks and playgrounds, and at museums and aquariums and puppet shows. Pretty much all of us were under the same type of entertainment duress. Getting the kids out of the house for an hour or two was our only relief.

As my kids graduated to elementary school, their ability to play alone did not improve much. My fellow school-moms and I frantically texted between ourselves to arrange playdates after school and in vacations. If we didn't, we were stuck with two choices—entertain the kids ourselves, or have them suck our souls dry with the complaint that they were "bored."

In my experience, apart from her baby's crying, the need to entertain her children is the single most crippling circumstance a mother faces today. It has arisen only in the last 20 years or so, as far as I can see. That feminism ignores this devastating intergenerational sea-change in mothers' lives is staggering. The need to entertain our kids wipes mothers out today in a way in which they presumably have not been wiped out before. Mothers desperately need research into this sudden development's causes, and research into solutions. Yet because mothering is women's experience, feminism won't come to her aid with that research.

Sleep(less)

Every moment that a mother is mothering, she is unutterably tired.

Mothers of young children don't just work all day; they work at night, sometimes all night. Not just for the first few months, unless they are lucky enough to have a baby that sleeps through. Possibly for years, certainly so if they have more than one child. For me, years of performing mothering work around the clock, mostly standing, 365 days a year almost without a single night's sleep, was a nightmare.

I was lucky, though, in that when Robbie turned 18 months old, he began to take a one-hour, 20-minute nap. To my boundless relief, this stretched out to two hours, then two hours, 40 minutes, as the months went by. By the time Lachie was out of babyhood, both boys often napped this long in the afternoon. Mercifully, mercifully, mercifully, they napped at the same time.

When they slept, so did I. After a couple of years of only broken sleep, and so little of it, an afternoon nap of two hours, 40 minutes was not enough. I needed five to seven hours. When the first child woke, I lay there in deep anguish, spinning out the seconds before I got up to extract maximum sleep value from each one. On a bad day, one child would wake after as little as 80 minutes. When that happened, I pushed myself off the bed in agonized despair, and launched back into the harsh routine of entertaining them, which mostly required me to stand up.

Much as I was deeply grateful for an afternoon sleep, sleep had a black side. It meant I got nothing done. Because my children demanded my attention every moment, every moment with them was an exile from my own life. My children's nap was my only freedom. To cast that freedom away to hurl myself into a different kind of oblivion, that of sleep, was itself cause for despair.

Incredibly, feminism denies that getting up throughout the night, for months or years in a row, is an obstacle to a woman putting in a full day's work like a man. Nor does feminism work to make society see a mother of young children as a Very Tired Person, and accommodate her accordingly—with a seat on the subway, say, or a go-to-the-head-of-the-waiting-list custom at the doctor's. Not only that, but feminism leaves the night-work to women. Were feminists the champions of equality they claim to be, they would have been shouting from the rooftops for men to meet an equal share of the night-shift. Instead, they stayed silent. Some men got up, some of the time. The majority of fathers I knew as late as the end of the first decade of the twenty-first century got up only on occasion, or not at all.

Certainly, there are times when a man should be allowed to sleep through. Any man with his own life or other people's lives in his hands—a bus driver, a construction worker at heights, a surgeon the night before an operation—needs full alertness. Most white-collar workers and many blue-collar workers, however, do not. No one insists that a mother of young children must sleep through the night to be rested for her paid work as an IT consultant or hairdresser or landscape gardener. Why should a man doing those same jobs be so lavishly excused from the ordeal of sleeplessness?

"Now They're in School You Can Go Back to Work"

As you may have noticed, despite all the tumult in a mother's life, we have only covered columns 1 to 4 of table 2. Until she also performs the career work in column 5, feminism locks a mother out of that coveted real estate of human experience, 'success'.

Our society likes to pretend that a mother is free to work once her youngest is in day care, or at the very latest, in school. Stay-at-home motherhood is an offensive state from which a woman must remove herself quick-smart. She is hounded back to work as soon as possible. Sooner than possible. Peer pressure is a near-irresistible force, and the mainstream media, which are overwhelmingly feminist, put peer pressure to formidable use, holding up the model of women who go back to work within a year, or six months, or even six weeks, as only to be expected.

Family and friends without children, and feminists with children, are then free to express critical surprise at a mother's 'prolonged' stay at home if she has a four-year-old and a two-year-old.

At lunch at a restaurant, our friends, child-free husband and wife John and Katia, looked across the table at me, while my boys, then two and four years old, went mad wrestling in a space beside our table (without upsetting the other diners).

"Are you working yet, Nat?" they asked.

I reacted with amazement and resistance. As it had so many times before, the difficulty of verbalizing a mother's workload to non-parent listeners cowed me.

"No!" I gasped. I had tended to crying babies or toddlers 365 days from before dawn until evening for four years. I had scarcely slept a night. I was not prepared to put the boys in care more than two days a week. On those two days, I hurled myself into a grueling morning routine to get them there. I cut my badly needed five to seven hours of afternoon nap down to two or three hours to collect them again, when I launched into the even more grueling afternoon and evening routine. By the time I left the day care center on those two mornings and got to a mall, it was 10 a.m. There I nodded over coffee, fearsomely sleepy in the middle of the morning, which is the high point on my body clock so things could only go downhill from there. From 10:30 a.m., I had 45 minutes before it was time to leave the mall at 11:15 a.m., to be home by 11:45 a.m., to make lunch and fling myself on the bed by 12:30 p.m. In those 45 minutes, I was supposed to live my entire life: run all my errands, clean the house, do the laundry, grocery-shop, see to all my household admin, exercise, eat right, and actually do something for me. And, according to the senseless feminist chronoscape, dovetail in a 40- or 50-hour paid working week, plus commute.

"No, I am not going back to work yet," was all I managed to say, and I tried to back this up with a facial expression that conveyed how impossible it would be to do so.

John's and Katia's faces tightened with disapproval. So did my then-husband's. He nodded in terse agreement with them that my at-home status made me a deadbeat, and shot them a meaningful glance of the 'You see what I have to put up with' kind.

"Loser," I could see them all thinking.

A paid job creates more work of its own. Now that she works, and if her children are too young for school, a mother must prepare them for day care. If she has a breastfed baby, she must express milk throughout the day at work, take a cooler bag to work and place it in the office freezer each morning and take the milk home at the end of the day when she must wash and sterilize all the pump's components (mine had 13 components to be washed individually), and wash out and re-freeze the cooler bag.

If the day care center does not provide meals, as mine didn't for the four-year-olds so they would be ready to handle their own lunch-boxes in the first year of school, she must make the kids' lunches, morning and afternoon snacks; sterilize and wash and make up formula bottles for younger kids; and pack a bag with diapers, two changes of clothes, water bottle, play-hat and sweater. In hot parts, center rules may demand she apply sunscreen to the child. Then she must make the journey to the day care center through peak-hour traffic, find a park, and get baby and wayward toddler into the building. Then she goes through the rigmarole of signing in, reading notices, and settling the children. She must place their news item in the news box, unpack their lunch into the fridge, and place morning and afternoon snacks in the appropriate tubs. Then she must peel crying kids off her legs. That primeval wrench of anguish at parting from their children that all good mothers feel can be one of the heaviest weights in a woman's day, but feminism says it is weightless.

If she has a child in school, she must journey on to school. If she has a child in high school, she makes a further journey to high school.

And into that impossibly overloaded morning, she must eat, dress, pack her work things, and get to the workplace.

She must also fit in personal grooming for work. She gets her hair cut and probably dyed, shaves or waxes her legs, paints toe- and finger-nails, shops for work clothes, takes work clothes to the dry-cleaner and picks them up again. Once I had children, I wore scarves over unwashed hair, used my blow-dryer twice in the first 13 years of motherhood, and let my hair grow long and the grey show. I wore knee-high leather boots or trousers almost every day of my life for the first seven years to hide my unshaved legs. After that, I gave up and went natural (and I am *not* the kind of woman who likes to do that). My toenails knew no polish until the kids were 10. Shopping for any kind of clothes, let alone work outfits, was out of the question. Until our kids were about eight, I suspect many moms at our elementary school were still wearing whatever was in the closet when our first child was born. Who can blame us?

Day care itself generates extra work. At my children's day care center, parents had to come up with a show-and-tell item for each child every week. Some weeks it was something easy, like a pretty stone your child had found. Other weeks, it took more work, like recording a CD. One week, I hand-drew and colored a beautiful big caterpillar we had found in the garden. It was black with orange spots. It was a lovely exercise to share with my son, but it took me about half an hour.

A mother may be drawn into the center's fundraising activities. She may volunteer to produce its annual profit-making wall calendar featuring the kids' artwork, liaises with the printer, and collects the monies from parents. She will make costumes for the Christmas concert, and attend it. She will write permission slips for excursions, draft asthma plans, write instructions to the staff for dispensing antibiotics for her three-year-old's infected cut, and answer requests for contributions like craft supplies or vegetable seedlings for the center's garden.

Feminism ignores all this extra impost on a woman's time.

To the matter of how children attend after-school activities when Mommy is at work, feminism has no solution, beyond an expensive nanny.

Take one of those after-school activities. A five-word task like 'take kids to swim class' looks simple when it's written on the page. But let's look at it for real. My kids whine and cry and moan about after-school swim class from the moment I pick them up at school until we get to the pool. As we get to the car after school, we discover one of them has left their school bag in the playground (who among us did that as a kid? No one!) and I chivvy them back to the schoolground to get it.

We're barely out of the car park before the car-screaming starts. I load CDs in a crazed attempt to mute their crying; they howl that they want a different CD. I refuse. They're screaming in protest about the song choice and going to swim class; I'm screaming in rage as we drive along.

Getting kids changed into swimmers is a brutal mission. My swim center is set in fields, with space to run and a football oval. It's great for the kids, but it generates exhausting searches for parents who traipse over the grounds and holler to kids to come into class, pushing up against the clock in a race to get the kids into their swimmers on time. Super-harried moms grapple with preschoolers in the change-rooms in a panicked few minutes before the start of class. Boys over six must use the men's change-rooms at the other end of the hall, so as Robbie turned six, I had to separate out his things, pack him off to that room and hope he didn't drop them en route, get Lachie changed in the women's rooms and then rush down to supervise Robbie from outside the door of the male change rooms. I learned the hard way that if I didn't do a surreptitious sweep of the male change-room as he left, he might leave his new swimmers behind.

Three times I left their school shoes behind, and had to make the 90-minute roundtrip back to the pool to get them. How did I do this three times, and not just once? Because they have so much stuff, typically five bags of it: a bag of swim gear, a bag of clothes to change into with maybe extra stuff like their coats spilling out of it, a bag for shoes (flip-flops to wear at the swim center, heavy formal black school shoes in the bag coming home), a bag of snacks and a flask of coffee for me and an apple for the horses in the field next door, my handbag (usually dragging off my shoulder with the weight of a book because the half-hour swim class was a rare chance to read) plus my coat and umbrella and a ball for the kids to kick while they waited for class to start. I always put their school shoes out of sight under the bench as they're expensive and tempting to thieves, and in the overwhelm of all that stuff, that's how I overlooked them.

Going home meant a harrowing reverse search of the grounds to round up kids who had rocketed out of class into the fields, and the unrelenting chivvy-trip to get them to the car. At home, I unload all the gear as the kids complain about helping me carry it to the house in three or four trips, where I hoist two clothes-horses out to the balcony to hang the swim-gear out. I rinse the chlorine out of the swim-gear first in the bathroom.

It is already past eating time. I launch into cooking, serving and eating dinner, cleaning up, bath routine, homework, bed routine.

Bath is a double burden of physical and mental debilitation. The physical is bending down to draw water, leaning into untenable positions to soap the kids up, the battle of drying and getting baby powder and pajamas on a wriggling body. The mental is the fortitude it takes to endlessly harry a child into the water, and to answer his philosophical bath-time questions when I badly need a reprieve from the day's demands. Then I do it all again with the second child.

Next, we launch into homework. Even my kids' early-years homework was taxing. I could not always understand the questions, which was frustrating for all of us. It needed active work from me, despite assurances from the school that homework was just about repetition of skills learned in class, and that children should complete it independently. I found myself under intense pressure to stop the homework before it was done, to give the kids time to wind down and enjoy themselves before bed. Giving into that pressure was a luxury I couldn't afford, although I sometimes did anyway. It meant too much homework rolled over to the next evening. If I had also given into that pressure the previous evening, we would have even more too much homework to do tomorrow night.

Watching TV, my kids ask for cut-up fruit, and before bed, hot milk. Just before 9 p.m. we brush teeth, another mini-military campaign of pushing them to the bathroom, setting a good example of brushing their teeth for them thoroughly so they will take it over themselves properly when the time comes, seeing to it that they rinse, not swallow. Then doing it again with a second set of teeth.

After that, it's bedtime. The magic of books melds with the frustration of kids who dislike that story, or can't understand it and need parts explained over and over, or who want a second and third story. Kids want to chat when Mommy is beside herself many times over with exhaustion, like a strew of Russian dolls ripped out of their housing and stomped on. Kids won't sleep, and re-appear in the living room 10 minutes later.

Only after the mammoth evening routine is done and the kids are in bed am I free to tend to the general housework, and to my own and the kids' administration—the e-mails, the forms to fill in, the phone calls, checking the school's app for daily announcements, the one-off household chores. But it is already past my bedtime.

Even if we end the day at 9:35 p.m. and I leave many household tasks undone, a typical afternoon/evening routine for me lasts from 12:30 p.m. (when I start dinner preparations) until 9:35 p.m. That is a total of just over nine hours, more than the standard eight-hour day worked by a man. If I didn't let my kids onto computer screens, I would also have to entertain them, adding many extra hours to the day. And that is only the afternoon rush; it doesn't count the before-school morning rush that jolts a mother to her bones, or all the errands she will do in the post-school-run morning.

This nine-hour afternoon work session is only part of what a mother is likely to handle every afternoon, however. If she has one, two or more children, she may ferry the kids to one, two or even more after-school activities, with all the gear that may entail: training shorts and T-shirt, mouthguard, socks and football boots for one child, tennis racquet, sporting cap and balls for another, plus snacks and sunscreen for each child in a separate bag, and any notes associated with that week's game like an enrolment form for the one-off coaching clinic the weekend after next. I know moms who fit in separate after-school classes for three children on one day.

A school mother's afternoon/evening marathon pales into a leisurely saunter if she has a baby and/or toddler alongside her school-age kids. Splice all the baby-work and toddler-work in columns 1, 2, 3 and 4 from table 2 with the over-packed afternoon/evening routine of an elementary schooler like my swim class regime above, and it seems inconceivable that we could ask an individual woman to take on so much.

All mothers with more than one child must overlay their school-kid system onto their baby and/or toddler systems, until the youngest is in school. Given most mothers have a gap of at least two years between children, most moms with more than one child will run a dual toddler/school system for at least two years. For women with more than two kids, or a bigger gap between children, they can be running this dual or triple baby/toddler/school system for many years. When all the kids are in elementary school, at least her system telescopes down to one school, albeit with more than one child to manage. Then, however, one child progresses to high school, and she scopes back out to a dual system across two schools.

To shoulder this titanic daily schedule, a mother needs to draw on a deep well of leisure in the middle of the day. It is her only chance for rest. Unlike a man, she has no early mornings, no evenings, no weekends, no holidays. Until her youngest is in school, she has not a single second's leisure, unless her husband relieves her of child care, which he may only do for short periods like a night at the movies with the girls, if at all. When her kids are all in school, she can only access that middle-of-the-day leisure in term-time; she is on duty 24/7 during school vacation. Depending on what country you live in, school vacation is around 12 to 16 weeks, or around one-quarter to almost one-third of the year.

Yet most at-home mothers I know do not take that sorely needed leisure in the middle of the day. In school hours, just about every non-working mother goes at a hurried clip, beset by errands, personal administration, and routine chores. Besides that, they help with weekly classroom literacy groups, or volunteer to supervise the class excursion to the planetarium, or sit as treasurer on the school bazaar committee. In fact, most at-home mothers *almost never sit down*.

Mothers Suck

To all a mother's eye-popping toil, feminists hold up a scorecard of zero. They assert that a woman is free to overlay a full-time paid career on it all. And when she does, feminists call her mangling schedule 'liberation'. What it really is, is extermination. Working that life, I sure don't feel liberated. I feel brutalized and punished and *disempowered*. Feminism is a ruthlessly disempowering force, for all the empowerment that it brings. It embeds mother-erasure into its core. Scarcely any woman can cope with a feminist timetable. And why should she?

We seem to like to believe that because a mother's love for her children is horizonless, her capacity to soak up the rage, the exhaustion, the ceaseless forced labor is horizonless, too. That gives society carte-blanche to tip hundreds of hours per week of child care and housework down the sump which is a mother's life. And then feminism tries to tip another 40- to 50-hour paid week plus commute down that drain, too. A woman's nature is limitless so her time and energy must be too, right?

As every mother knows, that is not true. A woman's nature might be limitless, but her time, energy and capacity for pain are finite. When she has to put up with a child crying, it is as painful to her as it is to everyone else. More painful because, unlike everyone else, she puts up with it every time the child cries, which could be every hour of her life, and unlike everyone else, she has to do something about it. When she foregoes sleep in 60-minute blocks three times a night for many months in a row to breastfeed, including when she most deeply needs it around 4 a.m., she feels as strung out as anyone else would. When she is deprived of a weekend and seven evenings and seven mornings a week, 52 weeks a year, for years on end, she is as zombified as anyone else would be. Society likes to pretend that mothers are biologically programmed to turn into some kind of worker-bee sub-species upon childbirth, genetically engineered to soak up suffering and the workload of two, three, four or more people with no trouble. But it isn't true. Mothers are not just drones in the hive. They are human beings.

One of feminism's most central tasks was to make women's experience as mellifluously, subtly, thoroughly and monumentally understood as men's experience already is. Every person on the planet had a mother. Every one of us relied on her for the first 20 or so years of life, or on someone who stood in for her. It behooves every single one of us—men, women without children, and kids themselves as much as they can—to have a solid grasp of the travails motherhood entails. Perhaps no one can understand a mother's love except another mother, but everyone should be able to comprehend its workload. Yet under feminism, no one has to grasp it. Everyone is not just entitled to remain ignorant of a mother's super-size contribution, but actively encouraged to be so.

Incredibly, a lot of that ignorance is right inside the mother's marriage or partnership. Almost every woman can tell tales of men's outrageous dismissal of the mega-loads their wives and partners face. My fellow school-mom, Jane, has three children, the oldest 15. She manages them across both an elementary school and a high school. When I casually mentioned men's blindness to mother-work one afternoon outside the school gate, she replied with ironic calm, "Oh yes. My husband thinks I have been on a 15-year holiday."

By shunting motherhood off to a parallel universe, not only has feminism stifled awareness of motherhood among men and in society at large. It keeps women who are yet to have kids ignorant of what's coming, too. For most mothers, that first child is a shock. It shouldn't be. It defies belief that motherhood, humanity's most universal experience (in that everyone had a mother), an experience that is wholly female, and women's most confounding and all-consuming experience, is hidden from women themselves by a movement that so vigorously defines itself as a friend of woman.

Once they become parents, mothers fare no better. Feminism turns its back on them in a very successful effort to mute mothers' vocalization of their experience. You would think that a pro-woman movement would bring the whole subterranean and unarticulated story of motherhood into the light for the first time in history by filling books and websites and TV shows and radio programs with its truth. However, when I was pregnant with Robbie in 2002, my bookstore stocked just one book on what motherhood was like. There were lots of pregnancy manuals, as if labor were the biggest hurdle, and a few mothercraft manuals about rashes and weaning, but next to nothing about motherhood's vast reality from the mother's point of view. This is astonishing, given that the majority of women are going to be, or are, or have been mothers at some stage in their lives.

I read that single book on motherhood, but it went in one ear and out the other. Like most non-parents, I lacked ears to hear, and feminism saw to it that I never grew them.

It was not until around 2008, some 30 years after the masculinist brand of feminism took over women's reality in earnest, that the mommy-blogosphere gave mothers a voice. For the first time, mothers slipped out from under feminism's oppressive silence and poured out motherhood's humor and horror in all its blazing detail. For the first time, mothers-to-be had a window into the parallel universe.

Even with all the fabulous feisty mommy-bloggers telling it like it is, though, the blogosphere has only made a dent in feminism's silence. Bloggers don't control mommies' place in society; feminists do. And whether it's the rigidly anti-woman timetable of the workplace; our social customs like the one that lets airline passengers get away with saying "Why doesn't she shut that baby up?" instead of offering to nurse the ever-crying baby; or our urban planning that ignores the need for public breastfeeding rooms, the feminist-perpetuated ignorance of motherhood still reigns.

The Real World

Motherhood is the planet's number one job, for three reasons.

Firstly, a mother works many, many more hours than anyone else. The person who works 275 to 307 hours per week (see table 1) in their paid job has never existed.

Secondly, those hours are more demanding than any paid job's. That is not to dismiss paid work's unique demands. Satisfying a customer is not easy. Nor is working outdoors in extreme heat or cold, as many men do, and some people, especially men, risk life and limb in the course of their job. That unique heroism on his part deserves our unflinching regard. However, except when a worker is risking their health or their life, paid work is just paid work. It can be stressful, but at the end of the day, all you have to do is satisfy your customer enough to make them buy your product or service. There is only so much that commercial activity can ever scoop out of you.

Not so motherhood. Motherhood draws on a woman to the limits of her being and *beyond*. Motherhood demands a super-humanity of her. It demands, no less, that she walk with God. Being invited by God to stand shoulder to shoulder with Him/Her to create humanity is the greatest privilege a human being can know, and it is a privilege to which only mothers have complete access. She gets to know God's love, not just as a recipient like everyone else, but as a giver. No one loves like a mother. In fact, a mother gets to shape a human soul even beyond God's power, for God delegates a lot of that immense soul-shaping power to her. Despite the privilege of walking with God—no, because of it—motherhood is the hardest job there is. Keeping pace with God is no walk in the goddamn park.

Thirdly, a mother's work is *more* important than that of anyone in the paid workplace, not *less* important. Paid workers just shape a piece of the economy or state. A mother shapes a soul.

Feminists say that if motherhood is something women do, then motherhood is demeaning. And motherhood *is* demeaning, or at least it can be. It can be drudgery. It can be tormenting and annihilative. A lot about motherhood sucks, at least for a good many mothers, at least some of the time. Motherhood might inflict many kinds of loss on a woman, but it is a task of which a woman can feel more proud than any human being can be proud of anything. A mother's self-renunciation is noble. Motherhood might suck, but mothers never do.

Feminists love to pretend that the formerly all-male world of commerce and government is the 'real' world, but they are wrong. Commerce and government is there to serve the realer realm of people, of families, of communities, of citizens, of life outside work. That realm of people is created and cultivated primarily by mothers, so that it may be lived in by us all, men, women and children. Motherhood is not some dispensable part of the world's daily affairs. It is the very source of the world's daily affairs. Motherhood is not only real, but hyper-real. Motherhood is a meta-reality that lies underneath and outside and above the reality of everyone else. Mothers know reality in a way that no one else knows reality. Theirs is the realest world of all.

3

"Get a Cleaner"

Putting the 'Work'
Back in Housework

"GET A CLEANER" IS FEMINISTS' response to women who try to articulate the daily demands of housework. What a contemptuously disingenuous thing for feminists to say.

Every woman knows that a cleaner is only part of the answer to the challenge of running a home. Every feminist knows how much work running a home is, but because housework is women's work, feminists pretend housework doesn't exist. 'Housewife' since the onset of the feminist era has been a byword for a failed human being. A word that used to mean 'a woman who runs a home' now means 'imbecile'. A housewife in feminists' eyes is weak, incompetent, unintelligent. Under-utilized. Un-self-actualized. Bored, and boring.

A housewife attracts sneers. Not from men, so much. From other women. "What do you *do* all day?" feminists ask in insulting mock-wonderment of the relatively rare woman who dares stay home today. Feminists avert their eyes from the genuine idleness of a man who may do next to nothing at home, but are masters at spotting the fictional idleness of the housewife.

A woman at home is not anything like as idle as feminism pretends. When I caught up for dinner with my old colleague and friend, Adrienne, a former marketing practitioner, she was in her early forties, with two elementary schoolers and one preschooler. She had not returned to work.

When I asked her how she spent her time when the kids were in day care, she groaned with resigned exasperation. "What do I do? I don't know how to explain it. What *don't* I do?" she replied. "There is always something. Today I was getting a tree in our garden cut down that threatened to fall."

Adrienne is right. There is always 'something' for housewives to do, but putting that 'something' into words is not easy. It is easy to put men's work into words. Men's work is visible. It has clear boundaries. He starts work when he shows up at the office, and stops when he leaves. Everyone accepts that when a man or a woman is at a paid job, he or she is working. We may not be familiar with every single task performed by, say, an auto tire factory manager, or a bakery health and safety officer, but we don't have to be to know and accept that the men and women in those positions are engaged in legitimate work. Even if he is not working very hard, such as when he is at a business lunch, or if his workload fluctuates so that at times he is only working at 75 percent capacity, we still give him a full 100 percent credit for working.

No such legitimacy attaches to running a home. Housework is hard to pin down. It's a kind of wallpaper with fewer clear edges, achievements and objectives than a man's work. No small portion of a housewife's work is repetitive 'maintenance'. Maintenance tends to be visible only when it isn't done. The place only looks a mess when she hasn't tidied.

A man's work, on the other hand, is more likely to be 'production' than 'maintenance'. He creates something that wasn't there before. For example, a man who pours the bitumen on a new road for the Roads department can point to the asphalt and say, "I poured that today." We can all nod appreciatively and be thankful that, yesterday, we didn't have a road, and today, thanks to his industry, we do. A housewife, however, points to our swept and mopped floor, upliftingly free of unhygienic stains, dust mites and crunchy bits underfoot, and we shrug. All she has done is maintain a pre-existing situation and stopped it deteriorating further. So we have a clean floor, we think. We had a clean floor last week, too (after she cleaned it last week). Who cares? Her work has got us no further ahead. A job that produces identifiable progress is more likely to win our admiration than one that only keeps us from going backwards.

Much of what a housewife does every day is anonymous. Some of her work is clear enough: say to someone, "I washed the walls today" and they know what you have done. However, a myriad of household tasks have no name. When challenged to justify her work to men or feminists, the housewife fumbles and stutters and sighs in the near-impossible task of communicating the complex and very real demands of running a household that tie her up much of the day.

Feminists put this inexpressibility to good use to pretend house-work doesn't exist. As it happens, most of the household tasks that do have a name are ones that can readily be palmed off to a cleaner (assuming a woman can afford one, and many of us cannot, or can better save or spend our income on other things). Discrete tasks like 'cleaning the bathroom', 'vacuuming the living room' and 'stacking the dishwasher' are all things that a cleaner can take over.

But many of the tasks with no name, I must do myself. Dropping the history magazines back to my neighbor after she lent them to my kids, and taking them back home again when she is not there, and trying again a second time later that day; running the quilts to the laundromat at the end of winter, and going back to pick them up; sorting through the kids' clothes at the end of the season, making a list of what they need for the coming season, running around the stores and shopping online and making bids online for those items and going to the post office three times to collect the parcels of pur-chases, getting the kids to try the new stuff on before I take the tags off and returning the stuff that does not fit or that they dislike to the store and shopping for replacements and repeating the try-on exercise with the new clothes, packing up last season's outgrown gear and taking some to the charity store, listing some on eBay, giving some away to friends with younger children—none of these tasks can be done by a cleaner, except maybe the laundromat visit if the cleaner is also a concierge.

Men's faces slip into a weird kind of unresponsive demeanor when a woman tries to convey to him how much work she is doing at home. It seems to be a conversation men think they can't have. Not 'can't have' as in uncomfortable, but 'can't have' as if the recognition that women have lots of housework to do is congenitally beyond them. That is because it *is* congenitally beyond them.

Sit around any coffee table with women, and you will hear complaints about men's blindness to housework—the stay-at-home dad who didn't know he had to report his sick daughter as absent to her school and so the mom gets a call at work from the school, the dad who played with the kids all Saturday but who had nothing ready for dinner, the husband who ran the warm-wash laundry through a cold cycle and shrank his partner's best woolen skirt, the dad who took his kids to the supermarket but could not compute his wife's instructions to hand in last week's grocery receipts to collect the free-toy-with-purchase from the service desk promised to anyone who spent $100 at the store, and so the kids missed out on the toy and harangued their mother to go collect it next day. Some women tell these tales in tones of condescending amusement or amazement, others in irritation or disgust.

Men's blindness to housework is a lamentable shortcoming. It would be inexcusable were it not hard-wired into them. What *is* inexcusable is feminists' wholesale exploitation of it to pretend housework does not exist.

Housework-blindness in men was God's gift to feminists. It suited their masculinizing agenda perfectly. It was a launch-pad from which to propel women into a full-time job alongside men, without having to pay heed to the job she already had running a home. When husbands made light of their wives' housework, and male employers didn't ever bother to accommodate it into workplace timetables, feminists cried to them in triumph, "You're right! She does nothing! You don't need to take any account of her home-running duties, because she doesn't have any. What a waste of space she is. You bad men have been keeping her at home in limbo, but now she is going to come to work alongside you. At last, she'll be gainfully employed in real work just like you!"

Feminists used to kind of recognize housework, to begin with. You may be old enough to remember the days when feminists called a woman's domestic workload the 'second shift'. It is hard to believe they could get away with so openly dumping a second load of work onto women and telling them they were 'liberated', but get away with it they did. If you're younger, you may not be aware that women in the 1980s and '90s, beladen under that double yoke of paid and unpaid responsibilities, used to laugh about it. "I need a wife, ha ha ha!" is what they used to say. They said this gaily, in a tone of cheery abandon, as if they would never dream of expecting a workplace schedule that accommodated housework, or husbands who pulled their domestic weight.

In fact, their preposterous double load seemed to afford them a perverse pride. It was as if a society that derided their contribution as housewives, prevented their access to a workplace timetable that allowed them time to make that contribution, and punished them with an additional paid job before it would validate them as acceptable human beings, was a society that treated them well. And that is exactly what feminists did think, and still think today. To perform the women's work of running a home is to be a failure, they believe. The only way to resurrect a woman from this state of failure, feminists say, is to make her do the paid work a man does and to delete her unpaid contribution from society's ken.

Home Ground: Why Homes Matter

Like most single mothers and many partnered ones, I cannot afford a cleaner. If the house is going to be clean, it's up to me. Whether I like cleaning or not, I don't want my children to live in an under-organized, under-cleaned home. But they do.

Despite my best efforts, a broken printer has sat for two years on the sideboard in the foyer because, as a single mother, I lack time to repair it. My car is parked permanently outdoors, because ever since moving in to this home three-and-a-half years ago at the time I write these words, I lack the time to make space in the garage for it. The place is messy. Dead flies dropped by the spiders in the cornices litter the floor, and as the spiders ate them, dark fly-juice dripped on the skirting boards. The walls have dirty marks. I am writing these words through a screen covered in dust.

I feel like I live in a state of semi-permanent semi-squalor. Apparently, I don't, at least according to the 14-year-old Indian boy down the road, Vivek. He is prone to making grandmotherly statements that sound charmingly incongruous coming from a strapping adolescent boy. "Oh, Mrs. Ritchie!" he exclaimed one day in his booming accent. "You are the only person in the street with a clean house!"

That everyone else lives in disarray worse than mine suggests our society is not living well. Beauty is essential to the spirit. A house of appealing rooms is one of life's most valuable pleasures. More than that, it is one of life's greatest *empowerments*. Homes, when clean and nicely decorated, radiate brightness, competence, possibility. They are a springboard to a higher place. They are a crucible for creativity, self-development, self-compassion, adventures both real and imagined. They are the place where we go deep into ourselves to revel in solitude's depths and heights, and where we experience the rich give-and-take of the company of friends, family and neighbors. Beautiful homes are both a departure point for discovering all these good things, and our arrival point when we have successfully journeyed through all these good things.

Feminism pours scorn on the primacy of a home in women's lives. A career is the overriding source of motivation, stimulation, and fulfillment in a woman's life, it says, not a beautiful home. Yet that is not the case for the majority of my female friends and colleagues. They go into the kind of raptures over a new line of removable wallpaper or strings of powder-pink bunting that I have never seen them exhibit about the latest sales figures or collaborative worksheet in the office. Taking delight in decorating, whether it's matching a vase to a gorgeous bunch of tulips, or playing with a rainbow of paint sample tags for a bedroom refresh, or sifting through a swag of modish fabric swatches to give a facelift to that armchair you inherited from your aunt—these are all sources of motivation, stimulation, and fulfillment for a good many women, just as career can be, and often much more so than career.

Maintaining a beautiful home is a form of deep *power* for many women. It is a power unique to women, mostly. Yet precisely because it is woman-power, feminists say home-making's joys count for nothing. Oh, really? If a woman doesn't care for 48-piece dessert sets or milk-washed sideboards, why isn't Martha Stewart's business a flop? If a woman cares nothing for a spiffily organized junk drawer any more, how come we soak up books, DVDs, apps and TV segments about decluttering? If home and hearth are so dispensable to us all, why do we pore over countless magazines, websites and blogs devoted to funky linoleums, metallic paint finishes, and verandah kitchens? And if swish pencil canisters and 64 ways with Mason jars are beneath us, what is everyone doing on Pinterest?

Of course, not every woman likes engaging with her home. For some of us, domesticity is just a drag. The last thing we'd want to do is go back to the days when society told a woman she 'should' keep a show-home, and that she 'should' find keeping house to be the pinnacle of life satisfaction.

What we need to do away with, however, is feminism's put-down of the home. Left to our own devices, few of us would genuinely disdain the value of the work we do as housewives, whether or not we actually enjoy it. However, we're not left to our own devices. Feminism inserts itself between us and our respect for our own connection to home-running, and tries to force us apart. Virtually every woman I have ever met diminishes the worth of her housework and under-calculates her housework-hours, to a greater or lesser degree, because she is swayed by feminism's discrediting of it. Many of my fellow school-moms, friends and female colleagues dramatically under-furnish their week's timetable with enough hours to get the housework done, and allot a booming over-supply of hours to their paid work, when I know those particular women well enough to know they do not need the money, and would rather devote their time to home-running than to work.

Even those women who hate housework, and there are plenty of us, want to have it in hand. "I need to feel on *top* of the housework," said my friend, Sharonne, a permanently harried stay-at-home mother of three very active preschoolers. She needs time to get that work done. And time is something feminism is resolutely out to deny her when it tries to push her into work. Pulling strength and a sense of accomplishment from a well-run household is a kind of empowerment that the great majority of my female friends and fellow school-moms want, whether or not they enjoy the actual housework. It's a power feminism does not want them to have, because it's a uniquely female power. Feminism only wants women to experience the kind of power a man possesses, the kind that derives from the workplace.

Housework sits more or less in the back seat of life. It is qualitatively different to paid work, which makes it formidably easy for feminists to dismiss housework as inferior to paid work. Because much of a woman's work takes place in the private setting of home, which we think of as a place of repose, beauty and serenity, it is all the easier for an insidious interpretation of housework as 'leisure' to creep in. The public setting where men work is seen as the opposite of these things. It is seen as a place of action, travail, utilitarian surrounds, aggravation and effort. He ventures out into the unforgiving world of work, with its taxing demands on his energy and skills and time, while she 'stays behind' and 'doesn't work'. Her housework carries zero credit points. If a housewife does venture out into the public world, it is to somewhere seen as equally cushy, like the shopping mall or the park. Our society filters out the grievous effort required to make these outings with crying babies and intractable toddlers in her care. All that is left is a picture of ease.

What makes it even more challenging to offset the perception that her housework is 'leisure' is that it may indeed be spliced with leisure. She is both 'off-duty' in her own home and 'on-duty' running that home, at the very same time. She may be putting the new Roman blinds up in the dining room ('work'), but enjoying doing it ('leisure'). That opens her up to accusations that she has it too easy. A man works at work so she should too, her attackers say.

The right response to them is that a woman should be entitled to enjoy housework, as much as a man is entitled to enjoy his paid work. No one accuses a man who enjoys his work of 'not working'.

Of course, housework is by no means always easy or enjoyable. It is menial and dirty and tiring and unrelenting. That gives it all the more dignity. Domestic tasks destroy us women to a degree, yet we do them willingly, and maybe extremely unwillingly at the same time. To step forward every single day of the year into a routine that prunes us back takes deep fortitude. To use another couple of metaphors, a housewife ploughs herself back into the soil, 365 days per year, to build the foundation on which everyone's lives rest, including her own life. A well-run home is the rock on which we all live. Her housework is below-the-line so that everyone else may live above the line. She steps down into the dark so that everyone else may be elevated into the light. That demands profound respect.

Menial it certainly can be, but housework can also be wonderful. It can be blissful to float clean sheets onto a bed in a sunlit room; to shop for glam picture frames to match the sleek white modernist chair in your hallway; to sprinkle pomegranate water on a freshly vacuumed carpet. Even housework's more mundane tasks can be rich and rewarding. To fold the laundry; to spritz-clean the mirrors; to whirl away the fuzz from the blinds with a lambswool duster—all can provide a double satisfaction in both the execution and the result. Feminism loves to pretend that only a career brings satisfaction, but it is not true. Housework, at least for some women some of the time, can be satisfying, too. It can be both less nourishing than career in some ways, and more so in others. Add in the power a housewife gains by being in her own home, her own life, working to her own schedule, free of career stresses, and housework can easily be a higher experience, not a lower one, than career.

Housework: Counting It Up

I have two problems with feminists' advice to get a cleaner. Firstly, a weekly cleaner is not with me the other six days. Even on the day the cleaner comes, I still have plenty of routine chores to do. Feminists won't admit this.

Secondly, I estimate that a weekly cleaner does only about 15 percent of all the work I perform in the home (and that's just the housework; that's not counting the fearsome motherload of directly tending to the kids). The cleaner does not go buy colored hairspray for my kids' end-of-term 'crazy hair day' at school Tuesday, or stay home to let in the plumber Wednesday, or shop for a new bed for the three-year-old on Thursday, or drop by the car wash Friday. In the logic-compressing way feminists have of assigning all these actions into one hermetically sealed hour with a cleaner, they pretend those tasks disappear. Incredibly, they have been getting away with this.

To show up feminists' 'get a cleaner' line for the anti-woman whitewash that it is, here in the pages below is a snapshot of the tasks I did at home in the past few months. Some are routine, and need to be done daily, weekly, annually, or from time to time. A good many, like Adrienne's tree-lopping mentioned earlier, fall into what I think of as the 'Tasks with No Name' category. Some are errands outside the home. Others are tasks of communication, planning and organization that I call 'Admin'.

I have left out gardening as many people live in an apartment today, but if you live in a house, you will know that even a fashionably 'low-maintenance' garden is work. And of course, if you live in an apartment you own, you will almost certainly have some building management responsibilities.

Back in chapter 2, in column 4 of table 2, I measured all my hours spent on housework in a household with two adults and two children. That column contained all the routine and one-off chores like cooking, cleaning and laundry, errands, administration, planning for festivities and social occasions, and 'tasks with no name'. It incorporates household tasks generated by the kids' presence like toys to pack away, medical appointments to make, or trips to the mall to buy new sneakers for them, but not any work spent directly on child care.

As you can see, I tallied my housework to 14 hours and 20 minutes per day. That's on a weekday. Allowing five hours for housework on a weekend day (mostly meal and snack preparation and clean-up), I reckon that I do 81 hours and 40 minutes every week on home-running. That is more than twice a man's paid workload of 40 hours. As I said in chapter 1, I both do and don't do that many hours. I double the hours up with child care tasks, or stuff them into too-short time periods, or skimp on them, or leave them undone and put up with the ramifications of that. The point is, there are 80-plus hours of housework to be done which, if we were resourcing a woman's job in the unpaid workplace with all the care we lavish on a man's job in the paid workplace, we would acknowledge and plan for.

Daily

Here are the routine daily housework tasks that I performed yesterday. I was a lot busier than this, for I have left out any weekly/monthly/annual/one-off tasks I did. I list those further on. This list of daily tasks excludes directly entertaining or engaging with the kids, but includes preparation of kids' meals, and administering their lives:

~ turn heater on, open curtains in five rooms

~ guinea-pigs: cut up spinach, carrot, apple, parsley and celery and take it to them; remove their overnight covering; put gloves on, shake out their blanket, refresh their hay

~ make school lunches x two: defrost bread from the freezer, make sandwiches; wrap crackers; wrap muffins; peel and cut up carrot sticks; pack fruit; fill water bottles

~ make breakfast for myself and eat it in a rush standing up, while hurtling around the house tending to children's demands

~ make children's breakfast. Children spill milk on table and floor. Run hot soapy water and wipe spill from table; fetch separate dishcloth I keep for the floor and wipe floor. Rinse cloths and take floor cloth to the laundry where I keep it away from the kitchen so it doesn't get mixed up with the dishcloths.

~ clear the counter and table of breakfast things; wipe them down

~ feed tropical fish; stick hand down into tank to remove catfish's daily cucumber stick which is weighed down with a fork; add anti-algae treatment to the water; cut new cucumber stick and lower that into the tank

~ turn off the children's computers if they forget (which the youngest almost always does)

~ as my rented home does not have a dishwasher, clear last night's full draining rack and hand-wash this morning's dishes

~ make beds

~ water house-plants

~ tidy entire house (which can take a long time with young children)

~ make lunch

~ tonight is Chinese fried rice; at 1 p.m., cook rice and spread on trays to dry

~ check e-reader is charged for this afternoon's soccer run

~ at 2 p.m., get the makings of dinner ready: cut vegetables, put pans on the stove waiting, get ingredients out (soy and oyster sauce, peanuts), place out a bowl ready to whip eggs

~ set table

~ clean guinea pig hutch: roll up soiled newspaper on bottom floor of hutch, sweep hutch, lay fresh newspaper, empty soiled hay and newspaper lining from top-floor cubby hole (they live in a two-storey palace), sweep cubby, shake out blanket square, re-line cubby with fresh newspaper and hay. Walk down the street and squat with the garden shears to cut them a bucket of grass from a wild patch by the side of the road (grass is their favorite food, good for them, and it saves money buying greens).

~ pack afternoon snacks for kids and different snacks for me and soccer gear (shorts, tops, shin-guards, soccer boots, track-top) and water bottles for boys' soccer class; also pack warm coat for me, and picnic rug as there is nowhere to sit at the field, and e-reader

~ have cup of tea and something to eat before boys arrive home at 3:50 p.m.; hurl them out the door to get them to soccer training in the next suburb over by 4 p.m. Feed them snacks in the car.

~ on our return, start cooking dinner

~ bring the garbage wheelie-bin in from the sidewalk

~ fill in a permission slip for an athletics carnival; show my son the slip is in his bag and remind him to hand it in

~ check e-mails while progressing dinner; make notes of tasks to action arising from the e-mails

~ clear this morning's dried breakfast dishes from the draining rack

~ call youngest to unpack his lunchbox and water bottle from his school-bag (I have done this every school-day for years now). Empty children's lunchboxes.

~ serve dinner. Stand up four times during dinner to get children a glass of milk, a second helping each, and a cloth to mop up a spill.

~ clear the plates

~ make and serve dessert; clear the dessert dishes

~ wash up lunch and dinner dishes

~ feed tropical fish again

~ turn lights on (three lamps in living room, two lights in dining room, two in kitchen, one on my desk)

~ at night in winter, cover guinea pigs with a blanket square in their cubby hole. Cover hutch with a sheet to stop drafts.

~ take shower; wash hair. No time to blow-dry hair, even though my hairstyle needs it.

~ make cup of herbal tea. Sit down.

~ children demand more snacks. Get up and cut up fruit for them.

~ before bedtime, make cup of hot milk for children

~ turn heater and lamps off; close curtains (my house is nearly all glass-walled so there are a lot of curtains)

A list like this can sound cut-and-dried. That's not the reality. Any one of these tasks can and often does consist of mini-processes that fray its edges, tease it out like a cotton ball, and expand it into more work.

For example, the trash bin I wheel in from the sidewalk may have plastic bags and food stuck in the bottom, so I haul it onto the lawn and rinse it out with the garden hose, fetch gloves to pick up the rubbish washed out onto the lawn, and pile the mess in a clean bin-liner from the kitchen.

Another example: covering the guinea pigs at night with a blanket can take two or even three attempts as they easily startle from underneath it, and spend the whole night shivering. Their hutch is outside the living room on the deck. I arrange the blanket into a tunnel to coax them back under, go back inside and sit for 10 minutes, and go outside again to see if they've made it. They haven't. They are sitting on top of the tunnel instead. I fetch a piece of cardboard from my office to block their exit from their inner hutch, where I lay the blanket, to the outer hutch. Repeatedly getting up and down from my desperately needed late evening rest as I search for tricks to get them to go under and stay under is exhausting.

And a third example, which should suffice to make the point: all mothers are familiar with the washing of hands that comes with so many tasks on this list—after feeding the guinea pigs (twice a day), the fish (twice a day), bringing the trash bins in, taking the trash out, after cleaning up the spills, and perhaps many, many times before, during and after meal preparations. Washing your hands might sound too trivial to mention, but do it, say, 20 times per day, every day, and it is wearing.

Feminism says it's not. Feminism says I can do all this, and put in a man's eight- to 10-hour working day, no wear and tear at all.

Weekly

Here are some of my typical weekly tasks:

~ menu-plan & write shopping list; shop for and unpack the groceries
~ laundry: about eight loads, plus hand-washing
~ change aquarium water and clean tank filter (a time-consuming and intricate task)
~ carry the heavy bin-liner of old guinea pig bedding outside to the main trash-can, fetch a new bag and re-line the garbage bin we keep specially for the guinea pigs' old bedding
~ polish children's school shoes
~ take out the trash

~ clean the bathrooms (two in my place, plus a separate toilet)

As with the daily tasks, a lot of these simple-sounding tasks are complex. 'Take out the trash' sounds like one task, but it is actually many: empty office, bedroom, bathroom and kitchen bins; empty refrigerator of old food; take trash to outdoor bins and wheel them to the sidewalk; take recycling crates of glass, metal, paper and plastic to outdoor bins, crush milk cartons underfoot to save space as requested by the local government authority, and wheel the recycling bins to the sidewalk. Wash out recycling crates and spray them with disinfectant. Leave them in the sun to dry and bring them in later.

With the possible exception of the trash routine if the cleaner happens to come on garbage day, cleaners do none of these weekly tasks.

These tasks total about 10 hours every week. With its dictate that I should ideally work full-time, feminism is saying that those whole 10 hours, or one long paid working day every week, must be crammed into the nights and weekends designed for a man to rest in and tend to his own affairs. Those nights and weekends for a woman are already full of routine work like meal preparations and mothering.

Occasional

I do these things below from time to time:

~ remove stains from clothes and furniture
~ wash grubby marks off walls
~ dust and wash skirting boards
~ vacuum window- and door-sills
~ clear out the refrigerator, take out all the shelves, and wash the interior
~ clean the oven, refurbish the burners with graphite polish, and attack the steel burner rims with lemon juice and salt to remove the black circle of burnt-on food

~ make various repairs to house and furniture
~ wash heavy bedding or take it to the laundromat
~ de-leaf the gutters
~ sweep and mop the bathroom, laundry and entrance hall floors
~ dust everything, including my many bookshelves
~ remove insect screens and vacuum behind them; wash windows inside and out; replace screens

At times in her life, a housewife will have larger occasional duties like:

~ moving house
~ yard sales
~ renovations
~ repairs after a storm

Add all these occasional tasks up, and I estimate they take a cumulative six weeks annually, or between one-ninth and one-eighth of the year. With its pressure on me to work full-time, feminism is saying that the whole one-ninth-to-one-eighth must be packed into the nights and weekends designed for a man to rest in. Just like we said of the 'Weekly' tasks above, those nights and weekends for a woman are already full of routine work like cooking and caring for the kids.

Festivities

Into a housewife's year goes a lot of planning for celebrations and other social occasions. In my household, that means Easter, Christmas, Halloween, two annual war-commemorative days, three birthday parties, and interstate vacations to see family, plus gift-buying for family, friends and neighbors.

Some years, a woman may have extra events to plan such as weddings, christenings, funerals or engagement parties. Add in buying gifts for and ferrying children to the birthday parties of all my sons' friends, plus sleepovers and playdates in school vacation and on weekends, and I calculate that I spend at least some time on festive activities one week in four.

As Christmas approaches, the workload lifts dramatically. Come September, I start to research gifts. I run myself ragged buying gifts over many shopping trips to many real or online locations, wrap the gifts, and post or deliver them. I write a circular for friends and family (at least in theory I do; I haven't had time to do this in years), try to style a fabulous Christmas table setting for the kids (no luck: it's the same nice but low-maintenance version every year because there's no time to do anything more), erect the seven-foot-high tree and decorate it (it's plastic, but we like it), decorate the house. I plan Christmas dinner and make the special grocery forays for it, sometimes to several stores. I buy gift boxes (or make them to save money if I have time, which I rarely do) and buy ribbon and shop for the ingredients to make edible gifts of *panforte* or passionfruit shortbread and wrap them up prettily.

On Christmas Eve, I do the milk-and-cookies routine (or sherry and gingernuts, which Santa seems to prefer), watch a Christmas movie with the kids, hang the stockings and read *The Night Before Christmas* to them. I lie awake shattered with tiredness as I wait for them to drop off so I can retrieve the gifts from the top of the wardrobe and arrange them under the tree. Santa leaves chocolate reindeer and snowmen and gold coins in little gold wire baskets on the tree, and is so worried that one year she will forget, that she leaves a large note inside her bedsheets to remind herself, though that means she also must remember to write the note.

On Christmas Day, I do the whole gift unwrapping routine, help the kids assemble their new toys, play with the kids, cook and serve Christmas Dinner, and clean up afterwards.

After Christmas, I do some of that work in reverse. I dissemble the tree, haul it all off to the garage in boxes, and take the decorations down. It takes half a morning. One year when the kids were pre-schoolers, I was so overwhelmed by single motherhood's exhaustion,

I left the tree up until Easter. I seriously thought about leaving it up all year.

I don't mean to sound sour about all these preparations. I love doing them. I still get a bit spooked on Christmas Eve thinking Santa is out there in the sky somewhere. My point is, planning all this meaning and joy is work. And my point also is, that all this work is meaning and joy. The festivities women arrange are some of the high points of life. They are more important, not less important, than earning a living. The point of earning a living is to live and love with our whole souls, and one of the highest ways we do that is by celebrating at festivity-time.

Feminism refuses to accommodate festivity-planning in its masculinist vision, because planning festivities is something women do. If women plan Christmas, say feminists, then Christmas sucks.

Errands, Admin and 'Tasks with No Name'

When feminists dismiss a woman's housework with the words "Get a cleaner," they treat a household as if it were the relatively simple home of the 1970s. Running a home used to consist of mainly cooking, cleaning, shopping, laundry, sewing and maybe gardening. A home today is a veritable mini-enterprise of people coming and going to various activities and jobs, a huge amount of correspondence, technology to wrangle, and a lot more stuff to buy, insure, learn how to use, clean, repair, and dispose of. Feminism has not kept pace with the new domestic reality.

Here is a snapshot of the many errands, administrative chores, and 'tasks with no name' on my list on the day I write this page, or that I have completed in the last week:

~ start on my tax return
~ ring my son's sports teacher to request permission to change his off-campus sports program from ten-pin bowling to football. Sign the permission slip and write a check for the football class.

Write a reminder note to check I receive the ten-pin
bowling refund.

~ renew library books online; return library books due now

~ I receive notice for jury duty. I read the documentation, research
what proof I need to supply that I qualify for an exemption as a
mother of young children; search online for statutory declaration
forms and search for confirmation that a form printed off the
Internet will be admissible (the last thing I need as an overworked
mother is for the Court to return the form to me saying I need to
re-submit on an original form which would need a visit in person
to a post office to obtain); search for notaries (perhaps known
as a Justice of the Peace in your country) and ring the notary to
confirm their availability; visit the notary at the local municipal
office and wait my turn before he can see me. Check what ID I
need to supply to him and take that with me. Send in the signed
stamped form. Make a note to check that I receive an exemption
slip well before the Court date. If I don't, chase it up.

~ research gift ideas for my mother's seventieth birthday. Shop
for the gift. Shop carefully for a card, wrap and ribbon, as my
mother takes great pride in the presentation of her gifts to us, and
has particular taste. Discuss celebration plans in several e-mails
between my brother and my father. Make those plans happen.

~ my old university college requests donations of plantings for a
memorial garden in honor of the college principal, who was also
my much-loved high school French teacher. I pore over the list
of suggested plants, research the best one (I go for blue ginger),
and write her a hand-written note to update her on my life since
school days. I fill out the donation form and send it off.

~ re-assess my health, household goods, and disability insurance
policies, and my retirement investments, something I do
annually

~ search for and buy swimmers online for my son when he left the
last pair behind in the swimming pool change-room—again

~ set up another visit to a notary, this time to have him sign an application form for a bank account

A cleaner performs none of these tasks.

Tasks Not Done

Undone tasks come back to bite. If nothing else, they are enervating, the last thing a weary mother needs. Enervation is the least of it, though. Undone tasks have consequences that hurt.

A good many errands and tasks in my life have been building up for not just months, but years—ever since I had children, to be precise. Here is a list of the perpetually undone jobs on my list as I write this page today. For each task, I list the time each one has been hanging around, and the consequences of not getting to it:

~ buy expanding foam glue to fix my son's broken plastic toy sword blade back into its handle. Find a repairman who can fix my sons' broken rocking-horse, wooden garage and wooden airport. *Time undone*: Between one and five years. *Cost of not doing*: The sword has been cluttering my task table for 12 months, and the horse, garage, and airport have been taking up space in a closet for five years. All that time, my sons miss out on using those toys. And having broken stuff around is plain bad juju.

~ sell an unused spare battery from my old computer. *Time undone:* Two years. *Cost of not doing*: The battery's life will wane, rendering it unsalable.

~ my Neighborhood Watch group has purchased an ultraviolet pen which we may all borrow to invisibly label our valuables. I am yet to borrow it. I also mean to photograph and write down the serial numbers of my valuables for insurance purposes. *Time undone*: Three years. *Cost of not doing*: A much reduced chance of recovering my goods if they are stolen. Home burglaries are common in Australia, where I live, as few households have guns.

~ get two prints framed. *Time undone*: Four years. *Cost of not doing*:
When my boys were little, I bought inexpensive prints from the
state gallery of two iconic paintings so the kids would be imbued
with high-quality art of national importance. Art that surrounds
us in early childhood stays with us forever. It saddens and
frustrates me that my children may be too old to appreciate these
works by the time I can frame them.

~ a blood test prescription from my GP is for last November. It is
now July. *Time undone*: Eight months. *Cost of not doing*: My health
and energy levels suffer.

~ re-write my will. I separated from my husband four years ago as
I write this page. My will needs minor updating from that time.
Its executor is a long-standing friend. I feel I should remove him
from this onerous duty, as he has moved interstate, and has no
real knowledge of my next of kin, my assets, or my current circle
of friends. *Time undone*: Four years. *Cost of not doing*: There
is a slight risk my money and goods will not be assigned quite
as I wish. My executor will bear the burden of sorting out my
affairs, not a task he needs when he has a business to run and two
young children.

~ I have not granted anyone power of attorney, nor the right
to make medical decisions should I become permanently
incapacitated. These are important arrangements that everyone
should have in place. *Time undone*: Four years. *Cost of not
doing*: Obviously, the consequences of not planning for possible
disablement, especially as a mother of dependents, are potentially
very negative.

~ two pairs of children's cycling gloves I bought for my sons as gifts
last Christmas are too small. I am yet to take them back. *Time
undone*: Seven months. *Cost of not doing*: I am embarrassed to
take them back after so long, so instead of getting a refund, I will
eBay them and recoup only a few dollars, or give them away and
recoup nothing. That is not money I can afford to lose.

It goes without saying that the consequences of not doing some of these tasks are much more serious than others. Appointing a power of attorney obviously ranks ahead of fixing my son's broken toy sword. I also realize that I may sound inefficient. But I'm not. My list of 'done' tasks is much, much longer. I have prioritized mothering and running a home and earning a living and career re-training and completing a postgraduate degree and writing this book and volunteering for a charitable institution over the undone tasks above.

What About His 50 Percent Share on the Home Front?

It is a mathematical law of an 'equal' universe that in a two-adult household, where each does 50 percent of the paid work (assuming their jobs are equally demanding), that each is responsible for 50 percent of domestic duty. Whether men can handle their 50 percent of the housework and parenting is another matter. The trouble with an 'everyone should do an equal share of everything' attitude is that it treats men and women as if they were genderless, like anatomically blank dolls. It denies women's contribution as mothers and house-wives beyond whatever home-running and parenting ability he may possess, and accords him kudos for a home-running and mothering contribution he hasn't actually made.

Feminism refuses to acknowledge that a woman has a committed relationship with a home that a man does not have. If men and women were naturally interchangeable, anthropology would find all manner of societies with paid and unpaid work split in various ways between the genders. As we all know, it mostly doesn't. In societies across time and space, with a few limited and qualified exceptions, women do the cooking and tend the home fires and mother the children because they are better at it. They might not enjoy it, but that's not the point. Like it or not, we women as a sex are wired for domesticity and motherhood, and men are not, at least not so much.

The fact that we are better wired for it, however, does not mean a woman's place is in the home, nor does it mean that domesticity is more our responsibility.

When I point out men's woeful under-contribution in the home to my female friends, fellow school-moms and co-workers, the majority roll their eyes and agree, some with a laugh, some in resignation, some with grim annoyance, some with gusts of anger.

It is true today's man might no longer go fishing Saturdays or out to the bar Friday nights while she stays back with the baby, as his own father may have done. But it takes more than 'attendance marks' if we want him to be her equal.

It also takes more than contributing at a pace of one task to one person when his wife is working at the pace of two, three or four tasks to one person.

"Oh, my husband goes to Chinatown to pick up Peking duck for lunch every Saturday," one woman in my group assured us all archly one afternoon in the playground.

That doesn't cut it. A man may get lunch, but he may also leave the screaming baby and the whining toddler and the squabbling six-year-old and eight-year-old behind for his wife to look after. She is breastfeeding the baby, and cooking courgettes and potatoes in time to cool them down for the weaning baby's lunch, and tending to the toddler who has just pulled the DVD rack over on his head and she's picking up the DVDs and fetching an ice-pack from the kitchen for the head-bump and treating the tears while the toddler clings to her leg the whole time, and she's adjudicating the older two's dispute over whose turn it is to play shoot-'em-ups on the computer, and she is setting the table for lunch, and she is changing the baby's diaper and lifting him protesting and wriggling into the high-chair and puréeing his vegetables and spoon-feeding him, and casting about in her mind for what to have for dinner, and taking the meat out of the freezer to defrost, and setting a mental timetable for when she will have to start cooking dinner by counting back all the steps in the lamb pilaf she decides to make, and hand-washing her work dresses which take two days to dry so they have to be washed by Saturday morning for Monday, and she is chasing the dog which has dug under the side fence again and is terrorizing the neighbor's carp (and two weeks ago the dog ate one of the carp and left the entrails all over the lawn and the neighbor was understandably distraught and she had to forego her intensely needed afternoon sleep in order to clean up the mess while holding the screaming baby at the same time, and that delayed the toddler's nap so far that the toddler then wouldn't sleep so she had to stay awake the whole afternoon to entertain the toddler which was beyond a nightmare, and she paid for the carp which she really could not afford to do and she sure doesn't want a repeat of that incident), and she is setting up a diorama of farm animals on the floor in a desperate attempt to distract the ever-whining toddler, and she is scouting ahead in her mind for all the things that need to be done that afternoon like softening the butter to make the chocolate tart crust for tomorrow night's engagement party for her brother-in-law, and working out where she will fit in a trip to the store to buy a gift for that happy couple, and stretching in her mind for an imaginative gift and coming up with one possibility after another and discarding them until she hits on the right idea (a newly released whimsical novel about the philosophy of skiing worked into a love story and mystery, perfect as they are both powderhounds) and thinking do I have enough of the right wrapping paper and ribbon, and thinking, I don't have time to check the stationery box but probably no, I don't, so I will have to get that at the stationer's too this afternoon when I drop by to collect the eight- and six-year-olds' weekly 'rocks and precious stones' magazine installment which comes with the free mineral sample, and she is thinking what clever kind of card could we buy for the brother-in-law and his wife-to-be, it would be lovely to mark this key moment in their lives by making one with themed stick-on elements like skis and cute woolly hats and chalets and pine trees, so I will add the craft store to the shopping run this afternoon, during which I will also buy groceries and drop by the department store for new shorts for the eight-year-old and a specially requested pink baseball cap with a fairy on it for the six-year-old because her best friend has one so she wants one the same, and she is thinking if I add the craft store, stationer's and department store to my run how will I get home in time to unpack all the groceries and get dinner started, and if I want to stay out that long I will have to express milk at least once, if not twice, which means I have to take the breast-pump and I have to express milk in the toilet cubicle in the public restrooms at the mall because it does not have a purpose-built breastfeeding room, and I will have to take a chiller bag and frozen gel pack to keep the milk cool in the hot car as it's a warm day so I must remember to pack those too, and that means I will have to drop the milk back to the car park before I go back in to shop because the chiller bag will be too cumbersome to carry around and that takes time I don't have, and expressing milk takes the best part of 25 minutes and that's time I don't have and I don't need the practice at taking a screaming baby to the stores with me, and she is thinking of what four out-fits her children will wear to the engagement party tomorrow and do they have enough clean clothes to make up the outfit, and she realizes, no, they don't, so she plans to schedule their clothes next in the washing machine which goes all day Saturdays, and the tod-dler's shoes will need de-mudding from his play at the park to wear to the party and the six-year-old's shoes need new laces inserted and the eight-year-old's sneakers will need renovating polish, and she is noting that she must remember to put the how-to-self-publish-your-novel books she borrowed from her sister-in-law-to-be into the bag to return to her at the party tomorrow night, and she is straining her way through her mind-map of the next 48 hours trying to find a hole where she can find time to sweep the kitchen floor which she hasn't swept in seven weeks, and, and, and, and, and. And every moment of that, the toddler is whining and the baby is howling.

Meanwhile, Peking Duck Man is cruising to the Silver Dragon with his favorite music on, getting out of the car, crossing the sidewalk to the restaurant, picking up the duck, re-crossing the sidewalk, and driving home, all in child-free bliss.

Men have a superior physical capacity to women; you may disagree, but I will swear black and blue that women have a superior domestic capacity to men. We can be equal with men in the 'public' world of business and politics, but in the 'private' realm of the home, we outshine him. We women know not just how to found a start-up and design the airport and run the bio-tech corporation, but also how to run a house. A man might be physically able to stack the dishwasher the way a woman does, but he does not see and do all that needs to be done in the house in the way a woman does. He may be a house-husband but he is never a home-maker in the way she is—and that is so even if she hates housework. A woman has a relationship with a home that is absent in a man. She *communes* with the house; he does not.

That communing translates into a lot of work for her. It sees her reach and stretch non-stop, day and night, to perceive all that needs doing, to attend to it, to anticipate pitfalls ("If we go away on the weekend after next, I need to get the groceries in by Friday night, but I'll be packing Friday night, so shopping must shift to Thursday night, but that's the eight-year-old's piano lesson, so Wednesday but Wednesday night I'm on call at work, so Tuesday but my six-year-old has a 6:30 p.m. physiotherapist appointment, so Monday. Fresh food will go off if I buy it five days early, so I'll buy a double load of dry-goods to last two weeks this Saturday, and buy fresh food the Monday we get back in my lunch-hour. That will mean no time to eat lunch that day.").

Men don't dwell in this space of constant anticipation and planning in the home. That means that even if his quantitative contribution is the same—that is, even if he is putting in the same domestic hours—his qualitative contribution is usually less.

Men get to ply their physical superiority in their jobs (if they have a manual job, that is, and most men's jobs throughout history until very recently have been manual), while women have to ply their domestic superiority outside their job, leaving them with two jobs if they also want a career. That superiority is our glory and our downfall at the same time. Our superior domestic skills leave us in an inferior position. We pick up most of men's share of the domestic load, while they pick up a 'Get Out of Jail Free' card.

That said, though, men's inability to pull their full domestic weight is no excuse for the perpetual exemption feminism has given them ever since the 1960s. Whether or not you think a man can run a household as well as a woman, men still have a lot of slack to take up in the home before they can claim to be at whatever their maximum capacity is.

Nor is men's real or alleged inability to pull their weight an excuse for the way feminism lets men believe their wives do nothing in the house.

What could feminism have done to open men's eyes to housework? Plenty. For starters, they could have filled the media with articles about the value and myriad strains of running a home. They could have got out a bucket of white paint, painted a white line down the middle of the house, and stuck up signs saying 'Her Half' and 'His Half'. They could have painted a line down the middle of the laundry pile, the dirty bath-tub, the unwashed pans, the empty fridge, even the kids themselves. They could have left their half sparkling clean, his half an undone mess, and maybe even dressed the kids on one half of their bodies only. It would have made a great photo stunt in a magazine or on TV.

Another tactic feminists could have employed is to go on strike. They could have dropped the work and made men pick it up. This is what my natural health therapist, Ellen, did when her husband told her shortly after their daughter was born, "You do nothing. You just have coffee with your friends all day." This from a man who contributed little more than his 40 to 50 hours of paid work per week and slept eight hours a night, to a woman who ran his home, all while caring for his baby every minute of the day and through the night, who also had an elementary schooler to care for from an earlier marriage, and whose baby had cried so much, she admitted herself and the child to a residential mothercraft nursing facility for unsettled infants.

Next day, Ellen did 'nothing'. She set up a string of appointments with her friends, and spent the day drinking coffee with them, just like her husband said she did. She left the breakfast dishes on the table, washed no clothes, ran no errands, made no phone calls, cooked no meals. She took care of the baby, and got her elementary schooler off to school and back home again, itself a very large task. Ferrying a constantly squalling baby about all day from one strange environment to another where it probably won't sleep is a tough enough gig in itself. It's harder than slogging at a paid job. Beyond that, though, she did nothing else.

When he came home, he said, "What's for dinner?"

"Well, what have you brought us to eat?" she said. "As you say, I have coffee with friends all day. I do nothing."

He never accused her again. Of course, had Ellen truly done nothing that day, her husband would have been left literally holding the baby. He could not have gone to work. And he would have discovered the real meaning of the word 'work' for the first time in his life. That's not to disparage the good work he does at the office. It is to say that a scant eight to 10 hours of merely commercial activity, with someone else shielding you from all your domestic work and child care, and getting eight hours' sleep a night, is a lot easier than doing a 12-hour day of caring for a crying baby and a simultaneous 16-hour day caring for an elementary schooler (less about five school hours in term-time), doing both your share and your partner's share of running a home, and getting only broken sleep for way fewer than eight hours per night, night after night after night.

Here's another suggestion: feminists could have staged a 'change-over time' skit. At noon on Wednesday, precisely midway through the week, they could have marched into workplaces, factories, boardrooms, into Congress or Parliament, into government offices, ringing bells. "Changeover time!" they could have chanted, as they plumped the baby and a pile of food-stained baby onesies down on their husbands' desks. "We women have met our 50 percent of the weekly household load; now it is the men's turn," they could have announced to the watching TV cameras and newspaper photographers. "We're going to take up our right to do half of the paid 40 hours of the household load, which takes a mere 20 hours per week. Get out from behind that desk, husband, and get in the kitchen where you belong the rest of the week."

That bolshie approach might not be to most women's taste today, and I'm not suggesting we should address men in those bossy tones, but enough feminists of the '60s and '70s had the militancy to do that kind of thing. In fact, some early feminism did make a stand for housework. No one remembers it, though, because by the 1980s, the masculinist brand of feminism we live with today had stomped out any such signs of female valor. Those briefcase-toting '80s feminists tugging their forelock before the masculine 9 to 5 workplace timetable were a much more biddable bunch than their earlier counterparts, but had they wanted to, they could have crusaded for the housewife. It wasn't daring that was lacking. It was will.

WE ALL, MEN AND WOMEN, need a truthful grasp of women's work in the home. It is *work* in its own right. There is far more work to do in society each day than just the paid kind traditionally done by men. Housework takes place in the home, which is a higher-ranking place than the workplace, and that gives it a primacy over mere commercial activity. Housework enables everyone to function, and beyond that, to live in comfort, energy and beauty. The recurring mental and physical commitment it requires every day of a woman's life takes a unique *strength* of a kind a man mostly does not possess. If feminism wants to be known as a pro-woman movement, it needs to start valuing that primacy, beauty and strength.

4

9 to 3, Not 9 to 5

*Working Hours That Work
for Women*

FEMINISTS ARE AT THEIR MOST craven in their worship of men with the working hours they keep.

"A meeting at 8 a.m. tomorrow at such short notice that I will scramble around on the telephone this evening in the unlikely hope of finding a nanny who can drive my three-year-old to day care at 6:30 a.m., and book a last-minute 7 a.m. place at the out-of-hours-care center at school for the seven-year-old, all while I entertain bored kids in order to keep them away from screens, settle their arguments over whose turn it is to set the table, come up with skillful and heartfelt answers to their questions about the war on the TV news, scrub the remains of last night's chicken Canton off the pan and unstack the dishwasher and stack all the dishes I didn't have time to do last night because we attended a birthday movie night for my 13-year-old's best friend, prepare the makings of tonight's beef stir-fry and cook it, serve it and eat while jumping up five times to fetch a glass of milk (for one child) and a glass of water (for the other) and seconds on two different occasions for them and thirds for one child, clear the table and wash tonight's pans and add tonight's dishes to the dishwasher, prepare and serve dessert and clear those dishes, bathe and dry wriggling children one after another, supervise their homework, search on the school portal for the French assignment the nine-year-old left behind at school and it takes me ages to find because it's buried in some misnamed link and the pages of the portal frustratingly won't load, and go upstairs to turn the wireless printer on and come back downstairs and print the assignment off, search on the school portal again for the math methodology podcast the teachers uploaded to help parents help the kids do their math homework, listen to the podcast but still don't understand the math problems, harangue the 13-year-old again and again and again to work on her solar system project and spend 45 minutes helping her thread Neptune and Saturn onto an orbit made out of bent coat hangers which I rummaged in the garage for, and Neptune and Saturn are foam balls I made a lightning-fast sortie to the mall for today in my lunch hour, and I couldn't get balls the right size so I have to cut one down with a paring knife, and my daughter is unhappy with Neptune's unevenly pared surface so I have to find a way to get her to accept a misshapen Neptune with gratitude and good humor, and she wants to paint the planets the right colors so we research the colors online and I help her get out the paints and paint kettle and brushes and guide her in mixing a range of colors some of which go awry so we mix fresh batches, deal with my own e-mails, give the kids their pocket money but make a note that I owe one child $5 next week because I did not have enough $5 bills this week, take my own shower, wash and blow-dry my hair for tomorrow's meeting, work out what to wear tomorrow, check the school's note about tomorrow's sports carnival to see what the seven-year-old needs to take, and pack the sunscreen and extra water bottle the note instructs us to bring along with swimmers and a towel, and the note says they can wear something in their sporting house color of blue like blue tattoos on their face to get in the team spirit so I search high and low and hit on hair color crayons in the craft drawer which I'm hoping will rinse out first time (and if they don't, I will have to dress in my bathing costume and get in the shower with my son for a special wash-the-crayon-out session tomorrow night), sneaker-treat my son's running shoes with white polish, and do the kids' bedtime routine? And get up at 4:15 a.m. tomorrow and make school lunches for four kids and hurl into the uphill task of propelling my children out of bed at 5:30 a.m. and get them fed and dressed and packed as they cry and move extra-slow with sleep deprivation which is hellish for me on account of the guilt I feel compounded with the rage that a kid's crying generates, and hunt in the garage for a box in which to hand the solar system over to the nanny and I don't have a spare box so I unload a pile of tax documents from their carton and use that instead and the tax documents spill all over the dirty garage floor and I don't have time to pick them up, and I fling myself out the door at 6:35 a.m. to be here by 8 a.m.?

"Sure, no problem," says the feminist to her employer.

What mammoth self-repudiation.

Try suggesting that a woman should work hours designed for women, and feminists' faces take on a steely glare of opposition. A man's hours are the only hours, says feminism. His are the 'right' hours.

In feminists' quest for the Holy Grail of self-actualization-as-a-woman-by-emulation-of-men, anything that gets in the way of making women over into his image is a serious threat. That makes a woman's towering pre-existing domestic load like some monster in the closet whose existence must be kept secret. So what does feminism do? The only thing this incompetent movement knows how to do—it sweeps the giant monster under the tiny carpet of unworkable time-zones of very early mornings, post-work evenings, and weekends.

However, those 'non-working' time-zones are already occupied. They might be off-duty periods for a man, but they are periods of mountainous on-duty toil for a mother. Even for a woman without kids, those times are still occupied with routine chores, meals preparation and weekend errands.

Feminism doesn't care. Those marginal hours of early mornings, evenings and weekends in a man's life are 'private' time, invisible, out of the public's prying eyes. It would be intrusive for society to follow a man into his private hours. We do not consider it our business to particularly know what a man does in those hours. By stuffing a family-size workload of home-making and mothering into those same peripheral private times, feminism angles to use the 'private' nature of a man's early mornings, nights and weekends as a cover for its denial of a woman's workload.

"Oh, we shouldn't concern ourselves with how she gets it all done in those times," feminism hopes society will say. "A woman's private time is her own."

But we should concern ourselves with it. Her domestic work may be done in the 'private' domain of the home but it is *work*, and that makes it everybody's business. As a society, we should know about it, care about it, validate it, and accommodate it.

The most acknowledgement feminists give a woman's double life in the workplace and the home is to tell her to 'juggle'. An insufficient tactic like that is a wicked refusal to come to grips with women's reality. It denies the primacy, the 24/7 schedule, the enormous scale and draining nature of mothering's work. It takes a lot more than juggling to be in two or more places at once: to be breastfeeding the baby *and* sending the e-mail about the five-year-old's school enrolment *and* browning the lamb for tonight's Irish stew *and* leaving to pick up the seven-year-old from school *and* washing the dog *and* being at the office—all at 2:10 p.m. on a Tuesday.

Media images of professional women never depict her frantically trying to transition from home to office and back again. They do not show the fiendishly crammed weekends in which she rushes kids to 7:30 a.m. baseball games an hour across town and 2 p.m. playdates in the other direction, and drives home and then back to pick up the kid from the playdate at 4pm, sorts old toys and delivers them to the school jumble sale, dispatches a heap of home chores, does eight loads of laundry, gets in the groceries, fixes meals and snacks, and ferries the 14-year-old to a party at 6 p.m., collecting two of his friends on the way, and then goes back to pick them up at 10 p.m. and drops them all home.

And it is impossible for any camera to capture the misery of all her experiences left undone: the cookbook manuscript she promised to proof-read for her neighbor but hasn't got to for the ninth weekend in a row and is feeling guilty about, the gym session her body hankers for but has no time to attend, the silk dress on the floor in the bedroom corner that she can't hand-wash and drip-dry and iron before tomorrow's upscale barbecue with the new people who moved in next door so she'll probably have to wear the boring work trousers she's worn three times to the office this week already, the terrace that has six months' weeds coming through the bricks which she lacks the time to get to, the e-mails piling up from her third cousin seeking memories about their shared great-grandmother to include in the family history the cousin is compiling for the first family reunion in 35 years this coming summer, the surplus kids' bed leaning up against the garage wall that she doesn't have time to sell online and the kids can't open the car doors on that side until she sells it and so they bicker about who has to be the one to get in the back seat first and move over.

Nor does the camera snap all the riches she has missed out on by working full-time: the uplifting Wednesday morning get-together she never had with the girls, the way her seven-year-old's face would have lit up when Mommy came to help with Thursday reading-rounds in the classroom, the strength and truth her Friday afternoon yoga class would have delivered, the ideas to be encountered in her town's Saturday art gallery trail that she longs to walk but never can because Monday to Friday's domestic work gets shunted onto weekends.

Instead, media images capture her sitting coolly at her child-free desk. Her beatific smile is meant to let us know that she is fully satisfied by workplace activity alone. She appears as unwarped as a man by the weight of an eight- to 10-hour working day on top of her stupendous at-home load. Not only that, she is smartly groomed, as if there were nothing lunatic about expecting a working mother to have time for highlights and lowlights and eyebrow waxes and the scouring of stores for that well-chosen outfit that took time, thought, online searching and pavement-pounding to put together.

These media stories sometimes mention her children, but always with an insultingly light touch, as if a baby were just another facet on the brilliant-cut gemstone of her life. You know the kind of profiles I mean:

> *Ellie is managing director of a drill-rig supplier and travels around the globe 10 times a year in her partnership work with the Institute for Under-Sea Resources to explore new technologies to allow offshore drilling to depths of up to three miles to tap geothermal heat for electricity. She majored in organizational psychology in her MBA last year, and is excited about maximizing the skills of diverse scientific bodies around the world to uncover what might be a new era in sustainable carbon-free geothermal electricity supply for the entire world by 2025. She has four children, aged 1, 3, 7 and 12.*

Bios of working women like Ellie's routinely stuff lines with career achievements and then tack on a little one-line coda mentioning that, oh, and she's a mother too. That coda flicks away motherhood as a job in its own right, as her primary job, and demotes it to the same place in her life as fatherhood sits in her children's father's life. Sly, injuring, haughty, the 'motherhood coda' is intended as a putdown of the primacy, struggle and overwhelming schedule of motherhood, and ensures that the workplace never accommodates it. Those bios are a disgrace.

As we can see, the fictional Ellie has a baby, a preschooler, an elementary schooler, and a high schooler. That is four different systems to run, and four places to drop her children to and from every day. As table 1 calculates in chapter 1, caring for a baby and a preschooler equates to 6.8 40-hour per week jobs, more if a woman has no input from her partner in the home. With Ellie's two school-age children, we can add about another half-time job, or 20 hours per week, per child, onto that tally—for getting each extra kid to and from school, each extra child's homework and after-school pursuits, each child's snacks and meals (cooking for six is more work than cooking for four), sorting out more arguments, finding each extra child's lost tennis gear, each extra child's visits to the emergency room and the dentist and the speech therapist, each extra child's birthday parties and playdates and sporting fixtures, each extra child's illnesses, the ongoing work of being a disciplinarian and a role model for each extra child, and so on. An extra 20 hours for each of the two older children equates to Ellie working 7.8 full-time jobs every week if she is the woman in table 1. That is an unworkable scenario for a stay-at-home mom, let alone a working one.

A New Feminine Workplace Ecosystem

One of the most important kinds of 'equality' feminism was supposed to deliver was the formulation of a whole new economic eco-system that catered for women equally as much as it already catered for men.

When women entered the workplace en masse some 40 years ago, we were supposed to see a seismic re-calibration of the relationship between her 'private' world of unpaid work, and his 'public' world of paid work. Those two great theaters of human activity, the home and the workplace, were supposed to splice.

What would happen when we spliced the 'private' with the 'public'? To begin with, in households where women performed 50 percent of the paid work (that is, women who worked full-time with full-time working partners), 50 percent of the housework and child care would immediately transfer to the man's lap, where it belongs. Come the days when the female people who wash their socks are working alongside them, men can no longer act as if sock-washing is not their problem. It is their problem, 50 percent of the time. Those dirty socks are sitting in their in-tray, lookin' at 'em. Once male workers lost the back-up of a 24/7 stay-at-home wife, that cozy ring-fencing of the workplace from domestic reality should have come to an end.

As we all know, the ring-fence stayed put. Masculine immunity from housework and parenting duties in the 'private' theater pretty much sailed right on. So did the arrogant male belief that (men's) work in the 'public' zone of the workplace outranked (women's) work in the 'private' zone of the home, only now feminism encouraged women to join in with that masculinist snobbery.

The feminist made a great show of telling us what a big, strong, self-confident woman she was as she asserted her right to join the man's world. So great was her self-abasement, however, that she believed it did not have to change to fit *her*. She believed she had to fit *it*, and derived her sense of self-worth from how zealously she did so. The rigid masculine workplace timetable kept course without a waver, so ably championed by fawning feminists who showed up at 9 a.m. or 8 a.m. or earlier, and stayed until 5 p.m., 6 p.m. or 7 p.m., five days a week.

Feminists' insistence on aping men's timetables suited employers down to the ground. Feminism is a product of the left, but it plays beautifully into the hands of the right, whose big bad employers rub their hands with glee at the sight of serried ranks of shoulder-padded women marching with joyful determination toward an eight- to 10-hour day at the office, all flinging aside any claim to a day that accommodates their pre-existing domestic work.

This is what feminists should have said to assembled male employers and co-workers as they marched into the office for the very first time, back in the 1960s or '70s:

Make way, Housewife and Mother coming through! The big guns are here! The seriously hard workers are on the scene. Those wives and mothers who have been shielding you from the equivalent of 307 hours per week [see table 1] while you put in 40 are now beside you. Meet the female people who face up to their 50 percent share of their domestic and parenting responsibilities. They also face up to most or all of your 50 percent share of those responsibilities. If you want that cushy situation to continue, and you want to get accustomed to the second income she will bring, accommodate her with a woman-shaped workplace.

The fact that women carry so much more domestic responsibility than you makes them superior, not inferior, to the rest of you in the workplace. A mother arriving mid-morning after getting kids off to school, or going home mid-morning to care for a sick child, or taking school vacations off, is out of the office doing something harder and more important, not easier and less important, than you. She is not 'letting down the team'. If you are a father, she is going home to look after your children and cook your dinner. If you have no children, she is that same woman as your own mother who cooked your dinner and cared for you. Do not tell your mother who stayed home and sacrificed herself for you 24 hours a day, 365 days a year, for the best part of 20 years, that she can only join you in the workplace if she divests herself of the encumbrances of motherhood. Women clean your bathroom and shop for your groceries and run your errands and, most significantly, take care of your kids, so that you don't have to. That your wife takes care of your kids is the only reason you can be in the workplace at all. Do not shut her out, do not cripple her with conditions designed for a male employee with a wife at home, do not sneer at her, do not treat her like a man with nothing else to do but show up to work, and do not treat her like a problem. She is not the goddamn problem. More than anyone else on earth, she deserves your gratitude and accommodation.

This is what feminists actually said:

Don't move a muscle! We're going to fit right in with your world! Yes, we already do 307 hours a week tending to your children and running your home while you chip in only 40 hours, but we're going to wash your socks at 3 a.m. and wipe ourselves out doing it, just so we can sit at our desks alongside you by 9 a.m. Because you guys are the model of success and legitimacy with your 40-hour weeks of commercial activity. You are right to believe that it is only your paid activity that counts in our household. We are nothing until we are just like you.

We excuse the workplace from ever having to meet any needs a woman has that are different to yours. We mothers and housewives would be a liability if we left early to fit your six-year-old daughter for her concert tutu and we babysat your 10-year-old son the entire 12 to 14 weeks of school vacation every year, so we won't disturb the workplace's sacrosanct immunity from mothering's realities. The workplace always comes first over contemptible stuff like raising the next generation and wearing clean socks. Don't worry. We'll see to it that our shameful child care and housework never interrupts your seamlessly child-free, reality-free workplace.

No woman who sends the message to the workplace that women are free to work a man's hours and conditions deserves a reputation as a friend of woman. She may herself be willing to work a man's hours, and she may want to make that clear to her employer, and if she does, we can be glad for her and support her. However, if she wants to be known as a friend of woman, she also needs to make it clear to her employers that she is unusual in wanting a man's timetable and conditions, and she needs to strive to provide woman-friendly employment for all the other female employees in the business. That any one woman is willing to work a man's hours does not excuse feminism's wholesale presentation of women to the workforce as male-identical employees. No matter how wide the trail any individual feminist may have blazed into previously masculine territory, to blindside women's immense domestic workload as she goes is more than just rotten pioneership. It's an own goal.

Equal Opportunity is not supposed to mean, "You women too can come and work the same hours and conditions as a man!" It is supposed to mean, "This workplace accommodates women, who run homes and care for kids and possibly care for elderly or handicapped relatives, equally as much as it accommodates men, who mostly do not do those things."

The truth is that women's circumstances are very, very different to those of men. Our working schedules and conditions, therefore, should look very, very different to those of men.

So what might a truly feminized workplace look like?

Part-Time and Proud: Dropping the Stigma of Part-Time Work

In a truly feminized workplace, a wave of women starts arriving at 9 a.m., 10 a.m., 11 a.m. A wave of women starts leaving at noon, 1 p.m., 2 p.m., 3 p.m., 4 p.m. Some days they don't come in, because they can only work one, two, three or four days a week. They probably don't come in during school vacations, or if they do, they work reduced hours. A feminized workplace is not a workplace with as many women as men in it, who work an equal number of hours as men. That is a masculinized workplace.

Removing the stigma attached to part-time work is a milestone on the road to a woman-inclusive workplace. We need to dignify women's flexible part-time work with the same dynamically high status that feminists are so eager to accord man-identical full-time careers. We need to normalize it.

A crude tool feminists use to reach the 'top' is to match men's hours. Apart from fear of seeming 'unprofessional' if she works part-time hours, perhaps a feminist's greatest objection to part-time work is her panic that she will miss out on career success if she does not rack up the same hours as a man. In her eyes, if she only works 60 percent of his hours, she will only achieve 60 percent of his career success. In the man-fixated world of the feminist, that means she is only 60 percent of the way to self-actualization as a woman.

Do hours on the job and success work in direct proportion? A woman might spend 20 percent of the time on the job that a man does, and still acquire the same skills. She can be a GP working noon to 4 p.m. Mondays and Thursdays (a total of eight hours per week), and still be every bit as much a doctor as a male GP working 40 hours. He is working five times as much as her, but it is not true that a man who spends five times as many hours at his job will be five times as good at it, or be necessarily five times closer to success.

Feminists will reply, "Oh, that might be so for a humble GP, but jobs at the top demand a total time commitment, whether from a man or a woman." Says who?

Let's take an example of a top job, that of CEO. A CEO works, say, about 65 hours per week. The role ranges across a lot of turf. It needs all kinds of skills and knowledge from human resources, to management, to accounting, to law, to strategic planning, to specific industry knowledge, to IT, to psychology, to an ability to divine future trends and shifting customer preferences. How is it that we believe that that giant basket of skills and vision and tasks can shrink into a week of 65 hours? And oh look: 65 hours just happens to be the comfortable weekly limit of hours available to a man (when we excuse him from pulling his half of the weight in the home, that is). How about that? It must be pure coincidence, right?

Of course it isn't coincidence. We shrivel the role of CEO down to a man-shaped 65 hours by hiving off the company's tasks to hundreds, thousands or tens of thousands of employees until the male CEO is left with a single manageable job. Yet when it comes to hiving off just one more slice of the work in the CEO-ship to make the role available to a woman working, say, 25 to 30 hours per week, we say it can't be done.

If we tried, people would say, "Oh, a CEO has to be available at all times." No, he doesn't. A male CEO is unavailable to just about every one of his hundreds, thousands, or tens of thousands of employees at any given time; in fact, most of them will probably never meet him. He is unavailable to shareholders virtually every minute of the year except at the AGM and maybe to a handful of institutional investors at quarterly phone-in briefings that might take less than an hour each, and he is mostly unavailable to the board except at board meetings, because he is busy running the company. He is unavailable to pretty much all staff from the time he goes home at night until the time he shows up next morning, around 12 hours out of every 24. Yet, incredibly, the company still functions. That's because it largely does not rely on his presence for any given hour at all.

In any case, just because a female CEO is not present, it does not mean she is not available. She can be available for critical consultations 24/7, whether she is supervising her 11-year-old's geography essay, marinating the spare-ribs for dinner, or cheering on her nine-year-old's home run.

It is standard for CEOs of public companies to receive multi-million-dollar remunerations. Do we really believe that a company wants a female CEO, say, $10 million-much for a full-time week, but would shut the door in her face if she was only available for half the time at $5 million? What if we applied the Pareto principle, better known as the 80/20 rule, and argued that 80 percent of her value might come from 20 percent of her hours? In that case, it might be that 20 percent of a full-time week, which is one day per week, might be a CEO's best value for the company: 80 percent of the value for 20 percent of the cost. It would still be a good career opportunity for her, still a great income earner at $2 million, and would actually allow her time to be the mother that she is and run her home. Why not the eight-hour CEO? It's not as loopy as it sounds. It's not loopier than ejecting a CEO's skills from the company because she can't ply them for the same arbitrary 65 hours per week as a man.

If we truly believe that a CEO-ship requires 65 hours per week or more, then we are saying that CEO-ships and many other senior roles are not for women, but only for men, and for women who are willing and able (or craven enough) to emulate men. That is a fundamentally anti-woman stance. The real reason feminism wants women working jobs at 40, 50, 65 or even more hours, is not because the job demands that time commitment, but because feminism wants women to copy men.

Part-Time Weeks

In 2012, I was looking for a full-time job that offered two full days in an office on the Thursdays and Fridays my sons spent at their father's, and remote work from home Monday to Wednesday when the boys were with me. As a divorced single mother, I needed a full-time income, but working full-time in an office with an eight- and 10-year-old at school was impossible. Virtually no office I have ever worked in in Australia, where I live, shuts at 5 p.m., or even 5:30 p.m. For much of my career before I had children, *de facto* quitting time was 6:30 p.m. On the days I edged out nervously at 6:20 p.m., I felt like I was leaving 'early'. Commutes are long in Australian cities, easily 90 minutes or more, and almost all day care centers shut at 6pm.

Needless to say, my chances of finding a job that fitted my needs were slim to zero. This was the case even though the kind of work I do, media relations, is almost all the desk-bound digital kind that can readily be done from anywhere. If feminism had feminized the economy the way it claims to have done, a job like the one I was seeking would be eminently findable.

All the same, as I anxiously trawled employment websites, I was surprised to find an ingenious array of incentives parading its way through the jobs on offer. Jobs billed as "glorious" and "life-changing" solicited me with group functions, "high-spec offices," prize draws, casual dress code. Other job ads shouted "fabulous working environment," proximity to transport, free on-site parking, "fresh seasonal fruit to snack on during the day," daily free lunch, a break-out area in which to "refresh," hotel and car hire discounts, and gym memberships. I could even get anniversary leave. One PR firm in my city offers employees afternoon naps in a tepee. Yet none of these employers, apparently so keen to attract talent, showed the slightest interest in offering the female half of the talent pool the flexible hours and conditions they so desperately needed.

I opted to ease back in with a two-day part-time job instead. It did not take me long in my job search to confirm what I already knew—that almost all the media relations positions advertised were of the unnecessarily full-time kind.

Why, when plenty of work in my industry consists of short-term or ongoing projects that can be completed in two days per week? My field was tourism, publicizing clients such as airlines, hotel chains, tourism boards, and cruise lines. Because tourism is a low-margin industry and these clients must employ publicity consultants in the many countries in which they operate, budgets in any one country are modest. That translates to relatively low workloads for any one client. In fact, the majority of all the many accounts I have ever worked on require input of one, one-and-a-half or two days per week. A full-time media relations officer is a substantial waste of money for many employers. So why were all the jobs full-time?

In the case of my field of tourism publicity, the only real explanation for such inefficiency appears to be 'convention'. It seems employers are still accustomed to thinking of jobs as full-time. Our society used to accommodate a man with a family to support by allocating him full-time work, even when it did not necessarily suit his employer.

Now that the economy has women in it, why are we not shaping jobs for them? Virtually every mother, and a good many child-free women, needs regular, part-time work with flexible clock-on, clock-off times. This should be a boon to many employers, because it reduces their costs. A truly responsive market would draw these women into the economy. Yet culture is a powerful thing, and it seems our male-oriented workplace culture overrides even employers' economic sense.

Part-Time Days

A frustrating aspect of my search in the part-time job scene was how few part-time jobs offered part-time days. The majority of part-time jobs I came across were segmented on a whole-day basis: Tuesdays and Fridays from 8:30 a.m. to 5:30 p.m., for example.

That suits some women. We might feel we do the best by the job when we give it a whole day's unbroken attention. It might be less destructive of our own energy, already depleted by motherhood, to focus on the job for a day at a stretch without the interference of caring for kids. Perhaps it is more streamlined or cheaper to make child care arrangements only for two long days, not over three or four shorter days, especially as most of us pay for a whole day's care no matter how much of it we use.

However, for many mothers, an eight-hour working day on top of unpaid work is about as easy as swallowing an elephant.

Just why can a two-day job of 16 hours not be spread over, say, two five-hour days and one six-hour day, or four three-hour days and one four-hour day? In my field, many employers and clients need someone present to kick issues along every day, so to spread the work out over fewer hours a day, five days per week, is in the client's best interest.

Obviously, not all employers can offer a flexible job. Some can't offer any flexibility at all. If a mom is a retail assistant in a mall and the mall landlord requires that all stores open at 9 a.m., then she has to be there at 9 a.m. If she is the pilot taking the 10 p.m. coast-to-coast flight, she needs to be in the cockpit at 10 p.m. and stay there all night until she lands the plane. If a factory floor manager runs a suite of machines across three eight-hour shifts every 24 hours, he cannot shut down the whole floor so a mom on one of the machines can go buy her 10-year-old new football boots at 4 p.m. next Thursday.

However, if a mom is, say, a graphic designer for a fashion house, or an IT programmer on a telco's website, or performing any kind of work that is not tied to time-critical slots in the day, why are we demanding her presence at an arbitrary hour like 9 a.m. that is near-impossible for the average mother to meet? A woman should be able to dare to negotiate to arrive at, say, 9:40 a.m. or 10:10 a.m. and leave at, say, 1:20 p.m. or 4:40 p.m. without fear that just broaching the subject will jeopardize her job.

One reason we demand women work full days seems to be the inherent belief among employers and co-workers that everyone must be on board at the same time. In pre-feminist days when the economy was largely inhabited by men, an advertising manager at his desk at 9 a.m. could call his copywriter at 9:01 a.m. on Monday morning and expect to find him at work on the next campaign. A trampoline salesman on the road at 4:47 p.m. on Tuesday afternoon could call his contact at the toy store chain headquarters and speak to him to secure an order.

While that makes for maximum convenience for male workers, it makes for maximum *in*convenience for female workers who already have jobs running homes and caring for kids. Having everyone on board at the same time today should be seen as what it is—a luxurious relic of a time when the workplace was a woman-free zone.

Workplace protestations that if a woman is not at her desk eight hours a day like a man, productivity will suffer, are irrelevant. Humankind's maximum productivity is whatever we can extract from the time left over after we all take care of the kids. We could argue that, right now, productivity is only so very high because a woman partly or fully matches his paid work in the economy. If women who had no financial need to work retracted their paid work entirely from the economy, as they have every right to do because they already work way more than 40 hours per week in the home, productivity would plummet.

Nor will GDP necessarily suffer if women work shorter hours. If workplaces were to provide a more flexible schedule, it's true a lot of women might shrink their hours. So they should. Most women I know are already working too many. However, a more flexible workplace will also lure a lot more women into the workforce. I can point to mother after mother after mother in my own circle currently stuck at home because workplaces won't let her in on mother-shaped hours.

In any case, upholding productivity and GDP is not women's responsibility. It is men's. That is, it is men who have spare capacity, not women. Let's see men put in 6.8 paid 40-hour weeks every week to match the 6.8 unpaid 40-hour weeks that table 1 calculates a mother crams into every seven-day period, and we'll all sit back and watch GDP and productivity skyrocket.

There is no algorithm in play in the universe that says all work falls into increments of five dinky days. Nor is there an algorithm that says work must fall into eight-hour days. Work falls into increments of 40-hour weeks and eight-hour days because our society says it should, to suit men. Yet it should also bend to fit a woman's life.

A Porous Day—A 'Mothering Comes First' Policy

One day in 2013, my 10-year-old left his guitar on the train coming home from school. With the aid of the stationmaster who alerted staff down the line, we dashed through the suburbs to the next station hub to recover it. That side-trip ate an hour out of the afternoon. That was difficult enough working from home for myself, as I was then.

Had I been working in an office, the guitar retrieval would have spun out into a much more stressful situation, and mothers' lives are already over-maxed out on stress. I would have received a text at work from my 10-year-old to say he had lost his guitar. I would have used work time to track down the train station telephone number, and by then the guitar might have been stolen, or past the central interchange and outward-bound on a suburban line. A string of phone calls from stationmasters back to me would tell me the guitar was found, hopefully, and would be returned to the lost property bay. I would have checked the lost property bay's business hours, and made a special out-of-hours journey to it. If the bay didn't open out-of-hours, I would have applied for annual leave to go get the guitar, and dealt with the fallout of paid work undone while I went on my wild-guitar-chase. I may have had to make up paid work time out of personal time that I don't possess because that is already overloaded with mothering work. Had the guitar not been found immediately, I would be making and taking further calls to and from the rail network in work's time to track it down. That is all assuming, of course, that I had a job I could interrupt to attend to personal stuff.

Unpredictability is one of the features of a mother's life that workplaces need to accommodate. When a mother wakes up each morning, she knows there's a pretty good chance she won't be doing exactly what she planned that day. A spanner is going to throw itself into the works. Lots of spanners.

It is not just unexpected one-offs like lost guitars that throw a woman's ability to work set hours. Every week, she runs a variety of household errands. They change from week to week. Unlike child-free co-workers, a mother cannot necessarily do these chores in the evening or even at weekends, for she is already working as a mother then.

What a woman needs from her workplace is a porous day. She needs to be able to pop out throughout the day—to get the moving cartons delivered for the big house-move in three weeks' time, or to take the six-year-old to the dentist, or to let the central heating technician in to fix the ailing thermostat that left inside barely warmer than outside last night. She needs to take her vision-impaired ageing father to his ophthalmologist's appointment; she needs to pick up the car from the mechanic's which shuts at 5 p.m.; she needs to make phone calls or send e-mails throughout the day. She needs the workplace's blessing to arrive at and leave at floating times, subject of course to the demands of her work tasks on any given day. Perhaps she arrived at 8:16 a.m. last Monday, but next Monday can't make it until 12:16 p.m. because there is a school assembly that morning. Perhaps she needs to leave at 1:18 p.m. today to take her nine-year-old to the speech therapist, but can stay until 3:04 p.m. tomorrow.

Mothering comes first. A 'mothering comes first' policy, and to a lesser degree a 'home-running comes first' policy, are a signature element of a truly feminized workplace. They permit a working woman to be just that—a working *woman*. A woman is someone with children to mother and a home to run (unless she has a house-husband, which she probably doesn't).

Feminism has made scarcely any provision at all for working *women*. It only provides for working *imitation-men*. It expects a woman to attend to her great medley of errands in a lunch-hour. The lunch-hour harks from the time when a manually laboring man needed to rest. He needed no time allotted to him for errands, because he was allotted a 24/7 wife to run all those for him.

A lunch-hour can be adapted readily enough for small tasks a woman might do—performing her sight check to renew her driver's license if the motor registry is close by, or picking up medication at the drugstore. For many of her errands, however, a one-hour period is not enough (and let's not pretend she doesn't also have to eat lunch in that one hour). Nor can all these tasks be done at midday. Her ageing father's ophthalmologist's appointment might be at 9:30 a.m.; the car needs picking up from the mechanic's at 4:45 p.m. Forcing a woman to run a household ('women's work') in a one-hour slot in the middle of the day designed for a physically laboring man to sit down in (men's timetable) is to hammer a square peg into a round hole.

Other accommodations a woman needs will place a bigger impact on a business's operations. A woman may need to take two weeks off to move her ailing mother into a retirement home. Our workplaces need to absorb that, where possible. Employers can assign the mom's work to other employees; they can call in temporary staff; they can even postpone deadlines or deliveries, if need be. No, it won't be a perfect solution if other staff must take on a double load, or when the temp is more expensive and untrained and makes mistakes or can only partially replace the absent mom. Yes, it might compromise a business's service delivery if her absence means a delayed deadline. That is supposed to be *normal*. A business that incorporates the full reality of women's human responsibilities outside the workplace, and not just a man's human reality like the need for eight hours' sleep and his desire for evenings and weekends and vacations off, is *normal*. It is operating at the maximum level of productivity at which a business is entitled to operate.

The stress of conflicting paid and unpaid duties that women endure today is untenable. It has been going on for decades, and it shouldn't have been. Employers and male co-workers were supposed to greet a woman's domestic workload with calm goodwill. No quibbles. No groans or sneering comments. No threats of firing, implied or expressed. No refusal to hire in the first place, unless the business really does need a permanently present worker. Just gratitude and a ready, unblinking, respectful acceptance that she has pre-existing responsibilities which will take precedence over the workplace at times throughout the day, week, year.

Respectful acceptance and gratitude is not what women currently get in the workplace. Employers and co-workers typically reject her need for flexibility outright, usually with intense disapproval, as if she were not the world's supreme contributor, but a delinquent. The workplace gripes that she is 'unprofessional', 'uncommitted' or 'unreliable', has 'divided loyalties', 'puts her kids ahead of her work'. So ferocious is the belief that a woman who cannot keep a man's hours is a 'liability', that I know of a lawyer-mom in my city who does not dare tell her law firm employer that she even *has* children.

Feminism never points those disgusting attitudes back at men. It never points out that the 'uncommitted' and 'unreliable' person is that male employee or employer who does not commit to his 50 percent share of home-running and child-raising and cannot be relied on to do anything much in the home, whether it is to feed the children something healthy for dinner on the one weeknight his wife goes to her community college class in accounting, or to remember to pick up the gym shoes that his seven-year-old left behind at the sports center after athletics class last week. Feminists never point out that a male employee or employer can only have 'undivided loyalties' at work because he is not loyal to his home duties, rendering him a major under-contributor and liability outside the workplace. Nor do they point out that a man who does not 'put his kids ahead of his work' may well be a bad or indifferent father.

A mother is *never* a liability. A woman is a giga-asset. She is the person who meets everybody else's responsibilities for them, men, children and often ageing parents or others in need. She makes life *very, very easy* for everyone else. The only reason most employer and employee dads can be in the workplace at all is because a woman is doing their housework and parenting for them. Feminism was supposed to negotiate from that truth. Housekeeping and parenting may be 'women's work', but accommodating it is everyone's job.

A School-Hours Economy

After five decades of feminism, a school-hours economy should be part of the furniture. Yet it is nowhere to be seen. That is because feminism doesn't want it to be seen. Can you think of a single instance of a feminist campaigning for school vacations free for female workers?

In 2017, I ran a search of a leading national employment website in my country, Australia. It held a total 155,202 positions. How many popped up on a search term for 'school holidays' (the Aussie term for 'school vacations')? A cool 213. But wait—most of those were not advertising school vacations free, but jobs in school vacations at summer camps, busy tourist attractions or seaside cafés. Others did offer school vacations free, but only because they were school-based roles in any case, such as school psychologists, boarding school cooks and admin openings. The number of jobs outside the education sector offering free or adapted hours in school vacations was a mere 20, a little above .01 percent of all the jobs going in the country on that site that day.

The overwhelming majority of mothers need some or all school vacations free to care for their children. Plenty of families cannot afford summer camp (I certainly cannot) and what kid wants to spend almost their entire annual vacation at camp, however much fun camp can be, and no matter what a phenomenal job summer camp proprietors may do?

Plenty of the work performed every week in our economy can be scooped up into school terms, at least a good deal of the year. A lot of projects are performed to medium-term deadlines of a month or a quarter or even a year away. That might easily allow a mom (or dad) to take a one-, two- or three-week gap at the end of every school term to be with the kids. Even in my deadline-driven field of media relations, for example, the bulk of the work is completed weeks or months ahead. My kids' school year consists of four 10-week terms. Taking two weeks out after every term is actually quite workable.

If a woman must work during school vacations, solutions abound. She can work remotely from home. She can make herself available to come into the office for urgent matters. If she needs to come in, perhaps she can do so for, say, two to four hours per day, maybe only every second day. Perhaps a meeting room could morph into a kids' lounge during vacation. While parents are off-duty during school vacation, retired seniors, students, and women whose children have grown or who do not have kids might like to fill the vacation gap in the workplace. Just as there is no algorithm in the ether that says all work must fall into 40-hour per week blocks, there is no algorithm that says all work falls into 48- or 50-week years.

I cannot imagine sitting in a job interview in today's suppos-edly feminized economy, and asking for school vacations free. I wouldn't dare.

My friend, Georgia, did dare. She applied for a job as a sales rep in New Zealand, where she lived, for a five-star resort in Australia. Her daughter was in preschool, and she was planning a second child. "I asked for school vacations off, and I got it!" she exclaimed. Her eyes were like saucers at landing such a long-shot, and she showed a proud defiance at demanding her due. "Everyone said, 'Ah, you'll never get it, don't bother asking!' but I did ask. And I got it."

Georgia shouldn't have to 'dare' to ask for a job that accom-modates school vacations. An employer can say no with respect and regret, but the mere request itself should not get her turfed out of the interview. In today's feminist workplaces, it mostly would.

Incredibly, I know not one woman who secured school vacation-free employment, but two. My good friend and mom-of-three, Tania, works three days per week as a development officer for a church-based family education office. Her employer insists that she not work in school vacations. "It's school vacation? You stay home. Your child is sick? You go home. Families come first," she reported him as saying, mimicking his emphatic tone.

So it can be done. Jobs really can accommodate school vacations.

Splicing Work and Home Locations

It is not just workplace timetables we need to feminize. We need to feminize our workspaces.

For a man, the borders between his home life and his persona in the workplace are fixed and fairly impermeable. He might allow elements of home to intrude. He has a coffee mug over-printed with a picture of his kids on his desk. Occasionally he invites colleagues home for a barbecue. He chats Mondays about what he did on the weekend. He swaps notes with colleagues about that motorcycle he is thinking of buying. But mostly, work and home are separate.

A man can only separate his workplace from home because his wife holds up the home end for him. When a woman enters the workplace, however, that same work/home separation that is an asset to him can become a burden for her.

When women entered the workplace at the dawn of the feminist era, that strict separation between work and home that men took for granted should have instantly blurred. We can respect a man's need for that separation (to the extent that anyone who evades their half-share of domestic work warrants respect). However, we should also respect a woman's need for the borders between home and work to be permeable. In most households, she is already meeting her share of the burden of running a home and mothering, along with the best part of his share of that burden. Her inability to maintain separation between work and home is a mark of how *responsible* she is. It is testimony to her commitment to her other jobs as mother and housewife in the private domestic realm, to *all* her jobs, not just to her paid job. Her need to cross the work/home line to blend all her roles should impress us, not give us cause to disparage her as 'unprofessional'.

Yet 40 years after women entered the workplace in force, work/home separation is almost as rigid as ever. It is only thanks to the Cloud, not to feminism, that some women can finally work from home. The Cloud is doing feminism's job for it.

Even so, many home-based workers do not work in total geographic isolation from their work. A woman may still need to attend meetings at client offices, or to work on-site in some way, maybe at the warehouse to which she delivers the pajamas she designs, or at the greenfields development plot on which she is the environmental consultant, or at the café for which she is the interior decorator. Home-based workers still need those workspaces to accommodate children where they can.

And of course, not all women like working at home. They already do that caring for children. Many women treasure their escape to the workplace.

One of the most obvious ways in which a woman needs to blend home and work is the ability to bring her kids into the workplace. Needless to say, kids cannot go into the science lab or the steel foundry or the intensive care unit, but in plenty of workplaces, the presence of kids is safe enough for the kids and everyone else. Not convenient, maybe, and maybe not safe to the pristine levels required by overweening health and safety laws, but as safe as the world is entitled to get. The workplace is not entitled to dine like a princess on caviar-grade safety levels delivered by over-burdened mothers who shield it from child care's reality.

A mother's childless colleagues will need to learn to save their files before the toddler pulls the computer plug from the socket. Everyone will have to keep coffee away from the desk edge where tiny mitts can tip it over. We will all have to put up with shrieks and yabbers in the background while we're on the telephone to clients. We still see the workplace through masculine eyes as a child-free zone. We still think men (and now women) 'need' a child-free workplace when, in all but dangerous workplaces, and those requiring silence, and those that truly need to be an interruptions-free zone, they don't. The need lies with mothers, who need a workplace to which they can bring their children, at least sometimes.

A mother needs to be able to bring her kids to work without any hint of intolerance from her colleagues. She should not have to do what my lawyer did one morning when her nanny was sick. "I called 18 babysitters. *Eighteen*!" she told me. If her employer had been truly 'equal opportunity', my lawyer could have taken the kids into the legal chambers without that frantic and time-consuming phoning around, plus time spent waiting for the sitter to arrive. A mother should not have to de-motherize before she is granted entry to the office. Mothers are workers, too, and one definition of a mother is a woman who has children in her company, at least some of the time.

Feminism has never seriously faced up to child care as the biggest issue confronting working women. Child care is not just about the bricks-and-mortar of kindergartens and in-office day care. It's about the primary connection of a mother and child. It's about the unpredictable and exhausting demands a child makes at moments so inconvenient to a mother's working schedule. It is about the sheer unworkability of needing to be with her children and in the office but lacking the workplace's permission to do both. It is about the wrenching angst a mother feels at being apart from her children for sustained or frequent periods. So often trivialized by feminists as unnecessary 'guilt', a woman's impulse to be with her children is one of her most fiercely felt drives, and one of humanity's noblest assets. We need an economy that honors that impulse and allows us all, the kids included, to reap its benefits.

One easy way to envisage what a pro-woman workspace would look like is to imagine what would happen if it suddenly fell to men to take on the near-100 percent of domestic responsibilities that women currently carry. The world would transform overnight. Men would instantly negotiate forthrightly with their bosses for floating arrival and departure times to let them get the kids to and from school. This might mean leaving at 2 p.m., at least some days, to pick up the kids from school and working from home the rest of the day. They would devise a strategy to cover their full or partial absence in school vacations. Quick-smart, they would shift in a sofa, bean-bags, toys, games stations and TV in the office corner to make a play-lounge, and maybe install a swing or cubby-house outside, so the kids could come in to the office a couple of days a week during vacations or after school. Fathers would consider it a necessity to negotiate time in which to run errands and make household phone calls and e-mails. They might nominate one dad among them daily to run everyone's essential household errands and go pick up the kids for the other dads, and to fix lunch for the kids who come in to the office in vacation. They might share out the cost of taking less pay to do this, or retrieve the time from the unpaid overtime that is standard in many workplaces today.

Protests that a workplace is not safe for kids would be rapidly dispatched. Dads would have no truck with pious health and safety practices that got in the way of their needs as a parent. They would get to work in no time taping electrical cords to the wall, or coursing a scheme of safe housing for cabling around the skirting boards. A coffee-cups-out-of-reach protocol would be implemented in a flash. Dads would erect high shelves in the office kitchenette to lift the cleaning agents out of reach. Locked doors and toddler gates would go up on kids-no-go zones like the server room. Only those work-places that truly need to be kid-free—factory floors, airport aprons, construction sites, for example—would be so. In all other workplaces where kids could be accommodated, they would be.

In short, fathers would quickly work out a no-nonsense, honest formula with their employers that acknowledged the full gamut of parenting's demands on a man's time. This formula would pay parenting the compliment of acknowledging it exists.

How long do you think it would take before fathers got all these sensible arrangements under way? I'd give it 36 hours. The cubby and the swing might take a week, two at the outside. Men are competent. They are strategic and tactical. They're good at devising systems and solutions. When they want to get a job done, they get it done. What would take them a day and a half has taken feminism four decades and counting, with no solution in sight. The only shadow of a solution is the odd day care center in office towers, and the recent emergence of co-working spaces with on-site child care. Those make up a barely perceptible percentage of workspaces worldwide.

Meshing workspaces and home needs handling with care. Calling for children-friendly workspaces is not an argument for moving our beds into the office. Homes are sacred. It is crucial our kids don't see us treating the office as a second home.

That said, homes should not be prisons for women. When employers shut women out of the workplace, they shut women into their homes. Forcing women to engage in what is sometimes a desperate search for summer camp spaces or after-school care or occasional care; forcing them to contort themselves into crazy-shapes to pick children up from day care at 6 p.m.; forcing them to chew up much of their earnings in child care fees, all because we won't let children into the workspace—all those are anti-woman practices.

Why?

Some people, especially men, may ask why we should tailor our economy to women. An employer may argue that he has a business to run. Yes, he does. But mothers have children to raise. Actually, employers who are fathers have children to raise, too, but they don't usually raise them. They leave child-rearing to their wives.

Businesses may say they are not in the business of providing charity to women. But women are not in the business of providing charity to businesses, soaking up the unpaid domestic load so male employers and employees are free to work. And businesses do a very nice line in charity to men, by crafting them that pitch-perfect 9 a.m. to 5 p.m. day, with two whole days a week free, and an annual vacation thrown in. Businesses do this for a man, who meets neither his own nor his wife's half-share of the parenting and domestic work, yet they won't craft timetables for women, who meet both their own and their husbands' half-share of that unpaid load.

An employer who is a father has an immense debt to his wife. Moreover, every employer has a debt to another woman in his life, his mother, who gave up the best part of 20 years to care for him. A male employer may say he has no economic imperative to cater to women, but his mother had no economic imperative to cater to him as a child. Nor does his wife have an economic imperative to give up her income to care for his children. On the contrary, both his mother and his wife had enormous economic disincentives to forego a career.

It is not just mothers who need mother-shaped jobs. Our children need them, too.

The Mommy Wars will always be with us while there are mothers who believe they must be with their children and mothers who believe they don't have to be. There are masculinist factors we should delete from those wars, however, like man-shaped timetables and workspaces. No kid should be sitting out his childhood in a day care center from 7 a.m. to 6 p.m. five days a week, and spending all but two to four weeks of his glorious vacations in summer camp, just because we tell his Mommy that she sucks unless she works Daddy's hours, and because we won't craft workplaces that lets kids drop by at times. We should not be saying, "Hey, kid, your Mommy is a woman, and women can't come into the workplace unless they make like Daddy. She can either stay home all day and go nuts and you can go without all the great things her income could have bought you, like an iPad and drum lessons and season tickets to the game and a seaside holiday every year, or she can work from 9 to 5 like Daddy does, and you can never go home to your family except at nights and weekends and two to four weeks a year. Take your pick."

Mommy may genuinely want a career, of course, but kids genuinely want their afternoons and vacations. When we treat mothers' need for a mother-shaped economy with disdain, we treat our children with disdain, too. A society that doesn't care about the greatest gifts women bring—their presence as mothers, and their very ability to manifest life and love and meaning with that presence—is a society that doesn't care about its kids. It is a society without a future.

THE SUGGESTIONS IN THIS CHAPTER are not utopian. They are essential arrangements for the great majority of working women. There is nothing utopian about a woman who works 275 hours per week (as table 1 says she does) as a mother and home-maker demanding access to the economy on her own terms.

The growing workplace flexibility of the last few years is welcome, but it is not enough. It has a lot to do with the digital era's remote working capability, and the shake-out of some full-time positions to part-time roles after the 2008 recession, and little to do with any new-found regard among feminists for women's need for woman-shaped workplaces. A truly femi-flexible workplace is grounded in solid regard for the worth of mothers and housewives *outside* the workplace. That will never eventuate with feminists in charge. It will only happen when the rest of us, women and men, bring the contribution of housewives and mothers in from the cold where feminism put it, and warm it up with admiration and gratitude.

5

I Am Woman:
Hear Me Roar Like a Man!

A Woman's Working Style

"SPEAK UP!" "Speak in a low voice!" "Lean forward at the meeting table." "Shake hands with a firm grip." "Be thick-skinned." "Don't apply eye-shadow in front of your colleagues; it looks too feminine." "Control your emotions." "Don't talk about your kids or the house-work with workmates." "Don't smile too nicely or too often." "Never say sorry." And whatever you do, don't cry!

Those pieces of advice have been routinely meted out to women in 'how to get to the top' career manuals for the last 30 to 40 years, and are still in force today, implicitly or explicitly. That a man's is the only approach to work has never really been questioned by feminism since the start of the 1980s. Not robustly, anyhow. A 'successful' woman screens out her feminine sensibilities, feminism told women as they entered the workplace in huge numbers in that decade. Softness, empathy, thoughtfulness, humility, smiles and humor, a drive to put the personal before the system, inclusiveness and co-operation, emotional engagement—all these feminine qualities were considered obstacles to success. Hardness, clear-eyed assertiveness, an absence of concern for others, self-confidence, seriousness, a dedication to the system over the person, ambition, emotional detachment—all these masculine qualities were considered desirable. The only masculine attributes that feminists disavowed were violence, and that gift some men have for unrefined behavior.

We are all familiar with media images of the career-woman of the '80s and '90s. She is still around today in too-large numbers. She typically wears a suit, more often than not in soulless masculine hues like black or charcoal over a colorless white shirt. She is all crisp outlines, with little hint of feminine curvaciousness. She has largely expelled any noticeably feminine qualities from her body language. Her direct gaze dares you to find even a skerrick of femininity about her. Apart from her lipstick that tells us she retains her sexuality, which is the only part of her femininity she is not prepared to give up, her stare is the stare of a man. It may not be as flinty as his, but it carries the same no-nonsense prioritization of the job above all else. It conveys no wonder or delight in the world, other than a haughty delight in her own self-conscious 'confidence'. She seems to want us to understand that she thinks feminine strengths of delight, receptivity and empathy are for losers.

"I've left behind all that despicable feminine nonsense," she seems to say to us. "Women are a thing of the past. We women are all the same as a man now, which is as it should be. I approach the job just the way he does." Feminism thinks she is a triumph.

Few media articles profiling 'leading' career-women ever talk about how those women are leading by providing a feminine alternative to their industry's traditionally masculine conduct. On the contrary, these articles almost always speak favorably about how much she 'follows' men through imitation. Their emphasis is on replication of male practices and attitudes and capabilities, not on a wave of transformative new feminine energy entering the industry. The only uniquely female part of her experience spotlit by the media is the resistance she met from men within the industry, and how she overcame it. And almost always, it seems she overcame it through being as little like a woman and as much like a man as possible.

Women and the wider media are steeped in gender denial today. It gets expressed in comments like this: "It doesn't matter if I am a woman in this auto spare parts factory manager's job; it's just about getting the job done." "A male or female elevator mechanic; what's the difference?" "Asking whether I like being a woman in this heavy engineering rail car manufacturing plant is the wrong question. The fact that I'm a woman isn't the point."

These statements are not necessarily untrue. In many jobs, it truly does not matter whether the job is held by a man or a woman. A woman *can* navigate the war-ship. She *can* pump the convoy full of gas. The most glamorous girl from my ninth-grade class now drives a mining truck the size of a small building.

On the surface, gender denial sounds positive. It is easy to pass off a unisex attitude as active acceptance of women. However, the gender-denier's assertion of unimpeachable good intentions toward both sexes way too often cloaks an anti-woman sentiment. It's not gender itself they are denying. Nor the male gender. Have you noticed how gender-deniers are mostly very happy to leave the male gender standing? It's the female gender they are usually out to bash.

What the gender-denier is often really saying is this:

"It doesn't matter if a woman holds a job traditionally held by a man, because a successful woman is going to do the job like him, anyhow. There is no such thing as a woman. Women are just a cultural mistake. We need to correct that mistake by ensuring every woman can and does behave like a man. Discrimination is preventing her from reaching her true destiny, which is to be just like him. Once women have the opportunity to enter the workforce, they can step forward into the clean, pure light of masculinity which is the highest and natural state of every human being. Everyone is either a man, or a physiologically female person who thinks, feels and behaves just like a man, and has been forced to think, feel and behave like a woman until now. Isn't she lucky that we're all working to bring women into their true state of man-identicality now? We're closing that gender gap!"

This insulting denial of femininity now permeates our society. Feminism has reigned over the abolition of women's approaches and talents and priorities and sensibilities. What this woman-denial does is pretty much double the stock of masculinity in the world, and wipe femininity from the face of the earth.

Gender stereotyping undeniably exists, but feminists who argue that a woman is nothing but a man struggling to break free of a crippling female stereotype seek to cage women in a male stereotype. Women are real. We are a gender in our own right with our own qualities, vision and capabilities. A woman is not simply a man with cultural coding errors preventing her from reaching her 'full' potential as a man-replicant being.

A Woman's Working Style

A truly feminized workplace is not simply a workplace with as many women in it as men. It is a workplace in which women move like *women* instead of like men.

"But what's a woman?" we may cry.

Discussing a feminine style of work is vague and complex and controversial. It is controversial for at least two reasons. Firstly, and very obviously, it comes across way too easily as an attempt to pigeonhole women into 'ladylike' roles and behaviors, or to risk classing them as unsuited to the job. After millennia of getting dismissed as half-wits, we women are understandably resistant to that.

The second and more serious reason it is controversial is because feminism has taught women to be ashamed of their strengths. Feminism has a horror of espousing any feminine quality that is not also a masculine quality. If it's not masculine, it's not legitimate in their eyes.

Because of that shame, feminism has refused to craft an identifiably feminine *modus operandi* in the workplace that women everywhere can plug into and draw strength from. That is one of its big failings.

Nor have feminists made any effort to engage in the sometimes uncomfortable process of fitting the two male and female working patterns together. Men and women are far more alike than they are different from one another. But no matter what their individual personality, all men and women approach their work through the prism of masculinity or femininity. The differences between men and women are subtle but far-reaching. The male and female ways of working are like two spaceships that dock at slightly different angles. Over 90 percent, say, of their modeling and construction materials and operation might be the same; but to get the maximum utility out of the 90 percent of the spaceship that is the same, we need to build docking infrastructure in the workplace that interlocks with the 10 percent that is different.

I'm not out to prescribe my own view of what makes a woman here, but to say that a womanly working style exists. Behaving at work 'like a woman' is not about laying down behavior sets or relying on clichés (although there can be plenty of truth in clichés). It is about women feeling confident enough to let their own feminine qualities shine through. Working like a woman is whatever every individual woman knows it to be for herself. It's not going to look exactly the same for every woman, which only makes a discussion of a 'woman's working style' all the trickier.

However, all our differing views aside, we women have a lot in common. This chapter aims to outline some of those universalities. What it's trying to do is not so much to dissect women, although that's a helpful thing to do and feminism should have done it from the get-go, as lift the shame feminism makes us feel about doing the job our way. Definitively dissecting women is a very large task beyond this book. Partly, it's a task for high-quality, responsible, woman-friendly scholarship across many disciplines over a number of years. Partly, it's a task any insightful woman can do on her own. Every woman knows what it is to be a woman without the aid of scholarship. She is an expert on the subject.

So what are some of woman's unique qualities?

Some of the things I suggest we women have in common are: commonsense, a lack of bluster, a get-on-with-it work ethic, endurance, emotional and social perception, engagement with the customer. For most women, I would also add morality, warmth, humility, and hesitancy. And, of course, a quiet wisdom. Some of us have smarts as well as wisdom, which is terrific, but no woman should ever need to possess smarts to be admired as a woman. Wisdom is a key ingredient in the recipe for any strong woman; smarts are optional. No woman was ever more of a woman just because she had smarts.

You may disagree with some of those qualities, and you will almost certainly wish to add others.

Here in the following sections is my own idiosyncratic exploration of a woman's unique aptitudes in the working world. Some of this stuff will seem obvious, or simplistic, or will have been said before. It might also seem stereotypical. That's okay. Just because something is stereotypical doesn't mean it's false. On the contrary, stereotypes hold a lot of truth. They're not automatically negative. This chapter is hardly an exhaustive summary of how women operate. It's just a fly-by of my own experience and my observations of other women. What it's inviting us to do is see that we women have our own working style that is different to men's, and that it is nothing to be ashamed of. The opposite is true—it's something to be proud of.

Values and Money

In envisioning a womanly working style, I found myself speculatively using my mother as a proxy for what a truly female manager of a traditionally male institution like a bank might look like. Born in 1942 on a small farm, she fully escaped the feminist revolution. She has always been a housewife. She continues to see the world from an entirely feminine point of view, and does not know that this is no longer ideologically sanctioned. She breaks the unwritten rules of feminism's masculinist agenda. She has not been taught to divest herself of her feminine being, and to instead walk and talk and see the world in the hard economic tones of a man. Treating a bank customer as a fellow citizen first, source of income second, would be the only possible approach to her. The bank is there to serve people, she would say, not the other way around.

If my mother were a bank branch manager, she would get the teller to open the door for a female account-holder struggling with a stroller. She would swap a baby-care tip with that mother on the way out. If she were bank CEO, she would instruct all bank branches to plant flowers outside, because they look pretty, and economic entities like banks are staffed by and for people, who appreciate flowers and are not just economic entities.

She would resist the modern reliance for granting a loan solely on the basis of number-crunching, and rely more on her assessment of the character of her customers. She would do away with the automated switchboard and staff it with people. She would know that an economic entity that prospers by sucking a community dry is a destructive force, and with that knowledge she would act not just as a guardian of the bank's welfare but as a guardian of the community's welfare.

Imagine the disbelief and ridicule my mother would attract if she tried to make those feminine innovations as a bank CEO today. "Manning a switchboard with people instead of a machine went out with the *ark*! It costs tens of millions!" her board would say. "You want to size up your customers' *character* when deciding on a loan? What the—? Run the numbers! And customers don't want *flowers*!" She would be hooted out the boardroom door faster than you can say "collateral." Her board would treat her as an inconceivable naïfe, utterly out of touch with the modern (read 'masculine') public world.

But those same board directors (and not all of them are men) would not hesitate to take exorbitant city-center premises, when technology means that a bank can function just as well from a much cheaper provincial town. Their offices and branches might sport glitzy fit-outs replaced every few years long before their use-by date and costing tens of millions of pointless dollars, but my mother's much less expensive flowers outside the branches would be considered a waste of money. These same managers would approve multi-million-dollar expenditure on vacuous advertising of the "to us you're a person, not a number" genre to promote their customer service, but baulk at spending money on actual personal service by manning the phone lines. They might outlay hundreds of thousands of dollars for staff teambuilding events complete with interstate travel, while my mother's staff would operate as a well-knit team without these stagey unnecessaries, because she would only employ staff members who treated one another well in the first place.

All of this male-style expenditure is bluster. So while woman-style expenditure designed to civilize the daily lives of us all and deliver the best whole-of-customer outcome would be considered an embarrassment (in the case of the flowers) and a waste of money, wasteful man-style expenditure designed to self-indulge, self-aggrandize, and cover up the non-delivery of customer service would be considered legitimate.

Service

Women typically take responsibility for a good outcome in every part of their customers' lives, not just in the economic transaction itself. They know the world is made up not only of dollar costs, but also of non-financial costs like the aggravation and dissatisfaction customers experience with a bad outcome. These costs are typically 'off-balance sheet' for a company, because the company tips them into the lap of customers. Yet in a female-driven economy where customer service is seen as a priority, not a cost, everyone benefits. This more holistic feminine view of the economy might not always make pure economic sense, but it makes wider whole-of-life sense (and oftentimes what makes whole-of-life sense might very well translate back into economic sense). Women know that whole-of-life is ultimately more important than the economy alone.

Customer service is something women typically excel at, because they are emotionally attuned to the customer. They put themselves in the shoes of the person with whom they are dealing. A woman is usually sensible of the ramifications her advice will have in the customer's life, offers help with challenges before it is asked for, and does not turn away until a request for help is fully resolved. Her care can flow right through to the last molecule of that customer's experience.

A man doesn't do this, at least not particularly. His help is well-intentioned but is likely to be more cut and dried. A man is more likely to limit product delivery to delivering product.

Obviously, the idea that women are adept at good service is a big generalization. We have all encountered men who gave terrific service and women who gave terrible service. Nonetheless, it is true that women's leading role in the wider non-economic domain of home and heart can give their service-providing a whole extra edge a man's is less likely to possess.

Women in customer service roles often do their exemplary job in spite of, not because of, the customer service systems of the large institutions which employ them. Banks, phone companies and other big organizations keep you waiting in automated support lines, push you onto their website's FAQ which only infrequently answers your question, and grudgingly let you through to sometimes under-trained or under-empowered staff who cannot assist you. These impersonal systems are essentially masculine in conception. Genuinely helping customers is not what they are about. Providing the lowest level of help necessary at the lowest cost is what they are about. A male manager focuses directly on dollars. A female service provider is more likely to operate on the principle that if you look after the customer, the dollars will look after themselves. And that even if the dollars don't look after themselves, a smaller profit and a more satisfied customer is the right outcome to seek, for everyone. Including shareholders. After all, shareholders are customers, too. They may only own shares in one company, but every shareholder is a customer of thousands of other businesses. Isn't it worth foregoing a fraction of a percent on a dividend to get a better quality of service as a customer on thousands of occasions?

Volubility

Today's male-oriented workplaces make no real allowance for the validatory function of talk in a woman's psychology. Talk about anything except the business at hand is not really kosher at work. Yet for women, talk is a powerful enabler. Talk is *real*. It is exhilarating. When we women get together, as friends or strangers, we instantly strike up conversation, because that is the way women connect with the bright, dynamic reality of existence.

At my sons' school canteen, we moms volunteer on a roster basis to serve the kids. As we heat up banana bread, freeze watermelon chunks, melt hot cheese into potatoes, and assemble salad sandwiches, we talk. Mostly non-stop. Our talk is animated and exciting. Sometimes it's hilarious. Sometimes it's serious and confiding, or supportive and healing.

Does it interfere with our work? Yes, to a degree. Some of the time spent talking is spent not working. However, most of the time spent talking is spent working at the same time.

As we talk, we ask one another's advice. Do we need more grated carrot? Is it time to turn on the hot chocolate machine? Have we ordered enough noodle pots for the week? That talk results in the job getting done to its best. As a result of all the information inflow, we don't over-grate the carrot. We don't turn the hot chocolate machine on too soon and over-heat the milk. We spot the run on noodle pots and get more in.

That might sound like an extraordinarily folksy approach to efficiency. Systems in big business for maximizing productivity are light-years more sophisticated than tossing a few words about carrots over the canteen table. Male-style systematized big business is hugely efficient, for all that it can generate a lot of over-spending. It is not that it is an inferior mode of organization to something a woman might design; it is an overwhelmingly superior mode. All the same, my point in mentioning carrots is that there is operational value in the constant flow of information that women facilitate when they talk.

Not least is its value for women themselves. For women, talk is a tremendous energizer. It encourages. Fortifies us. Talk is part of the point of the day. A day without talk is probably a day wasted for a woman unless she has engaged in something that specifically requires isolation, like composing music, or writing her novel, or working on a speech. It may be that on its energizing count alone, talk is a big efficiency enabler for women, not a detraction.

It is also powerfully creative. In my current role as a features editor at a national parenting magazine, talk is the way we generate ideas. The magazine has a reputation for exploratory, informative content. I'd hazard two-thirds of that content springs from the ideas-swapping that goes on as the all-female editorial team quips, laughs, and hoots suggestions from desk to desk a good deal of the day.

Yet our workplaces tend to discourage women's drive to talk. Women are expected to work the less voluble way men do. His more limited command-style verbalization is the 'right' way and her conversational patter is the 'wrong' way.

What are some solutions? It may be that offices need express policies that permit women to talk at work. Maybe we need women's-only sections where women feel free to chat while they work. Maybe we need open-plan arrangements with clusters of desks close enough for everyone to talk without shouting and disturbing others. Maybe if the office ethos discourages talk, female employees need to campaign for a 'this office talks' ethos, and identify ways to demonstrate to their employer that talk does not impact work outcomes.

It may be that those are good ideas, or bad ideas, or carry both positives and negatives. Regardless, these are ideas to which feminism has not turned itself. Identifying those unique female attributes that enable a woman to do her job to the utmost goes against feminism's

DNA. Businesses in any case might be forbidden to introduce female work practices because it would be 'discriminatory', as if only one gender (the male one) were permitted on earth. The result is that women must live with the baked-in discrimination of working within male practices.

Emotionality, Tears and Laughter

Of all the non-masculine attributes a woman can manifest, perhaps the one with the most potential is her emotionality. Feminism has failed to harness woman's emotionality in the workplace. She laughs; supports; bolsters; takes delight in things; encourages; soothes; observes; cries. Her shimmering enthusiasm, her giggly pleasure in things or her dry or raucous humor, the swift perceptivity, a sweetness or a steady emotional availability, the girlish energy (which even a woman in her eighties can bring)—almost all women possess some or all of these attributes in large measure.

So much possibility is to be mined from those qualities. There is the surge of warmth she can inject into staff morale with her humor, and the output she can draw from those staff as a result; the teams she can bond with her observant compliments; the unhappy customers she can soothe. Her emotional perception lets her spot the worsening grief of a marketing officer who lost his wife to breast cancer last year, and defuse these troubles with empathy before they spill over. Emotionality is a tremendous asset.

Yet our workplaces remain largely masculine, unemotional places. Feminism assures the workplace that it is right to frown on a woman's emotionality as a liability. Unless she has a particularly overpowering personality that won't be held in, or works in an unusually accommodating workplace, or is in a creative field where emotionality is the stock in trade, a woman is not likely to get to ply her emotional strengths in today's workplaces. Not fully, anyhow.

One of the most exquisite facets of woman's emotionality that feminism leaves out in the cold is charm. Charm is one of humanity's most powerful qualities. It is timeless, but its uniquely person-to-person quality would have made it particularly efficacious in the pre-digital age of flesh-and-blood workplace relationships. That was the time in which feminism developed, so we should have seen charm come to the fore in those days. Yet after five decades of a supposedly pro-woman era, who puts the words 'charm' and 'feminist' together in the same sentence?

Charm when a woman uses it is a particularly potent catalyst. It is light-as-air yet spellbinding, intangible yet undeniable. Charm is a superb force for good. It is a whisper, a hint, of the highest that humanity can be. It is the presence of angels among us.

We're speaking here of a woman's wholesome, civilizing charm, not the debased conception of charm with its connotation of sexual entrapment. Instead of invoking this most heady and lyrical strengths of woman, feminism ordered women to quash it. Feminism sides with the male Jezebellian view of a woman's charm as dangerous. That is even though men can be charming, too, and some men use it liberally to good effect in business and politics. We Western countries should be stuffing our diplomatic corps with as much feminine charm as we can, but Western female diplomats everywhere strut corridors of power sporting the same drab suits and stern faces of every deadwood male diplomat that ever lived. Charm is a woman thing, their frowns warn us, so charm sucks.

Confidence and Integrity

Perhaps one of the biggest differences between men and women in the workforce is doubtfulness. Most women are self-doubting, timid, hesitant, self-effacing, easily daunted, at least to some degree. They are not those things in all parts of their lives and at all times and in all ways, but in some parts and at some times and in some ways, they are.

In the company of other women, just about all women I know readily admit to not always knowing what we are doing, to a lurking fear that a project will not come off, to a sensitivity to failure or insufficient skill. Laying our perceived limitations out in the open is a source of strength for a woman. Our fellow women know just where we're coming from, and they support us wholeheartedly. Honesty like this equips women with the integrity they like to bring to their work. It places our perceived deficiencies in perspective with the talents we know we also possess.

Feminism puts a negative spin on women's doubts, hesitancy and humility by labeling them a 'lack of confidence'. What feminism is pleased to call 'lack' is actually a 'presence' of positives. Doubts afford a woman the ability to step back and gauge the lie of the land, and discourage her from biting off more than she can chew, which might convert into a higher chance of success. Hesitancy is just another word for caution, which translates into prudence. Her humility allows her to accept criticism and correct mistakes, and engenders alertness to the concerns of others, potentially valuable traits. All these supposed 'weaknesses' are far-spreading advantages. The subtle but high-tensile strength in these qualities is something feminism was supposed to tease out, nurture and enmesh in a specifically female working style.

Once a woman has used these strengths to survey a situation for all its dangers and drawbacks, and she is satisfied it's safe to do so, she makes a move. That move is made with a confidence deep-rooted in a carefully calculated truth. It's therefore a pure, authentic confidence from which it is very hard to swerve her. Its basis in truth gives her confidence integrity, and that means we could argue that a woman's confidence is higher-grade than a man's.

That is because his confidence lacks that integrity. Rather than grounded in a rational and careful sizing up of the situation as hers is, his confidence is more a free-floating animal with a life of its own. It is somewhat detached from reality, inbuilt in his psyche. It contains more bluster, is more 'crash through or crash' than her considered approach.

No one ever says his confidence needs fixing to be more like hers. Feminism presents his confidence as the benchmark, and urges women to match it. This is unjustified, for his confidence could just as easily be seen in the negative as reckless, inauthentic, irrational, inept and more prone to failure.

However, that would be to disparage men's confidence when we shouldn't. It too is a positive, but a different kind of positive. Even if his bold self-belief might result in a higher failure rate than her, the sheer number of times he barges through might yield a greater absolute number of successes. Faced with a challenging situation, a man is more likely to pick the situation up and punch it in the face to make it suit him. Undoubtedly, his boldness will carry the day a lot of the time. Who dares, wins. A man's confidence is responsible for a vast swathe of the world's achievements.

It should be clear that the world needs both kinds of confidence, his and hers.

It is in her very doubts, her modesty, her tendency to 'hang back' that a good deal of a woman's intelligence and capability resides. Her 'hang back' capability is both receptive and perceptive. When she hangs back, she is watchful, open, a soaker-upper of information and truth. That humble quietude is the seat of a uniquely female decency. It is the source of her refusal to trumpet mediocrity as 'success', something many men have no hesitation in doing. It seems to me that women's 'hang back' tendency is one of our most marketable strengths.

Needless to say, a woman's 'hang back' orientation tends to hide her light under a bushel. Feminism can't handle the paradox that many of women's best qualities tend to not show. The only strategy it has come up with to reverse that feminine invisibility is to exhort women to stop hanging back and behave more like men. "Speak up!" and "lean forward!" and, of course, "lean in!"

Men in Suits

Feminists' obsession with imitating men prompts them to adopt an attribute of the male workplace persona, his 'professionalism'. There's a difference between providing a service professionally, and putting across a professional image. Obviously, women need to do their job professionally, just as men do. A female rocket scientist must run through the checklist before lift-off just like a male rocket scientist. A female doctor must preserve patient confidentiality, just like a male doctor. What we're speaking of here when we use the word 'professional' is not a worker's capacity to do the job properly, but that self-possessed, buttoned-up concentration of energized detachment that courses through a man's body when he is in 'professional' mode.

A 'professional' persona sits right on a man. It is a genuine element of his working character. When adopted by a woman, however, it can be just plain berkish. Women's strength is not our impersonal detachment; it's our warm engagement. A man tunes out from all except the job at hand, the better to give good service; a woman tunes in to not just the job but to the wider human context in which it sits, the better to give good service. A man offers his customer a focused dedication to the task; a woman offers her customer a diffuse, lateral, more all-encompassing dedication to the task. Neither's dedication is in question; the point is that there are two different kinds of dedication, his and hers. Virtually every task in the world can benefit from both kinds.

The sartorial signal of a man's 'professional' mode is the suit. Straitjacketing all the potential in a woman's warm engagement into that masculine garment of detachment is to mis-read what feminism was supposed to be all about. A woman's intuitive understanding, her perceptive and receptive personality, are supposed to offer an alternative to his style, not to replicate it. While a woman carries that same upright *intellectual* detachment as a man, her *emotional* structure is very different to his. His emotional structure is also upright and detached; her emotional structure consists of a fluid, abundant *engagement*. It's a crucial difference between men and women. A suit doesn't convey her uniquely female qualities; it blocks them off. What is a conduit for a man's energy is a cage for a woman. A woman in a suit is channeling about as much woman-power as a clothes-peg doll.

Every man on the planet has an emotional detachment at his core that a woman lacks. That is so, even in the cuddliest teddy bear of a man. No woman on earth can follow him fully into that place of emotional detachment, and nor should we ever want her to. Her emotional engagement is one of humanity's greatest assets. To lose her emotional engagement is to lose mankind's collective humanity, its very sanity, civility and closeness to God.

Every woman on the planet has an emotional engagement at her core that a man lacks. That is so, even in the toughest cookie of a woman. No man on earth can follow her fully into that place of emotional engagement. And while we might wish he could, to lose his emotional detachment would be to lose his dry-eyed rationality and practicality. That practicality is one of humanity's greatest assets. A man's emotional detachment gives his practicality a unique drive all its own. We owe the success of Western civilization to it. All the same, his emotional detachment is not something a woman should need to imitate to win society's approval.

Professionalism man-style involves a certain amount of front. While 'front' is, by definition, an inauthentic show, a man's use of professional 'front' paradoxically contains a good degree of authenticity. He uses front to create a genuinely committed, competent, trustworthy reality in his working self for his customers. Transfer that front to a woman, however, and it instantly takes on an air of unreality. That is because women are authentic already. When a woman wears a suit like a man, she engages in a front like he does, but it's an inauthentic one. Instead of 'professional', which is a positive thing in a man, the suit renders her 'professionalistic', and that's a negative thing. 'Professional' is essentially honest behavior.

'Professionalistic' is essentially dishonest behavior. That means not that women will lie and cheat, but that they are not sending a true message of their natures to their customers. 'Professionalistic' is not the behavior of a strong trustworthy human being; it's the behavior of a flawed human being pretending to be something she's not.

Things have changed in the last 15 years or so. Newsreaders have switched out of suits into shifts. Strappy sandals are the go in workplaces that would have decreed pumps before. Women are daring to look sexy at work, in an appropriate way. Fashion magazines that have cried "the suit is dead" since the '90s are finally closer to right.

However, none of this seems to be coming from a newfound feminist regard for womanly qualities. It seems to be coming from the great loosening of formality unleashed by the digital age. Were it not for the casual-wear ethos of the twenty-first century, feminism would still be leaving women stuck in double-breasteds. And things still have a long way to go. Look down any busy street in any Western city in the world, and you can't miss women in the male drag of a suit.

Roar Like a Woman

The differences between the two sexes are thrilling. They greatly *expand* the human footprint. They are a sensational asset, not a liability. As a society, we should be reveling in those differences, exploring them enthusiastically in every last detail, and extracting every bit of potential from them that we can.

Way too many high-profile women are still channeling masculinity in their working style, at least to some degree. That may make them successful masquerade men, but it makes them failed women, tin women in a silly masculinist parade. To claim 'success' as a woman when we walk, talk, work and think like a man is defeat. Those high-profile women at the top will probably be the last to change. We real women at every level throughout the economy will have to show them how it's done.

And we can. Wear the choker and dangly feather earrings to the office, if that's your style. Ooze niceness amongst your colleagues, if that's your natural personality. Don't even shake hands at all if you feel it's too blokey, let alone with a firm grip. Don't square your shoulders. Don't lower your voice. Don't swagger, unless that's truly in your make-up. Use your strengths of hesitancy, sweetness, humility at work, if those are part of who you are. Smile, when you want to. Laugh. And yes, cry. Let's roar like women.

6

The Life-onomy *vs.* the Economy

To Be or to Work?

ON MY MOTHER'S SIXTIETH BIRTHDAY a little over 10 years ago, she and her friend, Jennifer, celebrated one weekday with afternoon tea in Jennifer's garden.

A lace tablecloth draped to the ground. A floral centerpiece handcrafted by Jennifer picked up on the loveliness of the garden all around. Jennifer had baked and frosted a birthday fruitcake. She had wanted to wrap it in cream lace, but couldn't find lace the right hue, so she antiqued white lace with black tea.

Jennifer's daughter, Amelie, was there too. She had attended the same school I had, and her younger sister, who was my age, had been my close childhood friend. Amelie, a busy mother of three pre-schooler boys, had made not one, not two, but half a dozen varieties of pretty edibles, among them heart-shaped cakes, a range of tray-bakes, and delicate shortbreads. Real heart's-ease blossoms plucked from the garden twined their violet faces around the napkins. Tea was brewed with ceremony, and served in heirloom tea-cups handed down from assorted great-aunts. As they sipped and ate and chatted and laughed, my mother and Jennifer strengthened a friendship some 30 years old.

What a bunch of losers. There they sit, in the sunshine, steeped in the purposes of friendship, beauty, and creativity, when feminism tells them they should be toiling for an employer. At 2 p.m. on a weekday, they are in charge of their time, when every good feminist knows that 'successful' women's time is wrested from their grasp by work. Like women everywhere, including all the ones in the work-force, these three women had plenty of domestic work to do that day. Unlike women in the workforce, however, they had the time in which to do it. They were busy, but not to the point of insane overload. They had forged a rewarding celebration using resources under their own control, such as the backyard setting, their own special crockery, and raw ingredients purchased at prudent expense. In that one ceremony they had known so many joys—the joy of baking, the joy of decorating the table, the joy of giving purpose to a garden space Jennifer labored in every day to beautify, the joy of eating freshly baked home-made food, the joy of gift-giving, the joy of nature, the joy of leisure, the joy of building on an already very long relationship.

What working women would have done is shun the 'private' sphere where the garden party took place, and hand themselves over to the 'public' sphere of a venue in the commercial world. In outsourcing the celebration to a tiring after-work off-the-shelf experience in an impersonal café, they would have missed out on many of those joys and powers. They would have had no creative input into the decor of their surrounds or the table. The cakes would have been supplied by a wholesaler for a mass market, probably using artificial flavors or preservatives, instead of cooked fresh and tailored as an expression of love by the cook. The crockery would be the chunky kind toughened for trade use. The closest the women would get to nature might be a café courtyard. If they didn't meet after a day's work when they were very worn, they would cram the get-together into a weekend already twisted by too many domestic tasks pulling them this, that and the other way. And they would have debited their bank accounts to the café's bank account, handing over many times the cost of the ingredients of the food.

Yet those same working women would consider themselves 'liberated'. They would look down their noses at that little garden party and think, "Don't those women know how unempowered they are?"

The Private and the Public

One of the most damaging legacies of feminism's masculinism has been the lionization of the 'public' world of men and the denigration of the 'private' world of women. Before feminism, men primarily spent their day in the 'public' world. Paid work, politics, law, academia, forging humanity's commercial and civic structures, building its physical structures like roads and skyscrapers, practicality—these all belong to the public theater of action. Before feminism, women primarily spent their day in the 'private' sphere. Unpaid work raising humanity's next generation, home-running, building humanity's emotional infrastructure through a home and a connected family and a thriving community, love, color, beauty and creativity made up her world. He was more hardware; she was more software. His work in the 'public' theater required a degree of coldness and detachment; hers in the 'private' theater required warmth and engagement. He made reductionist and unemotional decisions to maximize economic efficiency, which is ultimately good for everybody. She operated in expansionist and emotional mode to maximize the well-being of all around her, what we might call social efficiency, which is ultimately good for everybody.

Come the feminist era, men still primarily spend their day in the 'public' domain. And so do women. Nobody is doing the stuff traditionally done by women in the 'private' anymore. When feminists swore vows to the previously male enterprise of career, they willfully migrated their approval wholesale to all things 'public', and rejected all things 'private'. Under feminism, the 'private' has become a place of ignominy and utter unimportance. It is woman's world, and so a place of shame. It is not just a woman's domestic work in the 'private' realm that is walled out of acknowledgement by feminism. The whole gamut of a woman's contributions and experiences and rewards in the 'private' is relegated to oblivion, too. Caring, whether for people, places or objects; linking up the community; delight in a gratifying hobby; working for a cause that matters—all are deemed meaningless alongside the great god, Career.

All the freedom and power a woman gives up in gaining a job is never noted by feminism. A woman who joins the 'public' sphere of paid employment is considered to have made no sacrifice in leaving the 'private' sphere of home, because she had nothing to lose there. She did nothing, felt nothing, valued nothing, enjoyed nothing, contributed nothing there. Feminists say her existence in the private world is worthless.

Feminism has got it wrong. A whole lot of crucial elements of a woman's life are to be found only in the 'private' realm.

Women have the right to be in the 'public' sphere, to be sure—and we can always count on feminism to fight for women's right to be wherever its beloved men are. But women also have a right to their place in the 'private' domain. They have a right to see their immense contribution in the 'private' acknowledged and catered for. Much of a woman's power derives from the 'private'. In fact, this chapter argues that the 'private' pulls rank over the 'public'—it is more important, and the power a woman wields there is greater than the power anyone, man or woman, wields in the 'public'.

The 'public' and the 'private' are the two great dimensions of human existence. They each have their own power and function, their own justifications and characteristics. They are so important to a full understanding of all that men and women are, that from here on throughout this book, let's refer to them as the Public and the Private.

Just to make it clear what we mean by Public and Private in the discussion that follows, here's a definition:

The Public is the economy and the workplace, the governmental goings-on of politics and public administration, law and academia. It is a relatively narrow place, devoted to the utilitarian business of breadwinning and keeping our local, state or national civic infrastructure running. It is by nature de-personalized.

The Public is the realm of Doing. It is a 'masculine' place in the sense that just about every man needs a central role in the Public to complete his masculinity and his validity as a human being. It is usually where a man demonstrates his leadership and makes his prime contribution to the world. That contribution is through his deeds, usually deeds of paid work. A woman may have a role in the Public where she performs the same deeds he does, but although plenty of women need a role in the Public to be fulfilled human beings, or just to earn income, they don't need a role there to complete their femininity or to be valid human beings (at least, they didn't until feminism came along in the 1980s to tell them they did).

The Private is the world outside business and government. It is the individual, the home, family, and friends. This book classes 'community' as belonging to the Private too, because even though we go out in 'public' when we enter the community, whether at a neighborhood get-together or on a charity project, we do so on our own terms as fully rounded individual humans, not as de-personalized 'professionals' representing a business or government department. The Private is the place of living and loving, laughing and crying, our multi-faceted experience of and response to the world, the full morality of right and wrong (rather than the merely 'legal' and 'illegal' we encounter in the Public world of business and government), the place of being all that we are. The Private is where every one of us, man, woman and child, steps into their whole soul.

The Private is the realm of Being. It is a 'feminine' place in the sense that every woman has a central role there as the heart of a home, family and community. It is a role that a man cannot fill. It is where she demonstrates a uniquely womanly leadership and makes her prime contribution to the world, which is to live, love and Be, not just to Do paid work. Essentially, she *is* home, family and community. The Public is *never* where a woman makes her major contribution. That might sound like a very anti-woman thing to say, but it's not. It's a very pro-woman thing to say. No matter how impressive her career achievements in the Public, she always makes an even more impressive contribution in the Private, as this chapter will explore.

Greed Is Good

Feminists' renunciation of womanhood, and the rejection of the Private that comes with it, has opened the door to the great marketization of our lives rolled out by neoliberalism over the past 40 years. Neoliberalism places great value on the free market as the ultimate guardian of our welfare. Markets, like justice, are blind, goes their creed. When money is the only voice doing the talking, formerly oppressed minorities (including women) can step forward and prosper. Once they are as economically strong as everyone else, those minorities can wield their full and rightful power in society. Thus, money is the great democratizer. Markets are the ultimate expression of people's will, so a 'market democracy' is the most desirable form of democracy. A fully free market makes for maximum wealth for every individual, which makes for maximum empowerment for every individual, which is for everyone's good. Greed is good.

It is not that neoliberals are wrong. A rigorous and free economy is a legitimate cause to champion. Freedom from concern for all the important things money can't buy, however, is not. Inherent in the greed-is-good philosophy is a disregard for non-economic treasures like the family, community, civility, good character, social cohesion, domesticity, joy, sensitivity, beauty, appreciation, creativity, leisure and caring. Neoliberalism strips these things away because they get in the way of making money. But these are the things that women live and breathe and value and bring to the world. They are more important, not less important, than money. Neo-lib proponents of the economy wage war on these elements of our non-economic lives—what we might call the 'life-onomy'—not by declaring them an enemy as such, but by rendering them collateral damage. They are justifiable casualties in the laissez-faire economy's great onward march to supremacy.

It is no accident that the masculinist brand of feminism we all live with today arose at the same time as greed-is-good capitalism, in the 1980s. Greed-is-good is an essentially masculine philosophy. It is driven by money, by commerce, by the economy, which all belong to the Public turf of human activity where masculinity is sourced. Money, commerce, the economy play a central role in a man's life that they do not play in a woman's life, no matter how much she loves her job, how many hours she devotes to it, how much money she makes, how much she needs it, and how much she likes accruing or spending that money.

The kind of woman who floats to the top in the greed-is-good political economy is a masculinist woman. She is the one who will collude most readily with the essentially 'male' Public world of Business and Government, and stand up the least for the essentially 'female' Private world of life outside work. She places a phenomenally higher value on the power she gets from her merely commercial or political job in the Public than she does on the power she gets from her own individual life and time, her home, her family and community, in the Private. She lauds the contribution she makes and the rewards she gets through paid work in the Public, while ridiculing and denying the much greater contributions and possibly much greater rewards of her unpaid job as a housewife and mother in the Private. She works a man's very long hours which the life-denying greed-is-good economy in the Public demands, thereby denying time and energy to Private importances like home, children, caring, hobbies, passions, causes, nature, her very soul.

The 1980s greed-is-good philosophy gave oxygen to this masculinist woman, and she has been pumping oxygen back to it ever since.

They feed each other. She and her man-crazed sisters have been sitting at the top of the feminist leadership that whole time. It is virtually impossible to budge them, because their masculinist version of feminism is embedded in our economy. That is to say, it is backed up by money. Pre-1980s feminism, which was a much broader church and contained a lot of genuine regard for women's worth outside the economy, was no match for the dollar.

Had women managed to stand firm against feminism's masculinism past the 1980s, they would have provided a padding of vital truth against this dollarization of the soul. Feminism is a movement of the left, but in its wholesale shift to masculinist values centered on commerce, it has handed victory to big business on the right that leftists so love to hate. Business is an essentially 'masculine' endeavor (notwithstanding today's many fabulous businesswomen) in that work is an essential part of every man's masculinity. Because business was a man's undertaking, feminism said it outranked a woman's non-business undertaking of upholding society's soul in the Private.

That is partly why we have become a society driven by overwork, over-consumerism, the fakery of commercial 'brands' over the authenticity of the artisanal, producers pushing style over substance and consumers willing to accept it, a two-dimensional life of midweek work and weekend hedonism over a richer three-dimensional array of relationships and thoughts and knowledge and experiences, a wholesale lack of purpose, what is being called a mental illness epidemic, and the infiltration of sex, drugs and alcohol into the lives of our children. These imbalances and wrongs are what you get in a society dominated by masculinist values.

Women have the power to at least partly remedy all these imbalances and wrongs. Through their leadership in the human zone of the Private, they can restore authenticity, and thereby counter over-commerciality, and dispel the brutal work/play duality that flattens us all into two-dimensional cartoons of real people. Through their social connectedness, they can heal much of the mental health 'epidemic' which is probably just a disconnectedness epidemic. Through their morality, they can banish or at least minimize the wretchedness of drink, drugs and casual sex from our teens' lives. Almost every woman today is too busy replicating a man's paid activity to manifest all these woman-powers. And that means, in a very real sense, that women are no longer with us.

Greed-is-good feminism twists everything a woman values and contributes in the Private down to the 'male' level of business. Here is just one example. My mother is a skillful floral arranger. At a community lunch in a church hall in our town when I was a child, she styled table settings of crimson roses and trailing ivy in white Greek urns, placed at intervals down the center of the long trellis tables. She has the knack for placing every bloom and strand of greenery with classical perfection. They were breathtaking, even in that modest weatherboard venue. Everyone got the benefit of their beauty, including my mother, who had the additional privilege of providing beauty for others. Arranging those flowers may have had no strict commercial value—the luncheon didn't 'need' flowers— but lunching with splendid flowers is nonetheless a valuable thing. Providing that beauty is a kind of work that mostly only women do.

Feminist ideology says the beauty enjoyed by everyone at that lunch was of no account. "You should start a floristry business," feminists would instruct my mother. I suggested the same thing to her when I was a child. "Then I'd be stuck in a little store all day," she said sensibly. She rightly saw a floristry as a big diminution of her power as a non-working woman. In feminist ideology, a woman is only supposed to enjoy roses through the prism of the economy—as a producer (the florist) or a consumer (the florist's customer)—because the economy is where the men are.

That is a masculinist way to see the world. It's a values system that puts the essentially 'masculine' endeavor of creating money on a higher level that the essentially 'feminine' endeavor of creating beauty. It's a values system that is certainly good for the economy, and the economy is a very important thing. It's great if women expand the economy. But it's not a values system that's good for the soul, and the soul is supposed to outrank the economy.

Enjoying roses the 'female' way, as one who generates and appreciates beauty in the Private outside the economy, is supposed to be a higher-status experience, not a lower-status experience, than enjoying roses the 'male' Public way as a buyer or seller of flowers inside the economy. After all, arranging roses in the church hall allows my mother to give and receive more power, not less power, than arranging roses in a business. She calls on friends, who knew the powerful pleasure of growing the roses outside the economy in their own gardens, to pick the blooms. That way, she 'owns' the blooms in a more connected way than if she had bought them by the bucket at a wholesale flower market. It imbues the blooms with more meaning, and enjoying that meaning is a privilege and a power. She enjoys the power of creating the table settings according to her own taste, not to the taste of a client. Her rose-arranging schedule fits in with, rather than clashes with, her busy schedule as wife and mother, yielding her yet more power. Styling blooms for the community lunch outside the economy is a modest but hugely powerful way to make the world a more civilized place. Styling them for a customer who is a stranger dislocates her effort from the realm of the soul and the neighborhood to the realm of the economy, reduces her actions to a meaningless point on the money-exchanging grid, and drains it of its great personal and communal power.

Yet because business is the source of a man's power, feminism says it is the only source of power for a woman.

Good Things

A feminist's inability to value anything but work and the income and other benefits it brings is a shortcoming, not a talent. Strong women know this. Strong women know that life is about love and laughter and sadness and joy and caring, and it is about leisure and hobbies and spirituality, and a great many good things that have nothing to do with career.

Let's look at some of those good things.

Community

With the onset of greed-is-good feminism since the 1980s, women have retreated from the front line of defense of society's soul, which they used to do so ably in the home and the suburban street and the community hall, to take cover behind desks. A career-woman is largely excused from having to care about anyone or anything except her job. This is not to hit women over the head with all the blame for our deteriorated community ties. Nonetheless, feminism is making sure that community cannot survive. There is simply no time for it. Even if there were, feminism sees to it that community is so uncool, women don't want to nourish it.

Our neighbors, our elderly, the many disadvantaged kids who need adult help and guidance, anyone with a disability or illness, anyone in financial or emotional crisis at some stage of their lives, our schools, the myriad causes that benefit from fundraising—all need a strong community. It doesn't matter whether it's major help we offer, like creating a charity to help foster kids learn to read, or minor help, like feeding our neighbor's budgie while she's visiting family interstate. We all need a society made up of people who help one another, not just of worker ants.

Men can provide a lot of community help, of course, but it is heavily on women that the community relies. A woman's efforts, her particular bundle of skills, and her unique personality are what is called 'social capital' when she brings them to her community. The community needs *her*, not just the dollars she may donate to charity from her salary. Every woman has her own interests and motivations that can deliver a valuable contribution. For example, some of my fellow school-moms are running a 'just one' drive asking every school family to donate just one item (a pillowcase, a tin of soup) to a new women's shelter they've helped set up, the only one around for many miles. Maybe you are teaching yourself WordPress so you can build a site for your church's Bible study circle. Maybe you are founding a local conservation group to save an endangered finch. Or maybe you are just offering to collect a fellow school-mom's child from school when she is stuck across town in traffic.

Much of this work a woman does is not necessary to her, but it can be necessary to the recipient. The women at the crisis shelter need that tin of soup; the mom stuck across town needs someone to collect her child. Other community work a woman does might not be necessary at all, but is nonetheless deeply valuable to us all—documenting historic houses at risk of demolition for a local heritage group; or dropping some secondhand magazines off to a housebound elderly neighbor, watering their garden, helping them fetch their sweaters down from the closet, and keeping them company over a cup of tea, and finding out over that cup of tea that they need a new electric blanket and bringing over her spare one that she doesn't really need. There is a lot more work to be done each day than just the paid kind traditionally done by men.

It is not just a woman's community that benefits when she brings her social capital into play. She benefits, too, from the manifold and meaningful links she makes with others, and from her pride in forging a stronger, better world. Feminism likes to pretend that a career replaces and improves upon the community life that stay-at-home women used to enjoy. It claims that a working woman is doing something 'for herself'. Is she? Is leaping behind a desk and slaving for an employer doing something 'for herself'? Is she really overjoyed to leave her rich variety of experiences in the community behind for the uniform experience of commercial activity? Or is she working to pander to feminism's fetish with paid work when she'd rather be coordinating a working bee to build her daughter's school-yard chicken run?

It is highly doubtful that all women who work are doing it 'for themselves'. In fact, I am absolutely certain that many of my friends and fellow school-moms are working 'for their employers' and 'for feminism'. I am dismayed at the many women I know who turn their back on community, and work instead, not because they want to, and not because they financially have to, but to appease feminism's masculinizing demand that they do what men do. Feminism wins; their employers win; these women's bank accounts win; but they themselves lose out.

Feminism claims that work is mentally stimulating, and so it can be. However, work is a largely two-dimensional activity driven by a need or desire for income. If we weren't paid, most of us wouldn't show up. Work we do in the community is its own reward; we do it because it is inherently useful and meaningful. In the community, a woman can give of herself. That is a rich, irreplaceable and relatively effortless thing to do, effortless in that she gets to choose what she gives, and when. Paid work, by contrast, is often mentally impoverishing, readily done by another worker, and calls for effort aplenty. In the workplace, the employer does not want or need a woman's irreplaceable multi-dimensional personality. An employer wants her to do the job. Most of her social capital is wasted there. The exertions and unique abilities a woman brings to the job enrich her employer and the economy, but the economy's gain is usually the community's loss.

And the community's loss is ultimately her loss. The woman herself needs a community's helping hand sometimes. If she has a child in a wheelchair, she needs the local service club to raise funds for a bus to take her child to a school for kids with physical disabilities in the nearby city. If she has multiple sclerosis, she may need a neighbor to do her grocery shopping. She needs the local senior citizens' club to deliver meals-on-wheels to her shut-in mother, so she does not have to cook all Saturday and run a week's cooked meals over to her mother every Sunday.

It is not only these more necessary services she receives from a community. She benefits, and so do we all, from the serendipity of a flowerbed planted in a traffic circle by guerrilla gardeners at midnight; or by the glow from the Christmas tree raised by the Rotary club in the local mall; or by the block party organized by the enthusiastic new couple down the street.

In pre-feminist days, a woman's contribution outside the workplace was an accepted part of the warp and weft of everyday life. We used to greet women as three-dimensional beings who generated a web of contributions to society, many or all of which were not paid. Under feminism, we are shrinking women to a walking CV. We treat women as two-dimensional economic processors 'stimulated' by nothing but their careers, because men have careers. And only what men do counts, says feminism.

Feminism is wrong. What women do in the community counts, too.

Who Cares? The Value of Caring

It is not only communities that need women. Closer to home, her family and friends need the social 'mortar' her caring provides. Not just her immediate family, but ageing parents, siblings, aunts and uncles, cousins, nieces and nephews call on a woman's 'mortaring' skills pretty much anytime for aid, comfort, advice. A 17-year-old's chat with his mom about career choices as she washes and he dries the pans after a Sunday lunch; an aunt assisting a 21-year-old niece to write a moving-out-of-home budget; a 55-year-old who re-lives a childhood bereavement at a Thanksgiving gathering with his female cousin who was there when it happened; a daughter whose phone calls are a touchstone for her widowed father—these contacts with women can provide courage, direction, healing and hope for family members.

Those who benefit from this contact with women may not even be aware of what a help it is. That's because it is the matrix in which we live. This 'caring mortar' that women provide doesn't stand out like a man's paid work, any more than real mortar stands out on a brick wall. Feminism says man-made architecture, the literal architecture of roads and bridges and buildings and IT networks, matters because that is the kind of architecture a man builds. Feminism is busy right now exhorting women to enter careers in STEM (Science, Technology, Engineering, Math) because it is the stuff of which the architecture men build is made of. The kind of architecture a woman builds—relationship architecture—is dismissed precisely because it is the kind of architecture a woman builds. Nothing a woman does can have any value in feminism's eyes. A female architect of gas stations or coding protocols wins acclaim; a female architect of relationships (which is every woman on earth) wins sneers and invalidation unless she has a career like a man to shore up her acceptability.

Yet woman's 'mortaring' is one of the great constructive elements of humanity. It is a resource that nourishes the world. It is an enabling force that strengthens everyone who encounters it. It binds family members into something bigger than the sum of their parts. A woman's caring plugs people in to the universe.

What makes the 'work' in caring even more difficult to tease out is that it may be spliced with a lot of activity that looks like leisure from the outside. Think of a woman's *tête-à-tête* with a stressed sister at a family barbecue, or an e-mail conversation with a grandson to help him identify the best college course, or a chat with a daughter to help her resolve a disagreement with her friends. All these acts take place in what our society calls a man's off-duty time, which can disguise the fact that a woman is making a valuable 'on-duty' contribution.

Men provide aid to family and community, too, obviously. A man might mow the six-inch-high lawn for the old lady across the street; he will nail up the drooping gutter on the house of his 92-year-old grandmother; he will spend a morning building a play-fort for the local school for kids with visual impairments; he will taxi a neighbor with chest pains to the emergency room. However, men's 'mortaring' is typically performed much less frequently; it tends to come in short bursts of tersely worded advice and discrete practical action instead of unremitting warmth and empathy; and it tends to be offered only at times convenient to men.

Moreover, a man does not tend to take responsibility for seeing a problem to begin with. It is usually a woman who takes on the underlying responsibility for being alert to need in others. It is most often she who first perceives others' need, she who sizes it up, and she who informs her husband or partner what action he could or should take. That ever-present watchfulness for others' needs is a form of *work*. It is a responsibility she never puts down.

Nor does a man tend to see another's needs through to the end, as a woman does. Once the neighbor with chest pains is deposited at the hospital, a man is likely to return to his own concerns. A woman will stay tuned in. She will ring the hospital every day or two to check on the neighbor. She will think about what might need doing in his house (fridge emptied, heating turned off). She will go to the hospital to get his keys, and may make a special trip to buy him some fruit or to borrow books from the library for him. She will collect his mail, feed his goldfish. Unlike a man, who will likely segment his 'caring' work to weekends when it is convenient, she does all this mid-week too, whether or not it is convenient.

Moreover, a woman's 'mortaring' is generally motivated by consideration for others. A man's mortaring is sometimes motivated by consideration for others, and sometimes not. For example, he may genuinely care about taking the neighbor with chest pains to hospital, and building the fort for the kids with disabilities. However, his real motivation for mowing the old lady's lawn across the street might be that he doesn't want snakes setting up in the long grass.

Even when a man is motivated by a true desire to care, and notwithstanding the invaluable contribution he makes with his practicality, there is always one element missing from his aid that her aid has in bucketloads—tenderness. Tenderness enables a woman to absorb every hair's-breadth detail of a difficult situation, weave those details into a whole, and deliver that whole back to those in the scene with the suffering distilled away as much as possible. Tenderness makes everything as alright as it can possibly be. Even when things can't be made alright, a woman's tenderness enfolds all the raw contours of a painful situation in a healing balm.

Most of the cases of caring and community work in this chapter sound old-fashioned. That's because they are. Do you or your partner even know when your neighbor has chest pains, let alone take him to hospital? Even know where the nearest school for kids with disabilities is, let alone build a play-fort there? Maybe you fix the gutter on your 92-year-old grandmother's roof, but you probably ignore the ankle-high lawn of the old lady across the street. I don't know many women in the feminist era who do these kinds of things, and I don't do them either.

This book is not out to say that you or any woman 'should' do these things. How much we give to others is an individual choice, and the last thing we should be telling women is that they should do more for others. What this chapter aims to say is that one of the reasons women don't use their profound mortaring powers any more is that feminism has rendered them unfashionable. Feminism's decree that a career is the most important—and only important—activity a woman can undertake is a sleight of hand that relegates mortaring to the dark, where feminism wants all great, uniquely female powers to stay.

However, when feminism goads us into self-interest through our careers, it deprives us of the chance to be selfless. Being the selfless 'mortar' is a job most women have an inherent drive to do. We *want* to be there for others. We like to make everyone happy. Many women find the urge to care and help irresistible. I personally love being of use. I find community work more fulfilling, more empowering than any paid work I could ever undertake.

That is not to say that caring is always enjoyable. Like so much else in woman's circumstances, her ability to care is a double-edged sword. It is both an impressive force, and a force that weakens her at the very same time. In caring for others, she gives up herself. When she goes to fetch the key from her sick neighbor in hospital so she can turn off the heating in his house and throw perishables from his fridge, she renounces her own interests and purposes and time and energy and opportunities that day. She keeps herself small, to make others bigger. Caring is not a win-win situation, at least not always. Caring can feel like strands of a net a woman weaves about herself, entangling her in frustration and limitation and exhaustion. Caring can really suck.

With its mono-focus on career, feminism tacitly tells women that caring and helping is a shameful impulse they should cauterize. When was the last time we heard feminists extol the great feminine attribute of caring and helping? Feminism values disengagement and self-interest in a woman, not connectedness, because disengagement and self-interest are practiced by men. That is not to blanket-criticize men. Their disengaged self-interest can be a valuable tool to help them get ahead and provide for their families, which is in itself a way of caring.

However, feminism doesn't value a woman's career because it helps provide for her family. It values a woman's career because men have careers. Helping is what women do, says the feminist in disgust, therefore helping sucks.

But helping doesn't suck. Helping enables the helped and enno-bles the helper. Helping is what you do when you are more powerful than the helped. Some of us believe God helps us all the time, and we don't hear anyone sneering at God's power to help. Helping and caring is a form of tremendous *power*. Not the selfish kind of power wielded in the workplace and state affairs, that of power *over* others and sometimes making others smaller, but the power *underneath* and *among* others, the power of making others bigger. It is woman's power, one which men do not possess, at least not in such great quality and quantity. It is a form of superiority, not inferiority.

Feminism doesn't agree. It sides with the Biblical, dead-white-male view of helping, where a man is 'independent' and self-justifying, and his wife is merely a 'helpmeet', auxiliary, secondary to his primary-ness. He is front and center, she is periphery. Feminism never acknowledges a man's role as the recipient of all the help his wife gives him, never depicts him as someone who is therefore subordinate to his wife. Feminism instead portrays him as inviolate, unsullied by his dependence on the woman who runs his home and takes care of his children. To acknowledge his dependence would really spoil the picture feminism paints for itself of all valid human beings as essentially masculine, housework-free, parenting-free, caring-free, man-identical entities.

A woman's caring gene translates into heavy *work* for a woman. To be a woman is to feel a concern for others that a man doesn't feel. It's to feel a weightier engagement with the world. That is one of the reasons being a housewife and mother is more work than being a house-husband and father. Because caring is a subtle kind of work in comparison to paid work, however, feminists find it easy to deny that this extensive part of woman's job description exists. A woman's caring work is not included in the tally of her workload in tables 1 and 2 in the first two chapters of this book, partly because how much we care is a personal choice, but also because it is so difficult to identify and quantify. Obviously, however, caring should be added to the total sum.

'Secret Women's Business'

In the 1990s, a highly publicized clash arose over the planned construction of a bridge to a river island in my home country of Australia. Elderwomen of the local Aboriginal tribe opposed the bridge, claiming the island was a culturally important site. "What went on there?" the media asked them. "Secret women's business," one of them replied. This drew howls of derision from cynics who saw it as a cooked-up story to back a native people's land grab, and defense from those who believed we should respect an indigenous tradition. National opinion was divided, and the claim's legitimacy was never settled.

Whatever side of the fence you sat on, the term 'secret women's business' made a humorous entry to the lingo. A 'secret men's business' mental wellbeing program for men sprang up, as did a 'secret men's business' yachting group. A canine grooming parlor near my house is called 'Secret Dogs' Business'. But the term really comes into its own for girls' get-togethers. A friend of mine now meets up with her girlfriends for regular 'secret women's business' weekends at a luxury hotel out of town. No men are allowed, and they get up to whatever it is we women get up to when we are together. They laugh uproariously over a glass of wine in the spa, sample the local eats, book facials, and foray out to the quaint tourist towns nearby. Mostly, though, they get on with the serious business of talking about women's stuff.

It is surely a truth that all cultures have their 'secret women's business'. In English-speaking culture, we typically find it at that most delicious social locale, the girls' coffee morning. These might be in a café, or in a home. These get-togethers roll into one a whole lot of things with meaning. There is the love of cake, the pleasure for the hostess at home of setting a pretty table and the delight of the guests in that table, a thrilling opportunity for the preschoolers to play, a partial release for the mothers from the burdensome daily routine. Most important, however, is the talk. It is easy to dismiss secret women's business as gab-fests, a way of killing time. Not true. Conversation the way a woman does it is a kind of *work*. It is leisure too, of course—it's great fun, after all—but it serves a number of profound purposes.

Women need to talk. We validate our feelings and experiences by talking about them. That's one of the crucial things going on behind the chat at a coffee morning: validation. An experience in a woman's life has not fully happened until she talks about it. Talking not only completes us, it allows our experiences to overflow and spill into the lives of the other women we are talking to. By listening, our companions provide a structure into which we can send our experiences outside of ourselves, and mesh them into a bigger, stronger network of female humanity. If a woman has happy news to share, the joy is magnified and reflected back to her by her friends. If she has fears, she can set them in context by sharing, and then their scariest edges get contained. Some fears will shrink as the group points out that a worrisome situation is not as frightening as she thinks, or that there are ways to ameliorate it. Many fears may remain, but just by parceling them out to the group, a woman dilutes the fear and builds an army. The listening friends can all enlist as quiet soldiers in her fight. Buttressed by their sheer numbers and combined strength, she can leave their company with the moral support to get her through.

That is one of the reasons women's get-togethers resonate with a bond that is so rich and regenerative. Sharing ideas, good news and fears lifts us up and makes us safe, expands our universe and makes it both endless and graspable at the same time. At secret women's business meetings, the world is made sense of. There, women plumb down into the well of the universe, and fix on the truth.

Strength is not conversation's only purpose in 'secret women's business'. Conversation is also a productive source of information sharing. We swap recommendations for a dentist or a new frozen-meal delivery service. We lend a laminator for our friend's daughter's school project, and we give away outgrown bicycles to a mother with younger kids. We swap suggestions on the smartest time to slot homework into the day, and we refer one another to the latest educational videos on YouTube. The graphic designer mom whips up a new logo for the mom who runs a yoga school, while the artist mom recommends a color scheme for the chiropractor mom's waiting room.

Another purpose of conversation is to reinforce our values. On a recent sunny day at a verandah café overlooking the harbor, I temporarily joined that despised micro-group, the 'ladies who lunch'. I was meeting up with two wonderful retired friends for a meal. Even though I would put in far, far more than eight hours that day caring for children and running a house, I felt guilty. Not because I had done no work, but because feminism instills in us all an unspoken sense that to step into our woman-power in the middle of the day is forbidden. With its insistence on the full-time Monday-to-Friday working week, feminism covertly arranges women's lives so that they can only access their 'secret women's business' power at nights or weekends, peripheral time rather than the prime time of the working day. That subtly but, in my experience, deftly reduces me as a woman from a primary dynamic force in society to a side-lined wallflower.

I went to lunch anyway. As our conversation turned to books, two of us agreed that Louisa May Alcott's *Little Women* was our favorite novel. By giving the book's March family our seal of approval, and encouraging each other in this belief, we cement the Marches' reality into our own lives. No matter if you don't share our high opinion of the book, or if you take a dim view of that family's traditional structure; the point is that when women get together, one of the things we nearly always talk about is the way the world should be. By talking about the way the world should be, we help keep it there. We help resist more breakdown into the way the world is. We reinforce the morality of the universe, if only with our inner orientation. That reinforcement is a kind of work, and its effects can spread throughout society and last a lifetime. Standing firm as moral centers, however you perceive a morally ideal world to look, is one of the primary powers women possess.

A woman's power as a moral center stems from within her, not from her job inside the workforce. That is, it is sourced in the Private, not the Public. Had I lived out the feminist all-work no-play stricture that day and gone to work, I could not have met that womanly calling to identify and consolidate all that is right and good. Relatively little opportunity presents itself at work for women to infuse society with their moral presence, unless they work for a social enterprise.

When feminism turns its back on the Private, it turns its back on secret women's business. Maybe a working woman can find time to catch up with the girls outside her job. Maybe she can't. Either way, feminism doesn't care. Feminists like to pretend that a job gives a woman all the power she needs, but that isn't true. 'Secret women's business' is a pure, priceless power that a career can never give her.

Rest

There is another thing we need to value in a woman's life. Rest.

Despite the fact that women take on a far greater workload in the home than their male partners take on in the workplace, it is routine for our society to sneer whenever a woman takes a rest. A mother stopping for a much-needed coffee at the mall after the Herculean whirl of getting kids off to school that morning before she shops for Size 6 boys' underpants and blue-topped football socks and gets in the groceries and investigates beauty salon treatments as a gift for her sister-in-law's birthday and buys a gift for her three-year-old's buddy's birthday and drops by the post office to pick up her high schooler's textbooks she bought online secondhand before she heads back around 2 p.m. to pick up the kids from school and start the grueling snacks/sports/day care center pick-up/dinner/clearing up/baths/homework/bedtime routine that will go on until about 9 p.m.; a group of high school moms fitting in a set of tennis between the tortuous demands of providing consistent daily discipline to their 16-year-olds; a gang of preschool moms who have been awake all night with teething 18-month-olds and who are taking a precious 30 minutes out of their one child-free day for a treasured weekly power-walk after the storm of getting the toddlers off to day care—all may draw derogatory comments from passers-by about their 'easy' life.

Yet even in rare moments of leisure, a woman is hardly ever totally at rest. In the unlikely event that the mom at the mall has time to slump in a café over a magazine, her mind is ruminating on ways to improve her family's life as she leafs through the pages. As those moms we mentioned play tennis or power-walk, their 'improvement antennae' are out as they swap information between themselves on a new child physiotherapy business down the street, or an online tutoring service for their 16-year-old daughters, or a call from a charity seeking donations of old computers. A woman's mission of reinforcing the goodness in the lives of those around her is ever-present, woven in with her leisure in shifting, fluctuating, multi-dimensional ways. In a sense, she is always on duty. Her work has no distinct 'on/off' settings the way his does. Feminism makes no effort at all to alert society to this.

If we are ever to speak of a 'successful' life for women, that life must include some rest. A life without leisure is barbaric. It is in leisure that we are at our highest. It is in leisure that we meet God, however character-building work may be. When feminists succeed in goading a mother into paid work, they ensure her leisure is exterminated. A man can enjoy seven early mornings, seven evenings, two whole days a week, and two to four weeks of vacation a year. A working mother has no free time at all. You may have noticed that in table 2 in chapter 2, which analyses the time allotments of a mother-of-two's 24-hour day, there was column 1 for taking care of the baby, column 2 for taking care of the toddler, column 3 for a part-time 'extra pair of hands', column 4 for housework, and column 5 for career, but no column 6 for the woman herself.

If feminists want to be taken seriously in their sloganeering for 'equality', they need to show their commitment to a woman's equal opportunity to rest.

To Be or Not to Be?

Extolling the value of life outside the economy is not about saying to women, "Go back to the kitchen." Rather, it is to say, "Stay in the kitchen if you want to." It is to say, "The kitchen is a more important place than the workplace and we all value the work you do there." By the 'kitchen' is meant not just the literal kitchen but our function as wives, mothers, home-makers, and the heart of a family and neighborhood and community, our personal lives, our souls, all that we are and do in the full Private realm outside the economy. We women should be able to be and do all that, without censure for not also doing the paid stuff men do in the Public. Tremendous power is wielded in the Private. A vast width and depth of achievement occurs there. What happens in the kitchen, in our homes, in our communities, our individual and collective souls, is bigger and more important, not smaller and less important, than what happens in the office. The kitchen table ultimately trumps the boardroom table.

If women are never home, then no one is ever home. She doesn't have to literally be inside the four walls of her house to be home. She is 'home' when she moves about her extended family, the neighborhood, the community, when she is anywhere *outside* the economy, released from the workplace to be fully present for us all. In the Private, she forges a strong life for every member of her family. That strength grows outward into the community, and outward again into the nation. Homes matter. Homes matter in a way that nowhere else matters. Home is the root of our fullest selves.

For a woman to be the presence that keeps home and community alive is humanity's foremost power. Her presence is fundamental, not ornamental. Presence is a form of God. A world in which everyone is always absent is godless. And, with due respect to men, a woman's presence is a special thing that a man's presence is not. Women breathe life into humanity. When women are around, society's lights are on. Men traditionally did and still do our working, for which we should all be grateful, but women do our *living*.

185

And that leads us to what may be the most important observation anyone can make about women: that the 'living' women do is a form of *work*. Just *being* a woman is a kind of work. *Being a woman is a kind of work in a way that being a man is not a kind of work.* That is so important for all men and women to understand, that let's break it out onto its own lines:

Just being a woman is a kind of work.

'Being' when a woman does it is a thing in itself. Let's give it an upper-case 'B' and call it Being to signify that we're talking about a concrete thing of value.

What do we mean by Being? We mean a woman's uniquely feminine ability to burst above the low utilitarian clouds of work into the exhilarating golden sunshine of Existence. The point of human existence is *to Be*. A woman's presence carries with it a whole extra league of deep, roiling consciousness that a man does not bring to the world, and the point of human existence is embodied in that consciousness. In her resonant ever-readiness to perceive, to feel, to respond, to take in the signals from the Universe and relay them out to the world in the form of warmth, joy, love, light, laughter, appreciation, care, responsibility, watchfulness, tenderness, sadness, thoughtfulness and gratitude, she manifests the point of existence on behalf of every man, woman and child. I like to think of her as the Keeper of the Point.

When a woman is outside the workplace, she is performing the most critical task a human being can do. She is *witnessing* Creation, and in so doing, she bestows meaning upon it. By witnessing, she confirms for us all and reassures us all that the world has purpose. Even God cannot endow the world with meaning; it takes someone else to witness it to do that. After all, if no one notices and appreciates this amazing Creation that God has made, what's the point of making it? God needs someone to pick up this Creation thing and notice it to make it worthwhile, and that someone is her. In so doing, she fixes God's or the Universe's presence here among us on earth. What a majestic capacity. It's the ultimate power.

A woman's Being-work is not something she can do at work. At work, she gives up most of her Being-power in order to merely Do. After all, work is, by definition, a place where people renounce their personal lives to focus solely on getting the job done.

That doesn't mean that a woman outside the workplace isn't working. A woman's Being-work is just that—work. It is an *active* contribution. It is a towering three-dimensional energy with its own weather system, its own rules, exertions and contributions. Her Being-state is a kind of 24/7 vigil that is not trivial, selfish or lazy. Men might scoff and say, "Yeah, right! Being is work. Sure it is. All she's doing is staring at the walls. Nice work if you can get it." But a non-working woman manifesting her Being-power is not just staring at the walls, even if it looks like that's what she's doing (and it rarely looks like that, for few women ever have time to stare at the walls. Men, on the other hand, have seven nights and seven early mornings, two whole weekend days, annual vacation, and a whole retirement in which to stare at the walls.)

With her very consciousness and presence, a woman off-duty from paid work is on-duty at Being-work in a way that a man is not. A man off-duty from paid work is often goofing off. Chilling in front of the teev. Watching the game. Catching up with the guys at the bar. That's okay, but it's important to understand that a woman is virtually never just goofing off the way he does. Even when she is watching TV, or taking in a show, or catching up with the girls at the bar, she is doing something crucial that he does not do. She is Being, on behalf of all humanity. She never switches off from her alertness to the world, to the ever-present business of knowing, observing, communing, watching out for everyone, always receiving and interpreting and relaying those signals from the Universe.

A man is deaf to a lot of those signals. A man's value resides in *What He Does*; a woman's value resides in *Who She Is* (notwithstanding the extraordinary quantity of work she 'does' as a mother and housewife). He is primarily an economic unit (without wishing to minimize his fundamental worth as a human being, a family member and a citizen). She is primarily a non-economic unit, *and that is so even if she spends most of her hours at work.* A man's greatest gift to the world is his deeds, almost always those performed at work. No matter what her work means to her, a woman *always* brings a bigger gift to humanity than her career deeds. She brings her Being-power. Her Being-work doesn't show up in the GDP figures, but the Being a woman does outside her career is always more significant, more impressive, more *successful*, than whatever she does for a living. That Being-success stands clear of her career deeds. To Be a (good) woman is the ultimate success, and the only success society should ever demand of her.

Men have traditionally been the ones to keep humanity's body. Their income literally bought the food we ate that kept body and soul together, it bought the houses our bodies shelter in, paid for the medical appointments that kept our bodies healthy, bought the clothes that kept our bodies warm, and many other necessaries, besides. Not only that, but their physical labor built the bulk of our society's body, whether that be the factories we work in, the fields we plough, the cars we drive in or the roads we drive them on. Our society still relies heavily today on men's income-earning and physical strength.

However, if there were no women in the world, humanity would have no soul. Humankind would be nothing but a race of cyborgs. Men bring physical strength that no woman can match, but women bring emotional strength that no man can match, and it's through that emotional strength, her Being-strength, that a woman functions as *the keeper of humanity's soul.* A world in which women perpetually renounce their Being-power in order to merely work like a man is a world that has renounced its collective human soul. It matters not, how important her work is. Even if she is a doctor who finds the cure for cancer one night alone in her lab, or an astrophysicist who blasts away that Earth-bound meteor and saves the planet, that is not as great an achievement as manifesting humanity's soul through her Being-power. If she is so occupied in Doing at work that she never manifests humanity's soul by Being outside work, then that is not a world worth surviving in or saving.

With its obsession with the 'Doing' of paid work, feminism crushes woman's Being-power like a bug. Feminism cannot bear to think that there is an even more awesome contribution to the world than men's paid work, and that that contribution is made by women. 'Being' is the privileged role God or the Universe entrusted to women. 'Being' is not only humanity's greatest glory, it is God's greatest glory. Beyond all the Creative labor God or the Universe employs to make this wonderful world, His greatest glory is that He (or She) *exists*. Yet feminists would tell God to His face that Being sucks, that God's very existence sucks, that humanity's soul sucks, for no other reason than that Being is the power God gave to women. 'Being' is a power of shame, say feminists, simply because it is a woman's power.

Instead of validating Being-power, feminism shuts off its validatory oxygen supply. It re-routes all that oxygen to the Public dimension of business and government, where the men are. If you feel like your life is too controlled by Big Business and Big Government today, feminism's man-worship is a big part of the reason. There is no living, breathing alternative to those two essentially male dead zones, because feminism has shut down the Private, where the living, breathing humanity-power manifested by women resides.

And that means that women are no longer a force in their own right. When women use their Being-power, they manifest good values. With those values, our society could have stood firm against the social deterioration of the last four decades. With a thriving presence in the Private world outside work, women could have argued against the long-hours-creep that has bitten into the lives of so many employees, both women and men, since the 1980s. Women of all income levels could have stood up for a good life against the rich life that led to the 2008 crash. Strong mothers could have modeled a concern for others that would have at least partly drained the narcissism epidemic raging in our playgrounds before it began. Incredibly, mothers today are not even especially visible defenders against the appalling alcoholism, drug-taking, sexualization and early adultification of their own teenage children.

We women don't do these things anymore because we're all seeking a fake authority through man-identical careers in the Public arena of the workplace instead. We have lost the true, much more valorous, womanly authority we used to wield from within the Private. The leader in the Private is woman. A woman can replace a man's leadership in the relatively narrow Public world of commerce or government, but a man cannot replace her Being-leadership in the wider Private world outside it. Her authority as the ruler of the Private, the land of life, emotion and relationships, the place our very souls dwell, is supposed to be a powerful retort to the authority men wield in the Public, the traditionally masculine authority of kings and presidents and CEOs. It isn't, because feminism says this female kind of leadership sucks. Feminism portrays it as embarrassing, dumb, unsexy, or just plain irrelevant.

Work is a dehumanized activity. We do it for necessity's sake. No matter how engaging we may find it, work is ultimately about the business of *getting*; it is secondary to the business of *living*. We work to live, not live to work. Working to live is honorable. Living to work is unholy; you don't have to be a person of faith to understand that. Living to work perverts the purpose of life, which is to Be. Of those two great and equally necessary halves of existence, Being and Doing, the greater equal half is Being. Being trumps Doing. The Doing that is paid work is the means to an end; Being *is* that end.

What that means is that the Public is there to serve the Private. The commercial and administrative operations of business and government in the Public realm are there to serve us human beings in the much bigger and more important Private realm where we get on with Being-business, the business of meeting with our full selves, souls, experiences, feelings, liberties and responsibilities outside the workplace.

Feminism says it's the other way around—that the Private is there to serve the Public. That people live to work. That we Be in order to Do. That people are there to serve the economy and government. That womanhood (which is rooted in the Private and finds its highest expression in Being-work) is there to serve masculinity (which is rooted in the Public and finds it highest expression in Doing-work). Feminism is saying that we women exist only to hurl ourselves out at bed at 5 a.m., to tear around packing the kids off to day care and school faster than humanly possible, to dispense with our own and our children's humanity as rapidly as possible, in order to make a craven rush to the only place with any meaning, the temple of the workplace, wherein our man-gods dwell. At its most wholesale, what feminism is effectively declaring is that women are there to serve men.

This not only destroys us women. It destroys our kids. Our children are living souls, creatures who need to enjoy a wholesome breakfast at a civilized pace sitting at the table, little people who want to actively Be as they get dressed and joke with their siblings, who want time to talk to Mommy or Daddy about their not-quite-finished homework as they pack it into their school bags, who want to walk out to the car and get in at a manageable pace that allows them time to look up at the blue sky and count the poppies that have popped that morning in the flowerbed beside the car without shrieks of "hurry up!" from parents. By hounding Mommy off to be where Daddy is, feminism says that children are not to have these things. They're not to have their own souls, not to live in purpose and meaning.

Feminism's message to children is, "The purpose of life, which is to Be, sucks because it is your non-working Mommy who manifests that purpose, and she's a woman, and women suck. You suck, because caring for children is women's work, therefore children suck. Your existence doesn't count. Your family's existence doesn't count. Nobody's existence counts, except Daddy's. Beauty, passion and meaning don't count, because your mother brings us these things, and our masculinist society does not want anything your mother brings. Only Daddy's masculo-lode of career-power counts. Daddy is the Alpha and the Omega. Only men, and women who do what men do in the male domain of Business and Government, count. Forget about the future. There isn't one, except for a life of over-work, stress and pointlessness. Get used to it."

With that attitude from feminists, woman's role as the one who manifests humanity's soul scarcely stands a chance. And with the loss of humanity's soul, the purpose that Mommy would have pumped into the lives of her children dies, too.

To say that the Being-stuff a woman does outside the workplace is more important than the Doing-stuff a man does inside it, is not to speak in a spirit of female supremacism. A woman's power to actualize all humanity into being through her Being-state is the ultimate God-given privilege, and all strong women dwell in that gift with humility and a sense of responsibility, not with overbearing smother-mother pride. A man deserves ringing admiration for what he does in the Public world. We human beings need the fabulous things he produces and the income he earns at work. There would be no world without it.

But ultimately, it is life outside the economy and politics that matters, for both men and women. Most men and many women might need work for a sense of purpose, but work is not *the* purpose of life. To *Be* is the purpose of life. Our souls. Our friends and family and community and fellow humans. Our hobbies and interests. Our passions. Our causes. Our curiosity. The big, glorious, fully fledged world outside work, thrumming with mystery, clarity and meaning.

The Whole Woman

In answer to the question the sub-title of this chapter asks, 'To Be or to Work?', way too many women are answering only 'to work' and never 'to be'. Until we disinfect ourselves from the feminist belief that a woman must work like a man to be a worthy woman, we will continue to source our womanhood in the 'male' realm of Doing paid work instead of in the 'female' realm of Being. And that is to renounce our womanhood.

Our Being-worth in the Private dimension outside the work-place is a state we women used to exist in fearlessly, without shame, through all history before the masculinist strand of feminism took us over in the 1980s. We need to return to that fearlessness. Women should not need to work like a man a day in their lives to be worthy of admiration. In Being, they are life itself. They are a power all their own.

7

Who's a Strong Woman?

Pulling Off the Man-Goggles and
Driving Like a Woman

WHAT CAN THE FEMINIST LEADERSHIP say to accusations of masculinism? Here are three excuses they use:

Excuse One:
'The Fog of War'
When feminists are accused of behaving like men, their first retort is usually that they "had to" enter the world on men's terms. I think of this line as their 'fog of war' spin. It goes like this:

> *We were soldiers in the Great Feminist Liberation Army! It was war! There was all this smoke and fire, and bombs were going off, and visibility was near-zero, and there was no chance to care about women getting injured. All we knew was that victory lay on the sunny ridge-top in the village of Manhood, where everyone found status and power in a career! But the village of Womanhood was down in the swamp at the bottom of the ridge and it got in the way of our ascent to the ridge-top with all its demeaning mothering and housework and stuff, so we had to wipe out the village of Womanhood to save it.*

We had to send first-time mothers with six-week-old babies out onto the career battlefield eight to 10 hours a day plus commute, even though there were all these bullets whizzing around. We had to obey the village of Manhood's workplace timetable to the letter, and show up at 9 a.m. or earlier ("reporting for duty, sir!") and stay there until 5 p.m. or later ("Can we stay at our desks all day just like you do? Sir, yessir!") despite the fact it was killing us, what with all our work to do down in the village of Womanhood. We had to exhort every woman-soldier to imitate every man-soldier in the village of Manhood; we achieved that by blowing up her inbuilt self-worth, and replacing it with the drive to work like a man if she wanted to earn her self-worth back. We had to disguise her in the enemy's uniform of a business suit. There was no risk of her getting shot for dressing in the enemy's uniform, because men are blind to the fact that women have a whole other unpaid workplace to labor in, and are blind to the fact that women dwell in a whole extra league of emotional consciousness that does not sit well in a suit, and so men never recognized her as anything except a man anyway. We had to burn the homes in Womanhood by setting them alight with the accelerant of shame, otherwise some women might want to stay in them, and that would lessen our troop numbers fighting for the total occupation of Manhood.

The village of Womanhood was collateral damage. In any case, who'd want to live there? The village of Womanhood was for losers. Women are so thankful to us for wiping it out and winning them citizenship in Manhood. They know it was for their own good.

What bunk.

Feminists did not have to wipe out the village of Womanhood to save it. And they most certainly were not doing it for women's own good. Feminists wiped out the village of Womanhood *because it felt good.* Yet the self-styled Generalissimas of the Great Feminist

Liberation Army have hoodwinked us all into believing their strategy has been a great success. They point to women's near-total occupation of the ridge-top village of Manhood as evidence.

It is a Pyrrhic victory. The village of Womanhood has been gazetted off the map, while the workload of the village—the housework, the child care, a woman's work as an emotional center of family and community, her very existence as a She Who Is over and above her paid role as a She Who Does—remains. So do the female citizens of the village, only they are no longer permitted to think and act like women. Now they are trapped citizens of the village of Manhood, where feminism has won them the right only to prioritize and labor like their fellow citizens, men.

At the same time, without ever bothering the male citizens, women must run up and down the ridge, holding a job in both villages. Feminism did nothing to drain the flooding overload of domestic work in the swamp of the village of Womanhood by pumping some of it to men up on the ridge-top; it did not shine the sunlight of validation down on the village of Womanhood to dry it out and help it thrive; it didn't clear the tall trees obscuring the view of the village of Womanhood from the lofty vantage-point of the village of Manhood so that men could actually spy out the work that goes on down in the swamp; nor did it give tours of the village of Womanhood to educate the male inhabitants of the village of Manhood about what goes on there.

Excuse Two:

It's Our Right to Work (but only like a man, not like a woman)

A second defense feminists throw up against accusations of masculinism is to protest that women have a right to careers like men. And yes, we do. A woman's right to have what a man has is such a successful blind for feminists to hide behind, because it is woven from strips of truth. A woman's right to work like a man is undeniable.

But so is a woman's right to work like a woman. She has a right to a workplace timetable and labor laws shaped around her. Winning a man's rights is both a big gain and a disability at the same time. What use is a man-shaped career if she must stuff it into a woman-shaped life full of school-runs and kindy concerts?

A woman's right to a *woman-shaped* society is precisely the right feminism can't handle fighting for, because it means recognizing women as people *who are not men*. Feminists are appalled by anyone who is not a man.

Excuse Three:
It Can't Change Until Women Get to the Top

No matter how mutilating feminists' strategy for the 'liberation' of women has been, they seek to nullify women's protests with the assurance that it will all be wonderful when women get to the top.

Incredibly, a great many of us believe it. That is despite the fact that it flies in the face of the evidence. Can you think of a single female CEO who has dramatically feminized her company with a 'mothers come first' workplace culture? Show me the woman in charge who introduces individually negotiable timetables for mothers, schedules her business's essential activities into school term-time to free mothers up in school vacations as much as possible, provides respectful flexibility for emergencies like AWOL babysitters and the day your six-year-old tells you at 7:42 a.m. that they are supposed to go to school dressed as an earthworm that day, and welcomes children on-site, maybe with dedicated play-lounges or just a beanbag and TV in the empty meeting room. How many senior female managers do you know who set an optional 'go home at 2/3/4 p.m.' policy so that a woman (or a man) has time to cook dinner? Much more radically, show me the female CEO who divides all the jobs in her company into two-and-a-half day increments (that is, into 50 percent of the working week, or 20 hours per week), so fathers and mothers can spend an equal share of time in the workplace and at home? Much less radically, how many female leaders can you think of who set a loud and clear example by leaving work at 2 p.m. to do the Tuesday and Thursday soccer run? Right. None.

The last thing we need is more masculinist women at the top. A woman at the top who got there and stays there by behaving like a man is not an asset to womankind. She is a liability.

Feminism only cares about the top—the CEO-ship, the chairmanship, that ovaloid office in a certain white house—because that is the apotheosis of masculine power. The 'top' is a traditionally male power that is about having power 'over' others. While that is a terrific kind of power for women to possess, it is only one kind of power, and not the most useful kind I can possess as a woman. The power I need as a woman is power 'from' others. I need the power of regard 'from' others for the workload I carry as a home-maker and mother. I need the power of permission 'from' society to live as a woman instead of as a replica man, to live by my authentic womanly priorities, to put my own health, leisure, community, family and unpaid work ahead of career if that's what I want. I need the power 'from' employers who arrange the job around my mothering responsibilities, rather than expecting me to arrange my mothering responsibilities around the job. That power 'from' others is to be found everywhere. In a world that values women, it is to be found at the top, and in the middle, and at the bottom, inside and outside the workplace and government halls, not just by the handful of people in the political or corporate 'top jobs'.

A woman should not have to match a man's level of career success to be 'powerful'. In fact, she should not need a career at all. Feminism was supposed to create a world in which a housewife could move with the same dynamic ease as a man, whether or not she took a job. It was supposed to create a world where a woman's voice was heard equally loudly from the diaper change table as from the boardroom table—louder, actually, because the diaper change table is more important and more demanding than the boardroom table.

Turning women away from the diaper change table, from their homes, from their energized and high-contributing lives outside the workplace, and forcing them to sit instead at the boardroom table, will not necessarily increase their power back inside their families and homes and lives. Quite the opposite. It is likely to squash their power in their families and homes and lives by leaving them no time or energy there.

It is great to have women in positions of power in corporations and government if they act in the interests of the woman at the diaper change table; of the woman vacuuming the bedrooms; of the woman squeezing in a volunteering session to cover books in the school library before rushing off to buy pumpkin-hued hair ribbons for her eight-year-old's Halloween skate party; of the woman beautifying her front lawn by planting a jacaranda tree that will burst into a ball of mauve flowers every summer; of the woman donating her time to teach hip-hop to the local Down syndrome kids. But it is not great if women in 'top' roles use them to belittle, deny and prevent access to all those non-working powers a woman possesses—as the hand that rocks the cradle beside the diaper change table; as the vacuuming woman who knows the power of being on top of the housework; as the magician injecting pumpkin-magic into her daughter's party; as the fosterer of a tree of life in her garden that brings pleasure to all who see it or sit under it; or as the woman who manifests her formidable power to improve the world by helping the Down's kids know the joy of dance like all the other kids get to do. When feminists at the top offer jobs on a full-time 9 to 5 basis, they effectively block their female employees from manifesting all these awesome powers outside the workplace.

In any case, it is not power that feminists are seeking at the top. Self-actualization as a woman via emulation of men is what they're really seeking. Their unquestioned tenet that a woman is inferior to a man is behind their fetish with getting to the top. That is why they embark on that soul-destroying climb up the corporate ladder. They think that if they can just get there, then, and only then, will a woman be as good as a man. A feminist thinks that if she can just squeeze herself into the outline of a man's life, that suddenly her cells and shape will align with his cells and shape and—shazaam!—lights will flash, music will play, and she will switch on to the same status, power, transcendence and human worth as him! It's a puerile scenario that feminism has way too many of us believing in.

The Revolution That Wasn't

What could feminists have done instead of masculinizing the world? To answer that, I only have to channel my grandmothers.

My maternal grandmother, Joyce Lee, worked most of her life. She was a farmer's wife, café proprietor, bar-maid, grocery store proprietor, and bakery cook. She was business-minded, and loved working. Its daily action and purpose were indispensable to her. During World War II, she ran a café six days a week in her small Australian town for American soldiers, who were based nearby on my great-grandmother's farm, which was close to a military airfield. Joyce packed my two-year-old mother off in the jeep with the GIs each morning to spend the day in my great-grandmother's care on the farm, while she ran the café.

Yet Joyce always put her womanly work as housekeeper and mother first. Her home was unfailingly orderly and clean. Meals were cooked on time, every time. Even when Joyce and my grandfather took over the farm after the War, my mother tells me Joyce set a formal table every night with a linen table-cloth (stiffened with real starch, not the spray-on kind, and ironed by a kerosene-heated iron). She placed carefully frosted fairy-cakes into her two children's school lunchboxes. She sewed up pretty dresses for herself and my mother, and shirts for her son and husband. This she did on a remote farm where groceries were delivered once a month on the train from the next big town, and 70-plus cows were milked twice a day, and the only water in the taps was cold. For extra income, she boarded the local school-teacher and did his laundry. She reveled in womanly cooking, sewing and gardening. She once showed me the 72 first, second or third prizes or commendations she had received for her baking in the 73 categories she entered in the local agricultural shows. Her paid and unpaid work did not stop her being a central member of the community; she and my grandfather built a community dance hall and public tennis court with their own hands.

Joyce never saw her income-earning work as 'masculine' the way feminists do, and she never placed it on a higher pedestal than her 'feminine' work of housework and mothering. A functioning house; three substantial meals a day, and home-made cakes for morning tea, afternoon tea, and supper; and in later life after she had moved to town, a well-kept garden bursting with ultra-neat rows of high-maintenance annuals—all these mattered absolutely to her. They were an essential platform to an acceptable standard of living. She considered providing these things both a duty and a gift to herself, her family and community.

My other grandmother, Elsie Kruger, never worked and never wanted to. Her freedom and power as a stay-at-home mother were sacrosanct to her. Although she had complete and clear-eyed regard for my grandfather's work at the family sawmill, for its physical demands and risks, for its sacrifice, and for its obvious economic value, and although they lived in a happy marriage full of mutual respect, she knew her role as the mother of four to be the main game. She knew that the family did not live so that my grandfather could saw timber; my grandfather sawed timber so the family could live.

Elsie lived a fully independent life. Released from paid work's burdensome limitations, she was free to be a woman every minute of the day. Her pleasure in being with her children and grandchildren was like a deep, bubbling brook in which she swam all her life. Her initiative in staging regular Sunday evening barbecues kept our huge extended family of first, second and third cousins together. She would hand all us grandkids a balloon and a white paper bag of candy when we showed up at those barbecues, and we tore around the yard while the grown-ups chatted and ate. We chased wild kittens hiding in the drains, peered into the storeroom where she kept every issue of *Women's Weekly* magazine she had ever bought and, if she came with us, we ventured into the scary 'wilderness' area down the back where the custard apple tree grew. Her leadership in staging those nights provided me with memories that lift me into a higher, more exalted place forever.

Elsie was no prisoner of the 'a woman's place is in the kitchen' stereotype that feminism would make her out to be today. She felt plugged into all life had to offer precisely *because* she was career-free. She was adventurous and a sports nut. She was the first in the family to travel on an airplane, and in her youth in the 1920s, she was a local junior boxing champion.

Both my grandmothers were totally right in their attitudes to paid work. However, feminism tells us only one of them is right, and we all know which grandma that is, don't we? It's the working grandma, Joyce. In fact, even Joyce wouldn't cut it with modern feminists, because for much of her life she was the farmer's wife. To win credence with feminists, she would have to be the farmer. Feminists would have been particularly horrified to discover that Joyce never got a driver's license, though she could drive—she drove the tractor on the farm all the time—and instead rode a prim shotgun as my grandfather ferried her around town. In the eyes of today's feminists, my non-working grandma, Elsie, was a write-off. The only part of Elsie's life feminists would applaud is her boxing, because men box.

Both Joyce and Elsie would have adamantly rejected feminism's attempt to strip away their validity as women. Neither woman would have tolerated the idea that they must work like a man to be a worthy woman. Joyce worked because she loved it, and absolutely never to reference her womanhood off a career. Neither would have elevated the merely commercial activity of paid work over the exhilaration of being, living and loving that is the primary stuff of woman. Neither would have dreamed of sneering at their own domestic and mothering work that demanded so much of them and counted for so much. Never mind that much of housework and mothering is menial. They would acknowledge the drawbacks of women's unpaid work as readily as any woman, but to deny that the world needed that contribution from women, for no other reason than that it is women who make that contribution, would seem to them like what it is, a mad self-attack.

Neither grandma would have tolerated entering the economy on the masculine terms feminism offers. Both would have rejected the modern scramble to prostrate themselves before a 9 to 5 workplace schedule. Neither would have paraded down the office corridors in a preposterous suit, bristling in zealous emulation of men in a desperate desire to establish her self-worth as a woman. Neither would have preened about her career as feminists do, flaunting a man-identical job as a badge of worth. Joyce would never have dreamed of lifting herself up as a working woman by putting down her fellow housewives and mothers who didn't work. Neither would have stooped to playing a man's game by doing the job the way he did it. Neither would have sold herself wholesale to masculinity by pretending that a career sat in her life where it sat in a man's life. A feminist's life would appear to Joyce and Elsie as the life of the UnWoman.

So what would Joyce and Elsie have done to bring about the Great Feminist Revolution?

If no woman-shaped jobs presented themselves, Joyce would create them by starting up a business that ran on women's hours. If she ran a dress store, she might unapologetically close it at 2:30 p.m. so she and her customers could go home and get the afternoon chores under way. If she had wanted to be an architect, she would have set up not in a downtown office whose location broke her ability to be a housewife and mother, but in an enabling office attached out the back of her home that facilitated her ability to be a housewife and mother. Had she wanted to contribute to her country's defense by joining the Army, she would have clubbed together with other women to start a women-only unit in the Army Reserve, which would eventually make its way into the Army proper when their skill was proven, but their commander would accept with equanimity that they would drop out of training in school vacations to care for the kids. If she had wanted to take a job as a farm machinery salesperson, and the male CEO had said the job was only open to men on a 9-to-5 basis, she would have held him to account in person, woman to man, not stridently but robustly, and challenged him to recognize her fundamental female worth as a farm machinery salesperson who was also a housewife and mother, so that he couldn't hold out unless he wanted to make a total prat of himself (which of course plenty of men did, in the early days).

Joyce would have made all these sensible transformations by saying to her employer, "I am a valid woman as a housewife and mother and I would like a role in this workplace." By contrast, feminists say to their employers, "I am a non-valid woman as a housewife and a mother and I suck unless you give me a role in this workplace. I will do whatever it takes to get the job, and that includes denying the need to be there for my kids and to run my house."

That is, Joyce would have negotiated from within the Private, drawing on her self-respect as someone whose role *outside* the workplace was more important than the paid work inside it. Feminists, on the other hand, negotiate with the workplace from *inside* it, from within the Public dimension, as if those Public places they seek to enter—the world of commerce, the public service, politics—take precedence over a woman's unpaid work in the Private.

That is an important distinction to make. Joyce's primary tool for entering the workplace would have been the *presence* of her womanhood, demonstrating mothers' and housewives' right and ability to hold men's jobs. Feminists' primary tool is the *absence* of their womanhood, refuting their right to jobs that accommodate them as mothers and housewives, and assuring employers that the lowly 'women's work' of housework and mothering will never get in the way of the workplace where the big important 'men's work' gets done. That cedes an authority to the 'male' dimension of the workplace that it doesn't deserve.

As Joyce and her contemporaries made their way into tradition-ally male occupations, they would not have abandoned one iota of their femininity. They would have steadily developed a female working persona cemented in deep, rich, authentic femininity, not a tacky man-imitating feminist persona glue-gunned onto the side of masculinity like a spare rib. And as the realization that women could be soldiers and farm machinery saleswomen and architects gathered pace, a Feminist Evolution rather than a Revolution would have unfolded organically. And gradually, everyone would have seen that women could do the job, and do it their way, and on their terms. The Feminist Evolution would have embodied none of the detest-able rejection of a woman's non-working worth that we're all so used to now under feminism. We would have seen none of the slurs on women's unique aptitudes and sensibilities that is part and parcel of feminism's insistence that a woman responds in the same way as a man does to everything. None of the destruction of a woman and her family caused by an overload of paid work. Many fewer women shut out of careers because they can't work a man's hours.

This Evolution might have taken no longer than the 20 years or so that feminism's masculinist strategy took. And it would have got women to a place where they owned the jobs, instead of the jobs owning them, as has happened under feminism. Feminism has led us up a masculinist dead-end.

That's Joyce's strategy, but what about Elsie, my non-working grandma? An important part of this Evolution is what she would have done. Elsie would have contributed to the Evolution by remaining a resolute occupant of the village of Womanhood. She would have stayed away from a career in the village of Manhood altogether, and devoted herself to the wholly womanly work that is home-running and mothering and manifesting humanity's soul. That way, she radiates woman's worth, and invites everyone else to honor that worth. It's a simple and perfect tactic. Occupation is ten-tenths of the law. If the village of Womanhood lies abandoned because its female citizens were driven out by the self-loathing inspired by feminists, that's defeat. To occupy the Village is not just the fight. It's the victory.

Powered by Woman

Had feminism been sincere about ushering woman-power onto the world stage, we would have seen an explosion of academic and popular literature over the past half-century about women's unique capabilities. What we got instead was a monolithic suppression of exploration of female capabilities. Some scholarly work on the differences between men and women has been done, but it's very limited and mostly not mainstream. Even in academia, which should be ideology-free, it is largely taboo to point out any ways in which women are different to feminism's great god, Man.

What would it look like if women were unlocked to ply their unique strengths? What if they used their jobs to make life better for women instead of keeping the world shaped for men? Here is a sample of some ways I see woman-power missing in action. You can surely think of many more:

~ Female (and male) academics in many fields would identify in forensic detail every element of a mother's preposterously overcrowded day to shed light on its vast and intricate architecture, and to map her challenges. For example, psychologists might measure a woman's contribution in maintaining that intracellular

24/7 vigilance that calls her to incessant duty at 11:17 p.m. when the 15-month-old cries, or at 5:20 a.m. when she is breastfeeding and alert for the danger sounds of the 20-month-old about to clamber out of his cot and tip head first on to the floor, almost even before he has thought of doing it, or at 9:42 a.m. when the two-year-old is 300 yards from the duck-pond but could be beside the pond in a logic-defying two seconds.

Time management consultants might evaluate the highly concentrated labor 'credit points' inherent in managing multiple conflicting duties, and the added 'points' inherent in managing those unremitting conflicts with no rest, sleep or exercise. Then they would come up with smart ways to extract more value and rest from her motherhood minutes. Biologists and doctors would devise a method to gauge the torment of a crying baby. A crying baby is genuine torture, and it may be that one characteristic of torture is that it is unmeasurable, but that is no excuse to not try. Those same doctors would then seek ways to put a stop to the crying, for which every one of them should receive a medal.

~ All this motherhood-mapping would feed into work by female (and male) economists to develop sophisticated methods for measuring the true weight and value of the housework, mothering and 'caring' work that women pour into their families and communities. Don't say it can't be done; if accountants can hold a slide rule to something as nebulous as 'goodwill' and 'risk' on a company's balance sheet, they can measure a woman's much more concrete work in the home. Those methods would be popularized in mass-market books, blogs and media so that for the first time in history, a blazing light shone on women's immense non-monetary contribution. This was a hugely necessary task at the dawn of the feminist era. Instead, feminist economists stayed silent. The female economics writers I read seem to only ever report on the world the way a man does, by reporting on money. Sure, the economy is about money, but it is also about value, and that is where all the unpaid work women do comes in.

~ Female (and male) human resources managers would arm themselves with those economists' stats to campaign loud and long for female-friendly workplaces. Scarcely any HR consultants do this. Nor can I think of any female union reps or leaders who do this, not even in female-heavy sectors.

~ Female (and male) town planners would dot mother-and-child rest stations throughout town centers. Moms with young children badly need these. They might come with a fenced playground next to café seating where adults can sit to supervise in comfort, a hub for teens, breastfeeding cubicles with an armchair and a table for the water-bottle she will need to quench her thirst when the baby draws milk, microwaves, kid-size dining furniture, change tables with a sink and anti-bacterial soap beside each one, toilet cubicles big enough for strollers, and vending machines stocking everything bub from wet-wipes to spare outfits to healthy toddler and adult snacks. Going into the sixth decade of feminism, scarcely any city in the world yet offers this most basic and necessary facility.

~ Female (and male) accountants, financial planners and policy-makers would call for a radical re-working of the tax and investment systems to accommodate women's life circumstances. How about a lower or zero income tax rate for mothers returning to work? A differential treatment of her retirement fund to counter all those non-earning years? I have scarcely ever heard a feminist call for this feminization of our financial system. Yet I have been to four 'women's investment seminars' over the years, all delivered by besuited corporate feminists oh-so-proud to be a 'woman in the finance sector' and every one of them turned out to be offering . . . the same advice they give to men. In a financial system where women are treated like men, what other advice could they give except the lame tip to "save more"?

One dystopian manifestation of woman-focused financial policy is raising its ugly head in many Western countries, however. That's tax and other financial policy designed to 'nudge' women into—you guessed it—work. And not just a little work, but work full-time. Even with babies and preschoolers. It's grim policy designed to engineer a time allocation for mothering, housework and caring-work right out of existence, while leaving her with all that activity, and forcing her to match a man's work *at the same time*. Calls by feminists for these brutal 'gender equality' policies are everywhere in the media now. What these policies really are, is masculinization policies. They are designed to make women do whatever men do. What makes them even more offensive is that they are put forward not only by feminists, but by gormless male feminist-sympathizing scholars and policy-makers in government departments and think-tanks who consider themselves to be 'fully' contributing at 40 hours per week, and who have no plans to 'nudge' themselves or other men into 'equally' matching their wives' outsize workload in the home.

~ If feminists were serious in their calls for more women to enter politics, they would shape the role to fit women. Rather than shoving more over-busy housewives and mothers into super-full-time governmental positions designed for men, one elegant solution might be to create women's advisory panels attached to every government department. These could consist of women of all ages, from all walks of life, both working and not, who could voice women's needs and concerns, give input on the impact of policy on women (and children) as it is being formulated, and come up with innovations. They might be available online for consultation throughout their period of service, and meet to discuss policy for a day in person in their state capital at intervals of, say, once a quarter.

A structure like this would allow women a lot of influence. It would do them the honor of recognizing that they are too overworked as housewives and mothers to be burdened with the demands of a job in politics or the civil service—and that precisely *because* they are too occupied with raising us all as kids and cooking everyone's dinner to take part in government like a man, we need to hear their voices. Their unavailability is a sign of how important they are, not how unimportant they are. Perhaps the women could be elected, or selected by ballot, every one, two, three to four years. It would be relatively undemanding on the women themselves, and relatively inexpensive to run.

There is nothing stopping feminists at the 'top' from introducing suggestions like these, but they won't. And when feminists bleat that they couldn't possibly effect change away from the top, they deny the many kinds of power women already possess at the 'middle' and the 'bottom'.

One of those kinds of power is what we might call 'kitchen table power'. That is the power of women coming together to make change from inside their homes and communities. Feminism has created few charities or change-movements that draw on women's love, knowledge, skills and energy outside the economy or government. That is changing as a new wave of philanthro-mommies rides high on the groundswell of social enterprise. One example in my city is a collective which gathers up unused disposable diapers that families have left over when the kids outgrow them, and re-distributes them to women's shelters. From a moms' recycling collective renovating pre-loved cribs, strollers and other baby paraphernalia to donate to families in need, to daughters staging punchy dance-a-thon fundraisers for their mothers with breast cancer, to school-moms holding play-groups to teach English to newly arrived refugee women and their kids, woman-power is winging its way out across streets and neighborhoods, cities and countries, making the world a better place.

There is no need to do what men do, no need to take on a role in the traditionally male Public theater of business or government or academia or law, to be powerful.

Woman as the morally superior sex of peace is a profound power in herself. She is humanity as it could be and should be. In the feminine way of solving disputes, no one gets blown up by landmines, or bombed, or shot. Yet feminism seems to recruit women into the armed forces with more fervor than it puts into developing woman's capacity for peace. Female politicians and diplomats seem to rely on the same masculine tools of *realpolitik* and economic containment and large militaries that men do. Not that those tools are wrong, and not that they are only appropriate for men to use. All the same, women's moral authority as the sex of peace is largely ignored by feminist powerbrokers strutting the world stage. Sure, there were peace movements of the mothers-against-nuclear-reactors kind in the early days, but once masculinism got going in the 1980s, they died out or got relegated to the fringe.

Beyond mere diplomatic power, in any case, the most obvious untapped source of world peace is women's role as mothers. The hand that rocks the cradle rules the world. Every wacko dictator on the planet had a mother. Presumably, not all those mothers were wacko, too. A good many were possibly loving women. So what goes wrong? How does a loving mother produce an evil son? Where does a mother's power to shape her son end, and an evil father's power, or malign outside cultural or economic influences, take over? With the dawn of feminism, that should have been one of the most urgently investigated questions in history. What did feminists do? Let it lie, because mother-power is woman-power. And if it's woman-power, it's not power at all.

Why Work?

One of feminism's greatest deceits is to pretend that a career means the same thing to a woman as it does to a man. In feminist doctrine, work is supposed to feel the same to a woman as it does to him, fill the same function, take the same priority, bring her the same rewards. A feminist defines herself by how a man experiences the world around him. Whatever he recognizes and feels and understands and is motivated by, she throws her hand up in the air and says, "Me too!" If a man sees his primary activity in the day as going to work, a feminist avidly insists that work is her primary activity, too. If a man forges his identity through a career, so does she. If a man is motivated by ambition and money, so does she claim to be.

This insistence on assimilating a man's-eye view within herself is the subtle crux of feminism's disempowerment of women. A feminist thinks this masculinization makes her Superwoman, when it is actually Kryptonite to a woman's true power. By tying herself to men's apron strings, the feminist exists in a de-feminized serfdom. She kills off her own female power. Her very womanhood is deactivated. Men are her lords. Men rule.

We need to develop a truly womanly take on work. A career sits in a different place inside a woman's life to the place it sits inside a man's life. That key difference is this:

Work is the catalyst of a man's masculinity.
Work is NOT the catalyst of a woman's femininity.

When a man closes the door behind him on his way to work each morning, he has an appointment to keep with his masculinity. He would feel emasculated by a workless life. Masculinity and work coalesce. A man needs work's dynamic action to spur his masculinity into being. A kind of alchemical combustion happens in a man's life when he is at work. Sparks fly. An engine switches on. His masculinity kicks into life and he sets about making his primary contribution as a producer and breadwinner. This is something we should all be grateful for. A world without the fruits of a man's labor would not be worth living in.

When a woman closes the door behind her on her way to work each morning, she does *not* have an appointment to keep with her femininity. *She is already a woman.* A woman is not de-feminized by a workless life. Bored, maybe, but less feminine? No. Femininity comes free, without a paid job. She doesn't need a career to lock it in. The sparks of her womanhood do not fly when she goes to work because they were already flying. Don't get me wrong. Sparks of intellectual excitement or purpose may fly when she goes to work, but the engine of her womanhood was already humming. This is something we should all be grateful for. A world without the pre-existing sacred life-force of woman's un-work-related presence would not be worth living in.

None of this is to say that a man has more right to a career than a woman. It's just to say work means something to him that it doesn't mean to a woman, and feminism needs to stop acting like a woman is getting all the exact same benefits a man does from work. A woman and a man sitting at the same desk working the same job the same hours are not having entirely the same experience. Feminism says they are, and of course it is *his* experience that feminism insists they are both having.

That feminist pretense that a woman is meeting her femininity at work, the same as a man meets his masculinity, sets up an artificial galvanization around work for a woman. It sets her up to feel a drive to work that she doesn't actually feel. I personally find that draining and corrosive. It is false and de-feminizing. Crucially, I feel I have to give up a lot of my femininity when I am at work. You may not feel that way, of course. However, I doubt very much that I am the only woman on the planet who feels like work diminishes her womanhood. I don't feel that work takes everything away from me; I happen to love the sense of intellectual exploration and purpose that work brings. My current job as a features editor for a parenting magazine brings with it the joy of working with words, something I love. I get to explore loads of interesting new ideas, and I help make the world a better place with insightful articles for parents in my country's most respected parenting magazine. Nonetheless, when I am at work, I give up a lot of woman-powers that are essential to me, like control over my time, engagement with house and children and community, and the phenomenal Being-power that all good women bring to the world.

What a defeat for woman that is. Must I really defend my power and freedom as a woman by working, and thereby never possessing my power and freedom as a woman? A man does not have to renounce part of his masculinity to work in the same way I have to renounce part of my femininity to work. Sure, a man at work might lose the chance to goof off and head to the golf course, or add to that man-shack he is building, but he isn't giving up his fundamental powers as a man at work. He is gaining them. I *am* giving up some of my fundamental powers as a woman when I go to work, because so many of my feminine strengths and contributions and rewards lie outside the workplace, not in it.

For a man, his career is almost always the singular defining activity in his life. Work is the source of his identity. It is his main conduit to the outside world and the company of other people. It is his major, often his only, field of achievement.

For a woman, a career is not usually the defining activity in her life, or not the only defining activity. It is not the only source of her identity, or even a source of identity at all. It is not her only conduit to the outside world. It is not her only, or even her major, field of achievement. Almost all working mothers have three number one priorities: children, household management and work. Work rarely outranks her children as her first priority, no matter how much she may dislike motherhood and love her job. Nor is she necessarily willing to let work swamp her ability to stay on top of the housework. Nor is work necessarily a higher priority than any other aspect of her life, like personal projects, her social life, community connections, exercise and recreation. Work may be essential to her, but it is likely one of a number of essentials. She has more than one priority no. 1.

You might cry out in horror, "But I would go nuts without work! It's non-negotiable to me! It's part of who I am!" Of course it is, for a great many women. Work is indispensable to many of us, at least at some stages in our lives. Work can be an essential source of things that matter, whether it be mental stimulation, purpose, income, social connections, or creativity. Virtually all human beings, men and women, need those things and for a lot of women, paid work is the only place to find them.

Needing work to make us fully satisfied, however, is not the same thing as needing work to secure our *womanhood*. If those of us who felt we needed to work for satisfaction were prevented from doing so, we might feel under-utilized. Disempowered. Frustrated. Bored. Wasted. Angry. Beside ourselves. We might feel bitter, or outraged, that our birthright as a woman to work had been infringed. However, no matter how thwarted we may feel, we would not be less *feminine* if we couldn't work. Our femininity would not suffer like a man's masculinity would suffer in the same situation. Our sanity and satisfaction and sense of purpose and enjoyment of life may be sourced in our careers, but our womanhood is not. It is sourced *outside* the workplace. Work may empower us as human beings, but its absence has no power to reduce our femininity. No woman is one iota more a *woman*, just because she performed career activity that day. With or without work, our womanhood is always intact.

At least, intact until the 1980s. Women of the past 40 years are the first in history to think we need work to activate our femininity. That is because feminism has dislocated our womanhood from its true place inside us and in the full domain of life outside the workplace, and migrated it over to where a man locates his masculinity, the smaller, dehumanized domain of the workplace. Feminism tells us our womanhood swings on a career the same way a man's manhood swings on a career, and almost every Western woman under the age of about 70 is drawn in to believing it. In feminists' masculinizing reversal of the old proverb, what's good for the gander is good for the goose. And with that migration of our womanhood to the false place of career, feminism has crippled us all.

The Power of Validation

Everyone wants validation. It's a fiercely potent force. It is the difference between feeling like a success and feeling like a failure. It pumps us up. It makes us feel like we've *arrived*. Validation is what we get when society tells us, "You're doing great! You're where it's at. You've located the *truth*!"

It is usually society that decides what that truth is, not us. Some of us get validation by doing directly what society tells us we should do. Today, that means an impressive career, material goods, and sometimes fame. A growing number of people get validation indirectly, by rejecting the stereotype and going in the other direction, by adopting an anti-corporate pseudo-streetwise 'cool', or by seeking a tree-change sea-change downsizing counter-culture that is so popular today, it generates its own validation.

Men get validation just by showing up to work for 40 hours per week. For women, however, it's not so simple. That's because in women's lives, it is feminism doling out the validation. And feminism is not a friend of women. Feminism tells a woman that to earn her validation, she must do what a man does—show up at work full-time, or at the very least have a fully successful career on a part-time schedule. Doing 'only' home-running and mothering will not only earn her no validation, it will earn her *anti-validation*. It will earn her scorn.

Validation is something we typically get from others. It is pretty difficult to self-validate, which is why so many stay-at-home moms are unhappy, even though they may know in their hearts they made the right choice for themselves or their children.

They are in a double bind. Firstly, they do without the boost that validation gives to everyone who does paid work, man or woman. It is a breeze to go about your day when society tells you you're a success. Secondly, they put up with the active anti-validation that feminism beams at them. It is not easy to persevere as an at-home mom when society tells you you're a dud. Straining after validation but never getting it, especially when you're already overloaded with the demands of motherhood, is chronically exhausting.

Some of us are at-home mothers relatively unbothered by the scathing disdain feminism dishes out to us. We shrug our shoulders and get on with the mothering we love or believe we should do. And some of us are working women who are genuinely happy to accept the lifestyle feminism has engineered for us, finding the great mélange of conflicting paid and unpaid duties enlivening rather than burdensome.

Way too many working women are 'happy' with feminism's crushing lifestyle, however, for the darker motive of validation. The validation society bestows on a man is essentially positive. He goes to work, he gets his validation. Validation for us women is essentially negative. 'Stay home and you are a failure' is the message behind feminism's validation of women. His validation is carrot; hers is stick.

You might protest, "But I'm not working for validation! I work because I love my job. It's fulfilling!" or "I don't work for valida-tion. I work because I need the money!" Sure, many of us work for healthy reasons like love or money. However, that's only some of us. Just about *all* of us work for the unhealthy motivation of validation.

There is a subtle difference between working because the pleasure we take in our job satisfies us—that is, because we're working for fulfillment—and working for the satisfaction of validation. Yet there is all the difference in the world between those two satisfactions.

Working for fulfillment is the act of an empowered woman. A happy woman works because she likes the job (or its income).

Working for validation is the act of a compromised woman. She works not because she wants to, but because she thinks she sucks if her life doesn't contain the masculinizing element of career. That is a terrible reason to work. Plenty of us today claim to work for 'fulfillment' when in fact we are only working for validation. Validation can feel so satisfying that it's easy to mistake for fulfillment. Fulfillment comes from within. Validation can feel like it comes from within, but it actually comes from without, in women's case from feminism.

If we want to know if we are working for validation, ask ourselves this simple test question: would we dare to not work? That is, would we dare to remain a life-long full-time housewife and mother? The question is not whether we would *want* to remain a lifelong at-home woman, or whether we could afford to, but whether we would *dare*. Many of us would not want to be lifelong housewives, of course; it would drive us nuts. And in today's world where marriage occurs late, if at all, and those marriages often break up, relatively few of us have the financial freedom to remain outside the workforce all our lives.

But say, hypothetically, that we could afford to and did want to stay career-free all our lives—what then?

Virtually no woman today dares tread that path. We'd be too *ashamed*. We might take time out of the workforce to be mothers, but we rely for validation on the careers we used to have, and we scurry back to those careers as soon as we can. "I don't work right now, but I used to be a finance director," we say to justify our otherwise deplorable stay-at-home state. What should be one of the most empowering choices a woman can make, a uniquely womanly path of lifelong unpaid work and love outside the economy, is so contaminated by the virulent shame feminism has poured all over it, that almost none of us ventures along it. An all-womanly life is toxic turf.

And with that shame, feminism has broken women. What a thing to say, huh? We generations of women since the 1980s have been the first in history to feel *ashamed* of ourselves. Every generation of women that walked the earth before us had respect for their own womanhood. Sure, women throughout history were oppressed. They were belittled, condescended to, insulted, ignored, denied financial freedom, shut out of career opportunities, bossed around, treated as domestic servants, denied rights like property ownership. Until the twentieth century, Western women were literally disenfranchised in that they couldn't vote.

However, they weren't ashamed of themselves. Men might have despised women, but women didn't despise themselves, and nor did they browbeat other women to despise themselves. That freedom from self-rejection, that fundamental right to our own dignity has been denied us since the masculinist brand of feminism came along. Feminism replaced that freedom with masculine freedoms like a career (on a masculine timetable only), equal pay, and equal access to virtually every male sphere of human endeavor, even the military. We can respect ourselves for what we do that men also do, feminism tells us, but not for what we do as women.

And that seriously sucks. No woman should *ever* have to work for validation. A mother should have all the validation she needs right there, period. Likewise, a housewife should have all the validation she needs, automatically. A woman runs a home. That counts for a lot. She is the center of a family and community. That counts for even more. And most importantly, as we said in chapter 6, that 'Being-work' she does counts most of all. Her very presence, her love, her conscious communion with the Universe or God, the way she brings the Being-dimension into being, is humanity's supreme contribution. If that is not worth validation, nothing is.

So Who's a Strong Woman?

Feminists love to self-describe as 'strong'. Are they?

Let's look at some of the attributes feminists think of as 'strength'.

Their most common justification for their 'strength' is their 'achievements'. We need to drop this definition of womanly strength. Have you noticed how those 'achievements' are always career-related, always in the Public dimension of the economy or public affairs, where men dwell? A truly strong woman is not necessarily a woman who 'achieves' things. At least, her achievements are not inevitably the career kind, like founding an eco-tourism resort or building a new flu vaccine. Those may be wonderful deeds, but a man could have performed them. After all, as feminism never stops telling us, there is no difference between a man and a woman in the workplace. Deeds do not make her a strong woman any more than they make him a strong woman.

Nor is a strong woman necessarily a fulfilled woman. Feminists routinely claim to be fulfilled, but how is that a marker of strength? Plenty of women in pre-feminist history were frustrated by their missing careers, but that does not mean they were weak women.

Another definition of 'strong' that feminists love to employ is financial independence. Again, this has nothing to do with strength. While financial independence is a fabulous thing, almost every woman in history has missed out on it. Yet history is awash with good strong women, financially dependent on their husbands, who lived in a woman's steadfast truth and wisdom and purpose.

Yet another kind of 'strength' that has become fashionable is 'boldness'. I once heard a celebrity describe herself as coming from a family of strong women because they all had big, brazen personalities. Again, this is not a sign of womanly strength. Most of the silliest women I know are bold feminists who seek to secure their womanhood through doing whatever men do, and that is the opposite of strength. This is not to say that women shouldn't be or are not bold; it is to say that boldness is not in itself a marker of a strong woman. Some of the strongest women I know are quiet, timid and shy, in some cases painfully so.

A strong woman is not even one who stands up for herself, necessarily. Feminists love to trumpet their ability to stand up for themselves, but I can think of plenty of genuinely strong women who do not demand all they're entitled to, or who let others take advantage of them at times. A strong woman is one who knows what she deserves, but not necessarily one who stands up for it.

In place of respect for her own womanhood, a feminist feels shame. Shame is weakness. It is therefore possible to possess all the things feminism claims as 'strengths'—achievements, fulfillment, financial independence, a bold personality, a capacity for standing up for oneself—and still be a shockingly weak woman. The weakest women I know possess achievements by the score, claim 'fulfillment', are well off financially, have boldness to spare, and stand up for their right to be treated like a man (but not like a woman) very capably indeed. All these things count for nothing towards being a 'strong woman', if a woman is ashamed of her own womanly experience of the world.

And by the same token, a woman can be without career achievements, be financially 'dependent', be shy, and refrain from standing up for herself, yet still be a strong woman.

I would like to put forward this simple two-part definition of strong:

A strong woman sees the world through a woman's eyes, and she respects herself for it.

I suggest that those two simple things define a strong woman. A strong woman experiences and responds to the world 100 percent of the time as a *woman*. Unshakably. She values *all* that a woman is, not just her career. A strong woman never works like a man in order to self-actualize as a woman. She knows that a career doesn't make her a strong woman any more than it makes a man a strong woman. A strong woman never benchmarks herself against men unless it's right to do so. A strong woman respects her own work as a mother and housewife and carer, whether or not she enjoys it, and does herself the service of correctly prioritizing that work in relation to her paid work, as much as she practicably can within the limits of a workplace currently designed for men. She knows that the Being she does outside work is a greater power than any Doing she does in the workplace. She is moral, and committed to what she believes is good. All strong people, men and women, are good people.

By this definition of a strong woman, feminists don't come off well. When a feminist exhorts herself and other women to work like men in order to be a 'strong woman', she is weak. When she imitates a man's working style, she is weak. And when she sneers at the value of housework and mothering, and refuses to accommodate it in women's schedules, she is extraordinarily weak. But she is at her weakest when she rejects the primacy of her sheer womanly Being-value outside the workplace, and values herself only for her Doing-power in the workplace, as if she were a man.

When my grandmothers stood firm in their belief in the worth of their housework, mothering and Being-work, they were manifesting the confidence of strong women. Working or at home, we can all be strong women. All it takes is a woman's-eye view of the world. And respect for that view.

8

Choices, Choices

Making 'Choice' a Reality

IT'S TIME TO BREATHE a fresh new positivity into women's options. Feminism purported to give us lots of options, but it really only replaced our one available model of 'stay-at-home mom' with another single available model, 'career-woman'.

Both models were tremendously prescriptive and limiting and antagonistic to women, for all that many women got a lot of good out of one or the other, and for all that some women were completely happy living one model or the other. Both were ideological. Life choices conjured up out of ideology mix one part truth with several parts poison drawn from artifice, impossibility, denial and lunacy. They do a great deal of harm.

In its early days, feminism sought to cover up its coercion of women into work with the word 'choice'.

They weren't offering us 'choice' at all, really. Yet we all still pretend to believe in the myth of 'choice'. That sorry little sticking-plaster of a word is applied to the broken bones of women who make the go-to-work 'choice', struggling with unworkable lives as they madly try to shove themselves into an eight- to 10-hour working day designed for a man with nothing else to do, and then strive to cram their much bigger domestic and mothering workload into the marginal time-zones of early mornings, evenings and weekends designed for a man to rest in. Freedom to work like a man, without his freedom from child care and running a home, is not a feasible 'choice'.

All the same, we're all making that 'choice' because the alternative 'choice', to remain a lifelong full-time homemaker and mother, is an option scarcely any woman dares choose. Virtually every woman in the Western world swallows the feminist pill that says without a job, she sucks. And when we believe that, staying home is no choice at all.

This chapter offers up a happier and more realistic re-drawing of *all* the life models available to women, with and without career. It aims to redress the imbalance that feminism has set up in favor of career. Feminism puts a powerfully negative spin on all the downsides of giving up work to become a full-time mother: truncated career trajectory, loss of income and employability, loss of mental stimulation and purpose, loss of validation and status, and so on. A lot of these negatives are imagined, nothing but bogeymen cooked up to scare us. Others are real. Indeed, feminism willfully created two of the biggest downsides, the loss of validation and status, in the first place.

In addition, feminism actively imposes a lot of negatives on full-time career-women—insanely unmanageable schedule, loss of time with her children, loss of health and sleep, eradication of her outside interests and with it the erosion of her humanity—yet keeps up a ringing silence about these drawbacks. Feminism's stereotype of the 'successful' woman is fragmentary, with only its male-identical components in place to make sure a woman functions like a man, as feminism wants her to. The feminine components, the bits that support a woman to function differently to a man, are always missing.

We need models that celebrate female versions of success and power, not the male versions that feminism currently slams down on women with no modification at all. It would short-change women to trivialize the costs they incur as they choose their way through life.

It is essential that our models be honest. They need to fully front all the exhaustion and joys and complex scheduling and sacrifices of a woman's life. Giving up a career, or time with her kids, or her health, or her passions, is not a joke. Only models that openly admit the downsides help a woman craft a meaningful, empowered life path.

Discussing models assumes that women have options. It goes without saying that not all of us live the model we choose. A woman who yearns to be a married at-home mother may be a single child-free full-time breadwinner. A woman who wants a lifelong career without kids may have motherhood thrust upon her by an unexpected pregnancy. Financial need will naturally override a good many of our choices. It currently overrides mine, and there's a good chance it overrides yours. This chapter's discussion of life models isn't meant to be prescriptive, but suggestive, supportive, affirming. The aim is to do what feminism will not do: give ourselves a 360-degree view of every life choice we women have. And that includes the model that isn't a current choice—the model of a career-free life.

Mothers
Full-Time Mothers Who Are Happy to Be So

A female (or male) CEO shapes a part of the economy. A mother shapes a soul. That makes a mother's job the most important there is. Yet you would never think so from feminism's 50-year track record of dismissing it.

A stay-at-home mother enables and enlarges her child's very existence. Her presence is a profound form of work. Home is not a place kids camp at night and on weekends. A kid's afternoons and school vacations are for play, learning, joy, discovery, creation, for growing into their very soul. Kids need to do that formative self-discovery first and foremost in their own homes, and with the other kids in the street or from school, and maybe at extra-curricular classes in the community. Home is the place where children do their living in a way that it can never be done solely in a day care center or vacation program, however sensational the teachers and camp guides. A child is not just a sealed-off individual, but a soul who grows in concert with family members, his home, the wider community, and with the sheer time spent with all those people and in all those places. A non-working mother gives her child maximum helpings of that wonderful supportive structure.

Kids need *ordinary*. Ordinary is beautiful. Most of our sublime childhood memories will come from the ordinary moments, not the extraordinary ones. Ordinary times happen when we're Being, not Doing. A stay-at-home mom is likely to be the mom in the best position to deliver Being-ness to her kids. When we're Being, we're relaxed. The importance of 'relaxed' turns that old feminist chestnut of a parent's 'quality time' with kids on its head. The more relaxed our time with our kids is, chances are the higher its quality.

An at-home mother's value is likely to extend to providing a well-run home. That is a gift of civility to our children. Whether it's a topsy-turvy 'happy chaos' kind of well-run, or a serene and tidy kind of well-run, doesn't matter. Homes are where we grow strong and invincible as kids. They are places of profound *power*. A stay-at-home mother keeping a well-ordered home sends her child the message, "This family is made up of people who matter. The things women bring to the world matter."

Once her children are in school, a non-working mother is likely to be available to serve those around her. To see his mother serving as a figure of strength in the community can be a source of pride for a child. Feeling proud of our parents is crucial. I would not have been as proud of my mother's career achievements, had she had them, as I was of her community work and beautiful home. Community work manifests the truth that life is not just about friends and co-workers. A life in which we do nothing but socialize and work is a low-grade life of hedonism and commerce. It is pointless, and children know that. A well-lived life is about a much richer, stronger, more three-dimensional array of connections that reaches beyond mere career to the people, places and pursuits to be found all around us. A well-connected life is a life of humanity and purpose, and that is what all kids want their parents to have.

When a child sees a mother giving to the community around her and simply *being* there for others, that child sees a woman manifesting uniquely feminine power. It shows him that women bear assets distinct to those of men, and that her uniquely female contribution to the community is a form of leadership. The child learns that men are not the only leaders, and the domain of commerce where men dwell is not the only place where leadership plays out.

A stay-at-home mother's schedule is much more containable than a working mother's. A manageable schedule can be a marker of a woman's self-respect. It sends her child the message, in a way that nothing else can, that Mommy believes Mommy matters. It says a woman cares enough about herself to not warp and limit and crush herself with a damaging timetable. Even more crucially, a stay-at-home mother who resists feminism's goading to work for validation demonstrates to her child that a woman's importance and power have nothing to do with career. To see his mother not needing to work for validation allows a child to properly value a woman as a legitimate creature in her own right. That is an essential message to convey to our children.

Feminism is sending a different message. It is telling children that mommies are worthless beings who must punish themselves with a frenzy of colliding paid and unpaid duties until they come out with a nice shiny career like Daddy. Only then are mommies as 'successful' as feminism thinks Daddy already is, just by working his 40-hour week. That we send such a degrading message about women to our children is shocking.

The stay-at-home mother model benefits those around the woman, but what about her?

For starters, time with her kids is priceless for many a woman. Her relationship with them is the most profound and far-reaching relationship in humanity. Yet feminists have no compunction in pulping it.

Another of the obvious benefits of the at-home life is freedom from work. Feminists trumpet the attractions of career so loudly that to listen to them, you would think work had no drawbacks. But it does. Work is not always satisfying and fun and purposeful and energizing and enabling. It can be dissatisfying and stressful and pointless (apart from its income) and exhausting and compromising. That's not such a big deal if you are a man with little other contribution expected from you, but it compounds the oppression dramatically for moms who are already beset with a super-sized domestic workload. A stay-at-home mother's most prized asset may be her absolution from the wipe-out of 40-plus hours per week of paid work, plus commute.

Once the youngest is in school, at-home mothers get as much of their life back as motherhood allows. Their work-free life gives them time to exercise, to eat right, to see their friends, to pursue projects, to rest, to enjoy the aspects of their life that are important to them. They can keep an appointment with their own soul in a way a career-woman might never do. These are supreme freedoms. Instead of doing their darnedest to deprive women of them, feminists should be doing everything they can to ensure women get them.

If we take the feminist blindfold off, it should be obvious that a career-free life is a hugely superior model to paid work for many mothers. But what of the losses?

A career offers benefits like social contact, purpose, a chance to contribute to society, intellectual stimulation, and income. Even an at-home mother who is happy to be so stands to lose these rewards. Or so it seems. Feminists pretend to be attracted by all these pluses, but it seems clear that, in many cases, it is primarily validation-by-emulation-of-men that attracts them. We can say that because, apart from income, all these losses are sometimes easily replaced in a stay-at-home mom's non-economic sphere. Social contact with co-workers is replaced by more time (and higher-quality time) with friends, extended family, and community. Purpose and a chance to contribute can come from a project, say, researching her family tree, or selling T-shirts online to fundraise for kids with neurofibromatosis. Intellectual stimulation can come from myriad non-career sources, such as study, or taking a free online learning course, or hitting the sofa before school pick-up time and reading the world's great books.

Income is the one obvious advantage of work that cannot be replaced outside the workplace. Some women genuinely have to work (I am one of them). However, a great many mothers who are married or in stable financial partnerships do not have to work. Is selling our freedom and power as full-time moms in return for income worth it? Some moms will say "yes," particularly if they like the holidays, e-devices and clothes it buys, or they are saving for their children's college fund. Other moms, though, are saying "yes" because feminism has so schooled us to devalue the terrific power of a manageable life, so scorned a child's need for family purpose and a parent's presence, so derided the worth of a well-run home, so threatened us with humiliation if we dare stay home, that we trade these things too easily.

There is one other thing that cannot be replaced outside the workplace. That is employability. One of many at-home mothers' great fears as the months and years go by can be declining employability. It is a justifiable fear. That would seem a good argument for women to keep working even as they mothered babies and preschoolers.

Yet the notion that every mother of babies and preschoolers can keep skills current while she holds down the biggest job on earth is preposterous. Skill loss is only to be expected in motherhood. And if she loses skills while she mothers and then divorces, then that is a vulnerability both husband and wife should share equally. He needs to support her until she retrains. No woman should be forced to shoulder paid work on top of motherhood to preserve a man's freedom to desert her whenever it suits him.

Full-Time Mothers Who Wish They Weren't

Even if we erase the corrosive sense of failure that many at-home mothers are made to feel by feminists, not all mothers like staying home. Motherhood can be a transcendent pleasure, but it can also be hellish. It can be both those things at once. The heinous 24/7 schedule, the minute-by-minute renunciation of our own thoughts and actions, the agony of entertaining kids, the entrenched rage as they scream and bicker, the ceaseless demands for toys, drinks and snacks, the crushing thrice-daily meal-time drudgery, the sleeplessness—there are tremendous downsides to stay-at-home motherhood.

It is debilitating for a woman who suffers as an at-home mother to have to dwell within the constraints of a stereotype that broadcasts to her and to the world at large that her life is 'fulfilling', 'joyful' and 'easy'. It is important that we acknowledge that many moms who choose to stay home find it none of these things.

One reason she may stay home is that she is just too busy. Although she might rather be at work, willing does not mean able.

A second reason she might choose to stay home, even when she does feel up to working, is that she believes her kids need her full-time presence.

A third reason she might stay home is that she can't find mother-friendly work, or because child care costs negate or even exceed her earnings.

Moms who give up their lives to stay home with children for the first two reasons— because they are too busy or because they believe they should—need all the sympathy we can give. Motherhood is about gain but it is also about loss. Loss of sleep, health, time to eat well, social life, study, hobbies, leisure, the power of contributing to the wider world, rest, career.

Instead of bulldozing her with the cock-eyed tactic of 'having it all', where 'all' means working a career designed for a man with a 24/7 wife at home at the same time as she is that 24/7 wife, we can commiserate, and validate. Home is a much unhappier place than it needs to be for a lot of mothers, simply because we tell her she is a failure there. Our validation needs to be not a silly kind that tells women motherhood is only positive—"Oh, you must be so fulfilled taking a griping two-year-old to the park every day!"—but a sensible validation that engages unflinchingly with the not-enough-ness, the boredom, the agony of motherhood, as well as its profound rewards. It seems to me that much of the dissatisfaction of many moms I know stems not so much from motherhood's discomforts, although those are very real, but from the lack of validation they receive for putting up with them.

There is a difference between feeling 'successful' and feeling 'happy'. We might not be happy as at-home moms, but that does not mean we should feel unsuccessful. We tend to feel successful when society tells us we are doing something it admires. If feminist society started admiring the sacrifice and endurance of stay-at-home motherhood, instead of denying it, ignoring it or sneering at it as it currently does, unwilling stay-at-homes might at least feel a lot prouder.

None of this is to say that unhappy at-home mothers should grin and bear it. No mother should ever have to stay home for that third reason we mentioned—that workplaces won't let her in on conditions designed for a mom with young children. More than anyone, a woman who is enduring so much deserves a workplace designed around her. She should be able to have it all.

Mothers Who Work Part-Time

A medley of motherhood, time to keep on top of the house, and a satisfying job is the Holy Grail of 'having it all' that many of us crave.

Yet with its glorification of full-time career-women, feminism sends the message that a part-time working mother is only 'partly' successful. We need to turn that idea on its head and show that a part-time working mother can be doing 'more than' a full-time working mother, not 'less than'. A mother's part-time career should come with a dynamic high-status aura. Her multi-faceted life allows her the greatest exposure possible to the inward-focused richness of family and home, which is hugely prized by most mothers even if there is a lot they don't enjoy about it, and the outward-focused rewards of work.

A part-time working mother's life pattern also benefits her children in instructional ways. Her kids learn that mommies, not just daddies and women who match daddies' hours, are entitled to careers. Yet importantly, her kids do not sacrifice all their own happy home-based childhood. Kids of a part-time working mother learn to value not just Mommy's ability to weld boilers or sell bonds, but the work she does in the home baking the ginger crème brûlées the whole family loves, and painting the deck a gorgeous midnight teal that sets off the potted red geraniums so well. They see her as a fully equipped soul radiating woman-power in the top-ranking space, the home, not just a utilitarian unit radiating man-identical power in the economy. In them grows regard not just for the traditionally male realm of the economy that feminism is so keen to talk up, but for the more important and traditionally female realm of home and humanity that feminism is so keen to talk down.

Unlike a mother working full-time, a part-time working mother has a richer variety of experiences to call on. A full-time working mother sees almost nothing of the world except a desk-eye view of her paid tasks. She will liaise with almost nobody except colleagues during the week, and on weekends will be swamped by an avalanche of housework and child-related tasks. A part-timer, at least once her kids are in school, may have time to see friends, to visit the mall, to work on a save-the-local-river project, to join a Twitter fitness group, or to download a crafts app to knit a cute cup-cozy. She may even have time to read her favorite blogs. She is likely to be far better connected and active and aware and energetic than a full-time working mother beaten down to nothing but the two dimensions of work and children.

Does a part-time working lifestyle have any downsides?

Because it offers the best of all worlds, this model doesn't offer *everything* of all worlds. A mother working part-time will probably have to trim all her worlds to fit them in. She will spend time with her children, but perhaps not as much as she might like. She may miss orange-duty at football training when her nine-year-old son really wants his mommy to do it, and she may have to pass on serving as hiking-guide on her 12-year-old daughter's school camp. Her house may not be a dump, but it probably won't be to-die-for. She will valiantly struggle to wash the eight-year-old's baseball gear after training Tuesday afternoons in time for the Saturday game, and a lot of times she won't make it and her son will wear Tuesday's sweaty gear to the match. That old sepia wedding photograph of her grandparents that she found in the attic, and wants to display in a pretty silver frame she spied in the gift-store window, will probably go unframed, maybe for years.

In her career, satisfaction might mix with frustration. Projects she is excited about will only proceed at a partial pace. She may cede the most appealing parts of a project to a colleague. She maybe can't gain new skills, as she lacks time. And if she works, it is likely her leisure time that she swaps for career. Most moms have leisure opportunity only during school hours, yet this is when she is likely to be working. Not all mothers will be willing to make all these sacrifices. Some would rather do the orange-duty, supervise the hike, send the kids off in clean baseball gear, frame the photo, and maybe even sit down once in a while, dammit. The part-time model is the answer only for some women, not all.

Even if a mom is comfortable with her part-time hours, we need to acknowledge the very considerable workload that she is taking on. The sight of mothers at part-time work should not lull society into thinking that because she takes on, say, 20 hours per week, that the rest of her unpaid workload only equates to about a further 20 hours, bringing her up to an equal load with her husband's 40-hour week.

A mother at home already works far, far more than anyone with a full-time job, and that's before she takes on extra paid work. Society needs to grasp that a 'part-time' working mother is working 'super-full-time' when all her unpaid work is taken into account.

We also need to acknowledge how difficult it is to mix the responsibilities of child care and housework with paid work. Even if she did work only 20 hours at home and 20 hours outside, that is not necessarily the same thing as working 40 hours in a row. Those two jobs almost certainly overlay each other and conflict, at least some of the time, and that is a deep source of extra effort and stress for women. A woman's paid work almost always displaces unpaid work, that must be made up in another period, which itself probably already contains more unpaid work. For example, she may be at her job packing books in a warehouse for an online book retailer at 4 p.m. on a Wednesday afternoon, at the same time as she needs to get dinner ready. That means she must pre-prepare dinner early in the morning. But in the early morning, she is already frantic getting herself and children ready. Alternatively, she prepares the next day's dinner late at night after all the dinner/bath/homework routine is done, when she also needs to tend to her own affairs, complete household tasks, rest and sleep.

Of course, not all women are working part-time because they want to. Plenty of mothers work not because they like working, but because they are desperate for time away from their children, and to pay for day care, they need a job. They're shifting from a rock to a hard place. That is something society needs to recognize and appreciate.

Mothers Who Work Full-Time

This model of full-time working mothers has enjoyed so much glowing press, courtesy of feminism, that its advantages hardly need re-iterating here. Let's re-iterate them anyway: a full-time career can give a woman the maximum helping of satisfaction to be had from work. She will have the pleasure of producing the highest quality work of which she is capable, informed by the maximum years of experience possible. Her seniority may afford her the opportunity to sit on industry panels or boards. Her career may offer a high income, and even if it doesn't, it will probably give her financial independence, a sizeable benefit that most part-time workers will forego. Many mothers might add that freedom from the hour-by-hour routine of caring for children is a towering relief. These are all authentic benefits we can chalk up in career's favor.

Then there are the ideologized benefits. Feminism transmits an absurdly positive image of full-time career mothers as 'fulfilled', 'energized' and 'satisfied'. That will be the truth for a teeny number of full-time working mothers. All ideology contains some truth, or it would never stick. A full-time career really can make us fulfilled, energized and satisfied. Those of us founding a start-up with a new line in no-show pantyhose we dreamed up at the kitchen table, those of us averting possible climatic disaster in a policy-making role in environmental protection, those of us engaged in the intense intellectual excitement of physics research at a university—all of these things can fire us up to want to work full-time.

For almost all full-time working mothers, however, the truth is probably closer to 'tormented', 'exhausted' and 'squashed', at least a good deal of the time. No matter how much we love our jobs, that doesn't mean we love the price we pay.

So, what are those prices? We hear almost nothing of them, yet they are there in spades. One of the most obvious is time with her children. To miss out on most of her children's upbringing seems a nonsensical price to pay, even for mothers who do not enjoy motherhood.

A second loss is that treasure, manageability. A full-time working mother never works at a less than psychotic pace, except when she is at work, when her pace slows to a cruisy 100 percent or so, from the 200, 300 or 400 percent pace at which she works in the home. Unless she has a dream team of private chefs, nannies, cleaners, concierges and other bought-in services, the full-time working mother model is the least likely to offer manageability.

A third great loss, one that is almost never remarked upon, is time for herself. This can be an enormous sacrifice that ranks as high, or higher, than the loss of time with her children. She has no leisure. She has no rest. She probably has no time to exercise. She probably never reads. She gives up so many of the glorious facets of a woman's life. No creativity of the crafting/carpentering/making-stuff kind if she's into that sort of thing, unless her job provides it, and it probably doesn't. Scarcely any 'secret women's business' get-togethers with the girls, surely an unacceptable biggie on her growing list of sacrifices. No community connection outside work. No intellectual projects outside work. No time for Being, because she is so consumed by Doing.

Does her life look so 'successful' when we examine the whole truth? Seen in the light of all she loses, the full-time working mom might not be entitled to the unalloyed envy or admiration feminism urges us to feel. Pity, dismay, disapproval or contempt might be better responses.

It is important a woman knows she's working for the right reasons. Feminism loves to present stay-at-home motherhood as dull, stressful, demeaning. And so it can be, but so can work be those things. Is she working full-time because she truly, really enjoys what she does for those 40 to 50 hours every week? Or is she working those hours because she is referencing her womanhood off the masculine timetable? I personally find it suspicious when a woman claims to be very desirous of working eight to 10 hours per day, but cheerily downs tools around 5 or 6 p.m., which by odd coincidence just happens to be men's quitting time too. Is satisfaction really only to be found at the end of an eight- to 10-hour stretch? But not after, say, three or four or five hours?

Even if a woman is honest about the drawbacks of full-time work, many women will feel they are 'junior' to a man if they do not work as many hours as him. This is not entirely so. He may indeed pull ahead career-wise, but she has pulled ahead life-wise. She has spent more time with her children, something his full-time schedule denies him. He may be 'senior' to her at work, but she is senior to him at life. The business of life pulls rank over the business of work.

Nonetheless, women might still be tempted to work full-time in the belief that the most senior jobs will be closed off to them if they don't. As we said in chapter 4, senior jobs should come in part-time increments to suit women, not just in 40-hour blocks to suit men. That said, while seniority is not just a function of hours on the job, if a woman works fewer hours, it is true that her shorter experience is likely to keep her from some senior roles. So what? Are all the interesting or worthwhile jobs only those at the top? Really? Of course they're not. And even if they were, does a woman really want to swap the 'interesting-factor' and 'worthwhile-factor' of being with her children and living her own life for the 'interesting-factor' and 'worthwhile-factor' in a job?

That is something only she can answer. Right now, feminism does the calculations for her. It baits her by setting up a dynamic that says women who do what women do suck and women who do what men do rock. That way, she is reeled in to the man-loving answer that feminism has prepared earlier for her—that full-time work is perfectly manageable, right and the peak of 'success'.

And there is one more consideration. The only mothers who should be working full-time are those who can put their hand on their heart and assure themselves and everyone else that their children are happy. No matter what, rule number one is, the kids don't get hurt. That's not to say kids should have every little thing their own way, or that kids will self-combust if Mommy is absent sometimes. Nor is it to say that it's Mommy's role to give up work while Daddy gets to keep his full-time career; the sacrifice should be equally as much his as hers, however a couple wishes to divvy up the load. It's to say that the kids' welfare is never supposed to take a hit for the adults.

Looking at where childhood is right now, with epidemics of bullying, anxiety, poor nutrition, lack of physical exercise, 'nature deficit disorder' and the other challenges kids are experiencing, taking them even to the unimaginable point of suicide, it seems kids *are* taking a hit for the adults. Feminists have granted full-time working women (and, by extension, their husbands) immunity from accountability for their children's welfare. And that is not acceptable in any society. Ever.

The only mothers who should be working full-time are those who genuinely love what they do, and are genuinely willing to give up the bulk of their life-assets and power outside the workplace. If full-time working mothers are happy, and their kids are happy, then we can be happy for them. Enabling every woman to find a life that works is what feminism was supposed to be about. However, if she is mangled, and is only working this full-time gig because she buys feminism's belief that women are a sucky sub-gender who need to mainline testosterone via a man's timetable to be successful women, then she is no successful woman.

Women Without Kids

Working, Part-Time or Full-Time

Housewives work. Housewives taking a paid job work even harder.

Even without children, a woman is doing plenty in the home. She prepares as many as 21 meals a week, does daily, weekly, monthly chores, runs errands, administers her own and her partner's life affairs, and takes on all the preparations for vacations and special occasions on the calendar.

Back in chapter 3, I estimated that as a housewife with two young children, I faced over 80 hours of work in the home every week, even if I couldn't actually get to a lot of that work. A household without kids requires considerably less work. Meal preparation is much less complex, grocery shopping and laundry and ironing is quicker, errands are fewer, admin is far less intensive, and a lot of the social planning like staging kids' birthday parties and ferrying kids to playdates is something a child-free woman doesn't have to worry about.

Nonetheless, a woman without kids will still easily face, say, seven to 10 hours per day of home-running on a weekday, plus at least several hours of meal preparation and minor chores on a weekend. While allowing that a child-free housewife's weekly load might vary a lot from one household to another, let's estimate it at around 50 to 60 hours.

It might seem like that's too much. However, it is hard to see how we could make it much lighter. Assuming she has no paid help and makes most meals in-home, perhaps including her husband's lunch, with little in the way of restaurant meals or take-out for dinner, she might easily spend three hours a day on meals prep and cleaning up afterwards. If she works seven to 10 hours every weekday in the home, that only leaves four to seven hours each weekday for all the other stuff. One day might be for grocery shopping and some baking, one for laundry and ironing, and one or two for errands and admin, which only leaves one or two for cleaning. Four to seven hours across five weekdays is quite a scant allocation for all that.

Look at it another way. If we say she does seven to 10 hours of housework daily during the week, we are also saying that she has six to nine waking hours every weekday in which to twiddle her thumbs (if she's not working). Unless we swallow the feminist depiction of housewives as unoccupied, do we really think that home-makers float about for that much time every day?

And even if she did, why shouldn't she? Her husband is working only eight hours per day, leaving him floating about for eight hours every weekday and two whole 16-hour days every weekend.

Of course, a woman without kids who is also working is not floating about for those six to nine hours. She's working in them. That means her housework gets pushed into disempoweringly inconvenient time slots in the day. Clearing the breakfast dishes before work, remembering to defrost the veal chops for dinner before leaving home and running about in her lunch-hour to buy arugula and parmesan to go with them, paying the car insurance online at night when she is already cramming dinner preparation and household chores into evening hours and when a full-time housewife would have dispatched those meal preparations and chores and e-mails earlier in the day, offloading all the bulky household work like laundry and grocery shopping and cleaning onto the weekend—these are all big extra imposts on a child-free working woman's week.

That very struggle to manage the conflicting responsibilities of work and home is itself part of a working housewife's contribution. Conflicting responsibility is a stressor. A man mostly knows serene immunity from this stressor, because his wife shields him from it. In a typical household, he will pitch in to nothing like 50 percent of the unpaid work. If a child-free woman does 50 hours of housework, and 40 hours of paid work, then she is doing a 90-hour week. Her partner may do, say, six hours on domestic affairs (some yardwork, say, some e-mails, and a run to the hardware store for a couple of brackets to put up a new shelf in the laundry), giving him a total of 46 hours.

Yet in our supposedly 'equal' society, a woman without kids who does all this unpaid home-running *and* works full-time is considered to be contributing no more than her partner.

On top of her 50 to 60 unpaid hours and as many as 40 paid hours, moreover, a woman without kids (like many women with kids) is also likely to engage in 'caring work', the business of connecting with and supporting friends and neighbors and family, sometimes at inopportune times. Inside her own ambit, she will be on the look-out for ways to improve her husband or partner's life: she will bookmark a 'what's on' newsletter carrying a suggestion for a city tour coming up on the weekend, she will pick up their favorite pear flan Friday evening from the French patisserie, freshly baked late for the Saturday crowd, and she will swing by to pick up that set of golf clubs her partner bought on eBay.

Many child-free partnered women work full-time. Some of them will be quite happy, but just how many women truly think it is a great idea to work full-time when they also carry most of the home duties? It is likely that a good many partnered child-free women are working full-time simply because feminism has taught them to devalue their substantial non-paid contribution. After I and my friends married, but before we had children, we nearly all fell into this category. The only working timetable on offer was the masculine eight- to 10-hour day, and almost all of us took it without question. We worked full-time not because we wanted to or financially needed to or because it was comfortably manageable, but because it was not ideologically permitted to cut back. We lacked the self-awareness or the courage to value our unpaid workload.

It's time to reverse the feminist blanking of women's unpaid work. A child-free woman, like a mother, needs a woman-friendly economy. She needs better woman-centered workplace options, like time off for one-off domestic events such as moving house, or a 3:30 p.m. knock-off time so she can get home to cook dinner, or the potential to negotiate shorter hours for when her brother-in-law who is a father of seven has a bad accident that keeps him off work. She probably feels she needs way more help from her male partner. She needs a society that stops telling her that the paid work she performs like her husband is the work that counts. It's time for women to give ourselves permission to give ourselves the time to get our unpaid work done. It's time to treat ourselves well, after so many years of feminism treating us badly.

Women Without Kids, Not Ever Working at All

Well. No career, no kids? This model is pretty much extinct unless you're in your seventies. So ferociously has feminism persecuted women who choose this fully womanly path, that virtually no woman today dares tread it.

As we noted in the model above, a woman without children does around 50 to 60 hours of unpaid work in the home every week, give or take. Yet those hours are only her immediate contribution. Beyond that, she will probably do much more as a contributor to her community. Her non-working state may enable her to hand out leaflets about the walkathon her women's share-trading club is staging to raise micro-finance for budding businesswomen in Kenya, or to volunteer as a summer firefighter in her rural town. Even with no children of her own, she is still likely to be a family member— daughter, sister, aunt, cousin—which will take her time and energy. She may have elderly parents to care for, or a sibling with a disability, in which case she may have a heavy load indeed. Moreover, she probably goes above and beyond the 50 to 60 weekly hours of merely necessary housework to decorate and make comfortable a lovely home and garden for those who live in it, pass by or visit. All this contribution will add up to considerably more than the 40 hours per week her partner works.

But that's not all she does. Not only does a full-time housewife without kids contribute possibly more than a man during his working years, we must add into our calculations that when her husband retires, our man-loving feminist society says he is entitled to sit on the sofa and stare into space all day, every day, for the next 25 years or more. She is not. She is expected to keep right on working the same 50 to 60 or so hours in the home she always did, every week of the year. In that case, it flies in the face of the timesheet to say she has contributed less than him. Unless, that is, we assign her domestic work intrinsically fewer credit points than his paid work, which is exactly what feminists do.

How's this for irony? It may seem counter-intuitive to say so, but the lifelong stay-at-home child-free woman is the most 'equal' to her husband of all the life models in this chapter. That is because she is the one working closest to the mere 40 hours per week that he puts in. She still outworks him, but the women living every other model outwork their husbands by a w-a-a-y bigger percentage than the non-working housewife without kids does. Unless their husbands are pulling a true 50 percent of their weight in the household, and I know no men who do, then women living the other models are far, far more unequal to a man than the child-free woman who never works at all.

Just as the 1960s housewife was not nearly as under-utilized as feminism likes to pretend, nor was she as 'bored' as feminism says she was. Feminism did a lot to create the 'bored housewife' stereotype and has deployed it to great effect to deny the pleasures of full-time housewifery. It is true that many women were bored or frustrated or felt under-utilized in the pre-feminist era. My own mother was one of them. It is also true, however, that many women enjoyed the routine of home, sewing, gardening, and relationship- and community-building that was woman's world in the pre-feminist era, and my mother was one of them, too.

For society to tell women who wanted to be running a bio-tech company, or measuring orbits as an astronomer, that they could not, was inhuman. But for feminism to deny the fundamental value and joy of women's unpaid work as a housewife was also inhuman. The 'bored housewife' stereotype only ever applied to some housewives, not all. That all women work today because all women want to is one of feminism's biggest misrepresentations. The real reason no woman is a lifelong non-working housewife today is because feminism's insults have so discredited that life that no woman dares live it.

If women did dare to go career-free all their lives, what would their lives look like?

They could know maximum control over their day—what a prize! They could know the pleasure of tasks completed in a one-task-to-one-person ratio, instead of the multi-tasks-to-one-person ratio that working women with or without kids uphold throughout much of the week. They could create and live in functional, attractive homes, something most working women struggle to do daily, often in vain. They could tap their bottomless reserves of womanly strength and love to fill their lives with a rich mix of giving to their families, their husband or partner, their community and causes that matter to them. And they could do it without abrading themselves into a wreck as most working women do. They might study, whether with a full-blown degree in art history or a more manageable diploma in Italian, and that study might yield a keener satisfaction than a career could ever do. They could dip into the priceless well of their creativity, something working women have little or no time to do. They could tend to their own needs, their health, their need for *rest*—imagine that, working mothers! They could get on with the whole magical business of *Being* a woman without the de-womanizing yoke of seeking validation-by-*Doing* in the economy.

What of the losses? Ignore feminism's braying about how career-free housewives are caterpillars who can only morph into butterflies like men by joining the workplace. What are the real losses? The one serious pitfall for the woman who chooses to be a lifelong housewife (or a lifelong at-home mom) is employability. Should she divorce or separate, she may have no immediate way to earn an income. She enters the workforce at a junior low-income level. He has remained eminently employable, and the older he gets, the more senior and high-income he is likely to be. We need to formulate policy that irons out that huge inequality in a woman's and a man's vulnerability should they part ways. After all she has contributed, a woman should never find herself on the back foot after a divorce.

We need to come right out and say what feminists will not let us say—that some women do not ever want or need paid work to be happy. Life outside the economy can be a place of full-blown truth. The path of the lifelong housewife is a uniquely womanly choice, and that gives it its own special might. For some of us, that path may offer the greatest freedom and power of all.

9

Single Mothers and Little Match Girls

Why 'Single Motherhood' is an Oxymoron

WHAT DO UNSUPPORTED SINGLE MOTHERS and Little Match Girls dying in the snow have in common? Answer: Both should be relics of a primitive Dickensian age, but one of them is still with us.

My Story

As I endured the cosmic assault of my son Robbie's endless crying from his birth in January 2003, and the need to stand up non-stop to hold him to stem the flow of that crying, and the sleeplessness that accompanies getting up to a baby two, three, four times a night, my marriage began to deteriorate. That didn't change as Robbie morphed into a toddler needing minute-to-minute entertainment and care, a life I found unbearable.

A second pregnancy when Robbie was eight months old entailed six weeks of 24/7 morning sickness and the usual fatigues of growing an unborn baby, compounded by the super-load of caring for Robbie. As my second son Lachlan's arrival in July 2004 plunged me into a repeat round of sleeplessness while Robbie's night-terrors were still wrenching me out of bed once or twice a night, things didn't improve.

In July 2005, my husband said the marriage was over.

I had thought that, short of disablement, loss of a loved one, war, or crippling illness, life as a mother of young kids could not get any worse. But it had. I was aghast at the prospect of carrying out both a woman's and a man's work at the same time. I knew I would be incapable of getting by, financially and logistically. Robbie was two-and-a-half when my husband insisted we separate, Lachie 12 months old, and I had scarcely slept a night in that time. I had been occupied two, three, four person-times over every minute of the day in those two-and-a-half years. Much of that time had been spent standing, or bending down many dozens of times a day, or lifting heavy babies and toddlers and strollers and diaper bags and grocery bags and scooters and tricycles. Every day of the year, I was dragged out of bed as early as 5 a.m. or even earlier, worked all day and evening, and was wrenched out of bed to work several times a night. I was sagging with exhaustion, ravaged by my children's incessant crying, pulverized by the nightmare of entertaining them, driven mad with lack of exercise, and was under-weight and under-nourished due to lack of time to eat. Earning a living was going to be impossible.

I moved out to an apartment near our house. The boys spent half the week with me, and half with their father; we alternated parenting duty on Saturday nights. One morning, a week or two after the move, I bent over with sudden lethargy. Barely able to walk, I clambered on to the bed and lay there, wondering at what a strange place to be bed was at 10:30 a.m., usually the high-energy point of my day. Within days, patches of eczema appeared on my upper arms, which the doctor identified as a likely reaction to gluten. I was deeply fatigued. Medical tests diagnosed 'Crohn's disease' but in scare quotes, for the doctor admitted diagnosis was difficult. Stress was the cause, he advised me, something I already knew. My digestive system was inflamed, so that food wouldn't absorb no matter how much I ate, and my weight fell to 47 kilos.

I spent the first night in my new apartment awake until 4:45 a.m. Next evening, I expected a long deep sleep to make up for it, but spent a second night awake until nearly dawn. Then another. And another. I put it down to metabolic disturbances associated with 'Chrohn's'. The Chrohn's went on without relief; so did the insomnia. Struggling with two young children on such poor sleep left me in despair.

After nine months of living apart, my husband suggested we move back together. Move back in we did, but by 2008, he wanted a divorce. My sons were four and five.

We split our assets and care of the children 50/50. However, our situations were far from even. In the six years I had spent pregnant and working as a mother, his already very high salary doubled, more than tripled if you count an annual bonus. He was six years more senior. Not only had I foregone those six years of increased seniority in my own career, but in that time, my industry had been overwritten by the digital epoch. Media relations roles like mine were virtually a thing of the past, replaced by social media and other digital marketing competencies. Those vast new digital horizons were thrilling, in themselves. However, as a single mother, they were overwhelming. Not only would I have to catch up with the explosion of expertise in my field, but keep abreast as the professional ground shifted out from under me when new social media channels and other digital marketing tools sprang into life on an almost daily basis. My younger child-free rivals would do much of this professional development in a *de facto* manner on their own time, through their personal use of social media and other technology. In the pre-digital days of my pre-motherhood career, I had just about done all the professional development I needed; now, that development would be an ongoing upheaval. Not only that, but where I once publicized my tourism industry clients mostly through 300 to 400 traditional travel media only, I would now need to service them across countless websites, blogs and newsletters, plus any number of social media platforms and tools. And I would need to do all this for the same fee as before.

Inequality in the situations of me and my husband extended to the qualitative nature of our asset division. While we split our assets

50/50, he bought me out of our real estate investments, leaving me with cash falling in value through inflation, and him with three residential investment property income streams after he sold our fourth to buy me out, plus our own home. In my country, Australia, where real estate investing is a national pastime, annual capital gains on houses of 10 to 25 percent are routine. Anyone could see who had the better part of that deal.

A much greater inequality existed, however: my deep-seated maternal drive to be present for the kids, as opposed to a father's essential absence of that drive. To a man, child care is essentially somebody else's problem. Whose problem? His children's mother's problem. Grief for my children's loss of their family was eclipsed by my horror at the thought of shoving them into day care all week. Two days per week of day care was the max my sons were comfortable with, and therefore the max I was willing to tolerate. Their day care center was a superbly run and very inviting place, but the boys never really wanted to go. Of course, when I picked them up around 4:30 p.m. and they were zipping down the slippery slide, they never wanted to leave, but that doesn't mean they were thrilled about the prospect of living five days per week at day care. They wanted their own life in their own home. To banish them from their own childhood all day, all week, was unthinkable. I knew, and my husband knew, that I would stay home with them while he carried on earning a living. He was a good father, and he too would have thought it intolerable to send them into care five days a week. But he left me to carry the can. I financed their stay-at-home childhood out of my capital, while he preserved his capital and carried on earning.

On separating for the final time in October 2008, I moved into a rented house of my own. My digestive system disorders had not receded in the two-and-a-half years we spent back under one roof, but my insomnia had. On the first night I spent in my new house, an ominous familiar pattern returned. Despite not consciously fretting about my new circumstances, I lay awake until after 4 a.m. the first night. The next night, same again. And on it went. For weeks. Then months. Years. From 2008, I have not slept a single night. It took me some years to work out that what keeps me awake is the dread of needing to earn a full-time living coupled with the knowledge that I can't.

To earn a living, I needed to work from home, but running a business in the travel industry means travel. Business trips generate an overwhelming burden of excess work and pressure for a mother. There's not just the crush of projects to be completed for multiple clients before you leave. There's the house to shut up: arranging with neighbors or paid housekeepers to water gardens, collect mail and feed pets, buying pet food in and delivering it to the neighbors, clearing perishable food from the fridge, the usual household administrative tasks that need attending to ahead of your absence, and all the other things that go into shutting up a home that a businessman with a wife never has to do. There's the child care arrangements to alter and put into place: for example, if the kids are normally with me Monday and Tuesday, and they play baseball on Monday and have swim class at school and soccer after school Tuesday, but I am going away and leaving the kids with their father for a week, then the baseball, soccer and swim gear all needs to be transferred to Daddy's house, as do school uniforms for those days, and various other bits and pieces. Wrangling all those possessions is a further assault on a single mother's mental and physical faculties, already so overloaded with the conflicting double domains of child care and income-earning.

Then I must pack, perhaps get out-of-season clothes dry-cleaned or mended if my business trip takes me to the other hemisphere, and see to personal things like shaving legs or getting a haircut or dying my hair. On return, possibly jetlagged and definitely freaked out with exhaustion, I will have to swing straight into the fierce routine of mothering and housework, at the very same time as launching into the backlog of work that built up while I was away, at the very same time that I need to be resting. And I'll have to attend to much of the child care arrangements and household shutting-up in reverse—collecting mail from the neighbors and perhaps dropping them a box of chocolates as a thank you (having squeezed that chocolate-box-buying into my packed work itinerary), re-collecting all the kids' stuff from their father's house, re-stocking the fridge, and more.

The thought of grappling with all this left me flailing. I was convinced that I could not return to my old career on a consultancy basis. The only alternative in that industry was a paid job. However, a paid job was impossible. Even if I found a 5 p.m. finisher, which was extremely unlikely, I could not make it from downtown, where the job almost certainly would be, to the school out-of-hours-care center by its 6 p.m. closing time. A walk from the office to the train station of maybe 12 minutes, or longer; a wait of maybe 12 minutes for a train, or longer; a 42-minute train journey; a 10-minute drive to the school, parking and getting inside and signing the boys out by the strict closing time—it was not doable. If the job was in a locality on the edge of downtown that required an extra leg by foot, bus or train, and jobs in my field typically would be, then it would be closer to 7 p.m. by the time I made it to the care center. I could not afford a $20-per-five-minutes fine from the care center for every overrun, but much more importantly, I could not afford to have the center ask me to leave if I was habitually late, for what would I do with the kids then? The staff are not in the business of hanging back for latecomer parents at any price, and nor should they be.

My children spent Sunday to Wednesday morning with me, and Wednesday night to every second Saturday night or Sunday morning with their father. The closest I felt I could come to working full-time was to work Monday to Wednesday on reduced hours, coming in later than 9 a.m. and leaving about 1:30 p.m. on Mondays and Tuesdays when I could put in maybe another hour at home after picking them up from school, although that would be extremely difficult given a woman's afternoon load of after-school snacks, child-tending, homework, dinner, and bath/bed routines, let alone after-school activities; and then working from about 10 a.m. or 11 a.m. Wednesdays, and 9 a.m. to 5 p.m. Thursdays and Fridays. What I was going to do with them in school vacations, I had no idea. They would hate summer camp, and even someone very well-paid in my industry would not earn enough to cover a nanny.

My husband and I had settled our financial affairs the week before Lehman Brothers' collapse in September 2008 triggered the Great Recession. As I said above, his 'equal' share of the assets was in ever-appreciating real estate while my 'equal' share was in ever-devaluating cash. But as global stock markets went into freefall from October, having cash didn't look so dumb after all. Not many people had access to cash to buy stocks in the credit crunch, but those who did found themselves knee-deep in bargains. Looking to actively manage my money, I began to cautiously buy mining stocks around the Australian market bottom of March 2009. This I did for two years without much system, until a stock analyst friend suggested I do it full-time. Skeptical at first, I realized that this might be the opportunity I was looking for. And so, I became a day trader. I was later to learn that it is not uncommon for divorced mothers from high-income couples to do the same. I devoted myself to learning all I could about trading, and treated it as a full-time job as much as it could be, spliced in with the mothering work that my former husband insisted did not exist.

Starting from a knowledge base of zero, I soaked up as much stock market education as I could. I subscribed to financial newsletters, trawled online for scholarly articles on stock-pricing mechanics, pored over books on trading techniques and fundamentals analysis, signed up to price alerts on every commodity from tungsten to graphite, became familiar with the intricacies of buy/sell signals, borrowed high school economics textbooks from the local library, buried myself in government briefing papers on rare earths, and swapped notes in day trading chat rooms on whether we all thought the next

UN Security Council resolution would negatively impact our potash holdings in east Africa. I made a lot of money, though not enough to be completely self-supporting, and lost more than I should have, an almost inevitable result of a beginner's mistakes (although not all my mistakes were inevitable; I take the blame for some of them).

Despite the hope trading held out that I wouldn't need to work, or at least not full-time, my sleep did not improve. The terror that I might fail at trading was an ever-present strain keeping me awake. And then, I failed at trading. In early 2012, I missed a $300,000 profit. Two months later, I missed a trade that went on to become a profit of around $600,000. I greeted missing those two trades with the same emotionless calm with which all serious traders react (I discovered early that despair and elation are hallmarks of the amateur). However, whereas for most traders those missed trades would be disappointment, for me as a single mother they were disaster. The mining sector was stagnating, and while I was proud of my new-found trading skills, I could see that within about 18 months, my dwindling capital was not going to generate enough profit to cover my living expenses.

And my expenses were not low. Had it been up to me, I would have headed straight to the cheapest part of town, or even more realistically, moved back interstate to live with my parents. That would have been the financially responsible thing to do. However, the law does not require the higher-earning party to live near the lower-income party after a divorce. I had no legal power to force my former husband to move to a low-cost location where I had some hope of getting by. Instead, I was forced to stay in our city, Sydney, which is one of the most expensive cities in the world in which to buy a house. Even the 'cheapest' parts of town are out of reach for many, and I wasn't living in those parts. My husband lived in a triple-A suburb, and to be close to the kids, I was forced to chew my precious capital renting in a double-A location nearby. My much less glamorous house was worth half the price of his, but was nonetheless exorbitantly expensive.

It was May 2012. I decided to take an even bigger financial risk than day trading: to write this book. I figured I could get it done and produced in a year. Before I could finish it in 2013 as I'd hoped, however, my funds began to shrink. The supplementary trading I'd hoped to do on the side had delivered scant profits. In early 2013, I hit my 'emergency' level of savings at which I had promised myself I would pull the pin and take a full-time job. I moved us to the cheapest digs I could find, a run-down damp townhouse in a B-grade suburb in a C-location on a freeway that roared with traffic even at 4 a.m. It was about a 50-minute roundtrip journey to my former husband's home, which made transferring the kids very difficult for me. However, it ticked the essential box that the boys could walk from my home to school. That would do away with dropping them to school, and they would have to walk home in the afternoons and be latch-key kids.

I took part-time home-based contract work in my old media relations field for a time, and supplemented that with home-based writing piece-work, but still couldn't make ends meet. One year later, in 2014, a dream job opened up, that of features editor at the country's top parenting magazine. I took it. Here was a job in a sub-urban zone within an hour's drive of home, extremely uncommon in my field in my city. Founded by a mother (and now grandmother), it was that rarest of things, a job on at least some terms designed for women. The office closed at exactly 5 p.m. Staff could take the nationally mandated 10 days' sick leave as carer's leave to care for sick children. Many of the staff were women who worked part-weeks and/or part-days, and some who worked only about 10 days a month in magazine production periods. A female consciousness of the importance of the 'human' realm permeated the atmosphere and protocols, in contrast to the exclusion of the domestic and personal realms that prevails in male-led workplaces. No request for time off to attend a school concert or let the stove repairman in was denied. The whole office gathered for a short but civilized morning tea daily. Everyone got to choose a cake from a nice patisserie to share around on their birthday, courtesy of the company. The atmosphere was cheery, the business well run. And the team was terrific.

Even with these superb company conditions, the collision of mothering-work and paid work left me in a permanent state of brokenness—and that's before factoring in insomnia. Pushing myself out of bed at 5:10 a.m. in a screaming rush to make school lunches, make my lunch, feed boys breakfast, make my breakfast, dress boys and myself, pack bags, drop them to school and be on the road by 8:05 a.m. was too much. And I'm a 'morning person'. And I only had three weekday mornings of this. Many single mothers have five.

Evenings were much worse. Mondays and Tuesdays, I sat in thick traffic, or darted through it as much as the gaps and speed limits allowed, to get to the care center by 5:45 p.m. Had I needed to collect the boys Fridays, it would have been necessary to pay a babysitter to collect them, for traffic that night always extended the journey to about 90 minutes, half an hour past center closing time. And a babysitter was something I couldn't afford. I typically leave my center at 5:50 p.m., and do not walk in my door until 6:40 p.m., even though my house is only a mile away as the crow flies, for the traffic is heavy and the route circuitous. To be collecting kids at 5:50 p.m., when they needed to be already home and fed by that time, was bad enough. To then make a trip of nearly an hour home was worse. But to then get the kids inside and start cooking was impossible. They were starving, I was starving. My rented townhouse lacked a dishwasher; if I had been too exhausted to wash the dishes the previous night, I had to wash that 24 hours' pile before I even started cooking. And then wash the current 24 hours' worth after dinner.

That was only the start, though. After that came baths. Then an intense homework session for both kids awaited. Their program demanded a lot from both them and me. My younger son was required by the school to put in about 45 minutes of homework, my older son about an hour, plus 20 minutes of reading each. When they forgot to bring their assignments home, I would navigate the tricky school portal where the links had a maddening habit of getting stuck, and print it off for them. The computer was downstairs, the printer upstairs. I ran upstairs to turn the printer on, up again to check a printer glitch, up again to retrieve the printed page, beside myself with rage due to kids' demands and complaints, rage due to lack of sleep, rage due to the insanity of living in a society that says a woman can earn a living and be a mother at the same time.

Given that my former husband had 50 percent care of the children, you might think that his life was just as tough as mine. But you'd be wrong. He could afford a nanny. For most of the time he has been a single father, though, he hasn't needed to. Within a year of separating, he met a new partner who gave up her job to care for his two sons alongside her own two daughters. That relationship protected him from facing up to his full half-share of child care and home-running for about four years. Within a year of that relationship ending, he was engaged to a new partner whom he married. His wife now shields him from child care and home-running by looking after my two sons on weekdays, alongside her own three young sons all week. When a man re-partners, he usually finds a built-in nanny and housekeeper. A woman typically doesn't.

Desertion: It's a Crime. No, Wait—It's Not

In pre-feminist days, it was understood that raising a child was a full-time job. That's why falling pregnant outside marriage was recognized as a disaster. A mother faced around 14 years tied to a child too young to leave alone, while needing to earn a living at the same time. Unless grandma, aunty or another family member stepped in to take the baby, a mother was in an impossible bind. A man was under some social pressure to support his children's mother, whether she was his lover (however short-term that liaison may have been), unmarried partner or former wife.

In our feminist days, the picture is very different. A single father is now free to walk.

When I first entered the un-world of single motherhood, I was amazed at the reaction of many people around me. Their reaction was . . . no reaction. From other mothers to my own lawyer (herself a mother of three with a new baby) to self-appointed feminist spokeswomen to employers, many people never batted an eyelid. Holding down a job like a man while working as a mother at the very same time? They saw no illogic in that picture.

Others were saner. Many moms blanched when I told them my husband had left me unsupported. Some fathers disapproved of his desertion and were simpatico, as much as men are ever sympathetic to women's reality. But society at large, reflected in and shaped by the mainstream media and policy-makers who are generally in the pockets of feminists, radiated nothing but freakish denial that single motherhood breaks women.

That it is legal in this 'pro-woman' age for a father to drop his family like a hot rock beggars belief. Deserting a mother is supposed to be a crime. Yet it is no accident that single mothers' numbers have ballooned on feminism's watch. Feminists make florid feints of antagonism toward men in specific situations, like campaigning against domestic violence, or railing ostentatiously against rape. But at heart, feminists are pro-men and anti-women. It goes without saying that feminists are right to support battered and raped women, but those are a small segment of society. When it comes to the much more widespread and unrelenting, 24/7, years-long injury to women caused by deserting fathers, feminists don't side with her. They side with *him*.

This they do through an abiding silence and inaction that not only condones, but actively normalizes, single motherhood. "Destroying a woman is perfectly okay. You won't face any opposition from us. You're free to go!" their silence shouts to the deserting father's departing back, and to everyone else standing by doing nothing about it. "She is liberated, strong and independent! She can earn her own living! She doesn't need *you*!"

When I found myself separated with a 12-month-old and a two-and-a-half-year-old, the last thing I felt was 'liberated', 'strong' and 'independent'.

Feminism loves to perceive a father as 'independent' (and therefore superior) and a mother as 'dependent' (and therefore inferior). But there are other ways of looking at a mother's 'dependence'. One way is to acknowledge that a mother *is* dependent. She has the world's biggest job, and it doesn't pay. Her child care is the world's most important task. That makes hers a dependence of dignity and honor. It is a dependence of superiority, not inferiority.

Then there is a second view of her 'dependence'. That is to view everyone else—those of us who had mothers to raise us (which is everybody, or we at least had someone who stood in for her), those of us who are child-free but depend on mothers to raise all the people we will ever meet or love or buy goods and services from, and of course her partner—as 'dependent' on her. Because they *are* dependent on her. They rely on her to contribute those 300-plus hours per week we totted up in chapter 1, while she relies on her husband to contribute 40 hours. They all depend on her far more than she depends on them. Seen in that light, she is the most 'independent' person of all.

To be empowered and 'independent', I need to live in a world that operates on a woman-centered definition of 'independence'. As a single mother, I need financial support from my children's father, or from tax-payers (who are not responsible for me, but to whom I would have been very grateful for the support, had I drawn on it). That support leaves me truly 'independent' to do the work I need to do as a mother. Pulling that support from under me does not leave me independent. It leaves me helpless.

Parenting is a 20-year compact. Divorce or the end of a relationship is not supposed to mean that a father's responsibilities evaporate.
A deserting father should not be sitting evenings across town, or in
another city, or even in another country, with his feet on the sofa,
wine glass in hand, swiping right in dating apps, while his children's
mother spends every day thunder-struck by the cataclysm of living
two lives at once. She should not be hurling herself out of bed at
5 a.m. to get kids and herself ready, hurtling through peak-hour
traffic to school or day care, hurtling on to work, putting in the day's
paid work that we consider a 'full-time' contribution from a man,
rushing through peak-hour traffic to fetch kids from day care or
school, throwing herself into cooking/serving/eating/cleaning up/
household chores and admin/homework/baths, and preparing for
the next day, while he chills. Nor should she be forking out for a
two- or three-bedroom house or apartment in which to house them
all, while he takes a one-bedder.

He should not get to know the joy of two whole child-free days
every weekend, while she suffers under the burden of weekend child
care and sporting fixtures and cooking and housework and errands,
with no days free at all. He should not be free to beadle away blissfully
at his desk, while the mother of his children frantically frets that she
will lose her job as she begs time off work to pick up a sick daughter
from school, take her to the doctor, take her to the pharmacy, take
her home, wake the ill daughter just as she falls asleep at 2 p.m. to
pack her back in the car to go pick up the other children from school,
cancel arrangements for after-school activities and deal with the consequences of those cancellations (a band practice session to be made
up on a different day of the week; a special scene rehearsal to be re-
scheduled next week because the daughter missed the dress rehearsal
for the school play and that means negotiating with another parent
to take her daughter to the re-scheduled rehearsal because she can't
get time off work), stressfully ask for time off the next day because
the doctor wants to see the daughter again within 24 hours, repeat

the run to the doctor and the pharmacy and maybe make a third visit to a specialist which might become one of a series of visits, nurse the sick grumbling child, and do paid work from home to make up for her absence in the office.

Where a deserting father should be is not on the sofa, but in jail.

Why Isn't a Single Father 'Equal'?

Depending on the jurisdiction in which a woman lives, a deserting father is usually required to pay out-of-pocket expenses to cover the children's upbringing. He may even be required to pay a token percentage of his income as maintenance to her, but not necessarily so, and in any case, this is only a fraction of her needed income. Generally, a deserting father covers only costs, while the abandoned mother meets both her half-share of the child care duties, *and* some or all of his half-share of the child care duties, *and* is expected to relieve him of the need to earn her living. Few women would want to try to survive on single mother's welfare, and in any case, she will be forced to work once her children are past the age when single mother's welfare cuts out. In my country, Australia, that happens when the youngest turns eight.

How is it that the law does not require him to meet an equal 50 percent of the child care? That no one says to the single father, "Get a second job."? Yet she is expected to do as much as 100 percent of the grueling work of child care (which amounts to far more than the 40 hours he works) *and* she is expected to work a second paid job.

A man is entitled to buy immunity from his staggering time- and labor-intensive child care duties by simply handing over for out-of-pocket child-raising expenses. However, even that transaction is designed very much in his favor. His share of expenses may be calculated as a mere percentage of his one 40-hour per week income. When the former partner of my friend and single mother, Barbara, was unemployed, the law stated that he did not have to pay anything at all toward the upkeep of his daughter, for he had no income. The law also stated that his unpaid expenses did not accrue as debt to her, when they should have.

Why is his share of expenses calculated on an ability-to-pay basis? Yet her share of the child care and income-earning workload is not calculated on an ability-to-perform basis? His responsibility diminishes with his ability to meet it, our laws say, but hers does not. If the law states that she can perform the equivalent of more than seven 40-hour weeks (as I calculate a mother with an ever-crying baby and a toddler does in chapter 1, should her husband contribute no labor to child care and home-running) *and* put in a 40-hour week earning a living, plus commute, how is it that the law does not state that he can put in two 40-hour weeks—one to earn his living, and one to earn hers? That is only 80 hours per week, or five 16-hour days. Eighty hours is not 'working hard'. From where a mother is sitting, it is 'hardly working'.

To the protest that he cannot be in two places at once, our reply should be, "Exactly. So why do we expect a single mother to be in two places at once?"

However, the law in my country, and probably in yours, is even more lenient to fathers. Not only is his share of expenses limited by his 'ability to pay' at the low end of his income, but it is also limited by a cap at the high end of his income. I receive regular updates from the Government child support clearing-house stating my husband's income and mine, drawn from the tax office. On every statement, my former husband's income has never been less than half a million dollars. My income read as little as $5,434 one year, and it has never been as high as even the national average individual income, let alone as high as the average household income. Yet he has only been required to pay me an average of $7,999.50 per child per year. The most he has ever been required to pay me in support is $9,467 per child per year. The lowest he has ever been required to pay was $6,559 per child per year.

That leaves me with an average annual $16,000 on which to live and support my children for the 50 percent of the week they are in my care. Were the children with me the whole week, that would equate to a full-time income of $32,000 per year, when the average national income in my country was about $76,000, and the average household income was in the $90,000s. Clearly, I need to work full-time, with or without that $16,000.

And I go without that $16,000. Why? Because I waive it. My former husband already believed I was a burden to us because I didn't work. I was determined to give him no cause to criticize me as having an unfair share of our assets. We split everything 50/50, including time with the children, as I said. If I had then taken child support payments when he had 50 percent of the child care duty and I had 50 percent of the opportunity to work, he would have derided the arrangement as unfair. But as I said above, our situations were far from equal, and in hindsight, I should have taken the child support, even though it was not enough money to unlock the macro manacles of my circumstances.

It goes without saying that it would cost my former husband no pain at all to fully support me out of his income for the half-week the kids are with me; I could work the other half-week. Yet the law leaves me to endure the unrelenting pain of single motherhood, while protection for him from his 'pain' at paying more than an average annual $8,000 per child out of a very high income is written into policy.

Equality, Not Denial, for Mothers

A discussion of single parenthood and family break-ups is a can of worms. Morality, emotions, blame, finances, logistics—so much comes into play.

The single mother still attracts moral censure, and some of that can be deserved. She deserves criticism if she became pregnant heedless of the cost to taxpayers, but her partner is equally culpable in getting pregnant, and deserves equal censure. Much more, in fact, for a deserting single father is far more culpable than she is, both in deserting her and in throwing her onto taxpayers; she is not free to support her children because she's busy caring for them, but he most certainly is free to support them. Yet we hardly ever hear him get that censure. In fact, we almost never hear the term 'single father' at all, let alone hear it bandied about with the same low-rent whiff the term 'single mother' can give off. The term 'single dad' is heard on occasion, but it is used to denote the good single father who stays, not the far more common kind who leaves.

And of course, most single mothers are not moochers. Some fell pregnant despite contraception; some are widowed; the majority were married or partnered and legally abandoned by their children's father. None of these women deserve censure.

Obviously, the workability of getting fathers to meet their responsibilities in a failed relationship is fraught with difficulty. It's not the aim of this book to address all the tangled circumstances in which a woman might find herself alone with children. Many single mothers will say that getting the father of their children to support them is impossible. Some single mothers would rather grapple with trying to earn a living than engage with their former partner. Some are running from violence.

And some women—although we can bet they are far fewer than feminism likes to pretend—genuinely feel they can manage as a single mother. Those will be women whose day care center is a short distance from the workplace; who earn enough to get by as a one-income household in a two-income world and shell out for child care, too; who do not feel that awful guilt at expelling their kids from their company all day, five days a week, most weeks of the year; who don't mind that their kids spend their entire childhoods missing out on extra-curricular pursuits; who have at least some workplace flexibility; who are always in rude health; and who probably have extended family for support.

Nonetheless, no matter what any one woman's circumstances, the principle remains that a mother of kids too young to stay home alone is already occupied as a mother, and is therefore almost certainly not free to earn a full-time living. That principle should inform all our attitudes and policy-making around single mothers.

So should the principle that a man is equally responsible for his children's daily care. Yet feminists, those great priestesses of the Man-God, absolve him from both financial and child care responsibility. With feminists around to protect them, deserting fathers are untouchable.

10

A Woman-Shaped World

Let's Make It Happen

IF FEMINISTS ARE THE PROBLEM, what's the solution?

Many mothers, both at-home and working, value their contribution as mothers and housewives deeply. These are strong women who know their worth, but not all have what it takes to stand up for that worth. That is because going head to head with employers and policy-makers and the media and the public at large to make the world acknowledge a woman's hard-working reality in the domestic world is a hugely daunting task. It requires that seismic re-calibration of the relationship between the Public and Private domains that feminism was supposed to undertake decades ago. It takes a lot of know-how, courage and energy. It is the kind of task we normally leave to trailblazers. Trouble is, feminism doesn't have any trailblazers. All the feminist 'leadership' has is followers of men, masculinist groupies who tip-toe along in men's wake, putting their little feet in his big footprints.

It may be that no pro-woman leaders are going to step forward. And it may be that we don't need any. Every individual woman is a force in her own right. We all have ideas on how to build a world that values and incorporates *all* a woman does and is. Let's get to work sharing those ideas, at work, amongst our friends, at mommy-meetups, in our social media networks, at the school gate, by the baseball pitch, at playdates—wherever we meet other women facing the same battles.

Here are 10 things I suggest individuals can do:

1 *Ditch the Kryptonite*

Ditch the belief that you suck as a woman unless you do what a man does. That belief is Kryptonite to your Superwoman. It renders you a failure as a woman, no matter how 'successful' you may look on the outside or feel on the inside. No successful woman ever believed she sucked without a career. She might believe her *life* without a career sucks because she loves her work and doesn't want to be without it, in which case she should definitely work, but she never believes that *she* sucks without a career. She knows she is already a totally valid woman without it. Work because you like the work, or want or need the income. If you don't want to work and don't have to, don't.

2 *When Your Unpaid Work Comes First, Put It First*

My friend, Genevieve, runs her own public relations consultancy from a home office. She managed to have two babies whilst scarcely missing a beat. Although her clients think she works five days a week, she actually only works three.

"You need three days for work when the kids are at child care, one day for playdates and one to get things done around the house," she explained. When a client calls with a demand on a work-free day, she says, very professionally and obligingly, "It might take me a day to get back to you. Is that alright?"

Clients think she is busy on other work-related projects. They usually accept that. In fact, it probably makes her look in demand and therefore all the more impressive. What they wouldn't accept is Genevieve working as a mother and home-maker that day, because they think that paid work is paramount, high-status and 'permissible', while domestic work is dispensable, low-status and 'not permissible'.

Those clients are masculinist, arrogant and wrong. It is mother-hood that is paramount. The workplace's needs, not always but in general, come second to those of children.

That's not to suggest that it is fine to lie to our clients. However, until our clients acknowledge that a woman's reality of home-making and mothering exists, those white lies are Genevieve's way of circumventing their intolerance. Her clients do not suffer; she does a very good job for them, witnessed by the fact that they have stayed with her for many years.

While we don't all have Genevieve's leeway, hers is one example that we might be able to adapt to our own circumstances.

3 *Ask and You Shall (Maybe) Receive*

Now we get tough. At your next job interview, dare to ask politely for a timetable and conditions that accommodate housework and motherhood. Stand your ground when the interviewer declines your request, as she almost certainly will—for now. She can say no, but let's not buckle at the mere asking. If you keep laying a woman's job needs on the table, and I keep doing it, and every other woman keeps doing it, unfailingly, at every job interview in the land, women's authority as mothers and housewives will make its presence felt in the interview room as it never has in feminism's entire span.

Obviously, many of us are in no financial position to dictate terms to our interviewers, especially if we are single mothers. I have spent some years in considerable financial distress as a single mother. I have had to borrow from family to get by, and I have eyed home-less people in genuine fear that I will be joining them within weeks. Please understand that I am not suggesting you risk the job by fool-ishly throwing your weight around. I am suggesting that unless we are in immediate financial need and have to take whatever job is going, we should walk and talk in job interviews like we believe and expect that our housework and mothering work will be included and respected. That respect for our own contribution as women was second nature to my grandmothers; it is only in this spineless feminist era that we cower, too timid or ashamed to walk and talk like women.

4 Tell the Interviewer to Go to Hell (not in those words)

Now let's get tougher.

Quite often, and especially if a woman is one part of a two-income household, she has a choice. It may be that you are wholly able and willing to reject one job and take another. In that case, when the interviewer offers a job shaped for a man with a woman at home to do his child care and housework, you might express its unsuitability back to the interviewer. You might like to cheerfully say that, much as you'd love to take it, the job is clearly not able to handle the reality of the human condition, which is that children need raising and homes need running, work that is at least as important (and more important) as whatever work the job entails, and leave with a superior smile. The high ground is yours, so feel free to occupy it.

Or you might like to ramp up the pressure and very forcefully express your disappointment that you can't accept a job that denies something as fundamental as a mother's responsibility to raise the next generation. Your authority as a mother and woman is inalienable, regardless of how self-important the paid work might be, so use it. Refuse to back down in the presence of obstructionist interviewers. Make them look like the masculinists they are.

You might even want to challenge them by saying, "That job sounds like it's designed for a man." That might ring alarm bells with legal and HR officers in big companies with Equal Opportunity policies. They might feel bound to actually offer jobs shaped equally as much for women as for men, or retract their self-proclaimed status as an Equal Opportunity employer.

It takes courage. I am playing armchair general by suggesting you stick your neck out like this in an interview. I haven't done it to any significant degree, and I have worked in some relatively woman-friendly workplaces. However, you might be tougher than me. So tough, in fact, that you *are* willing to tell the interviewer to go to hell. In exactly those words.

And if you do, please share your story with us all.

5   *Are You an Employer?*

Do you employ people? Ah. Then the power to change the world lies with you. Will you do it? Will you create a workplace that welcomes the mother who renounced the best part of 20 years of her life to raise you? Will you shape a world that acknowledges that your wife (if you are a man) is grappling with her 50 percent share of running your kids, doing your laundry and fixing your meals, and probably also grappling with most of your 50 percent share of running your kids, doing your laundry and fixing your meals, while you sit coolly at the office on a 40- to 50-hour week?

I am not out to bite the hand that feeds us by insulting employers. It goes without saying that employers bring employees the gift of a livelihood. That demands our gratitude. However, the stark reality of a woman's workload as mother and housewife demands our gratitude, too. Our workplaces need to honor her reality. She is not a liability. She is the biggest contributor on earth. Not every employer can cater to their employees' pre-existing work as home-makers and mothers. If you can, however, please do so.

If you are a female employer and call yourself a feminist, we will believe you are pro-woman when we see it in action. Is there a single feminist employer in the world who offers jobs expressly designed for women? Almost none. Build your organization's jobs around the confounding, conflicting, debilitating and uplifting reality of house-work and motherhood. Then, and only then, will we all agree with your self-assessment as a champion of women.

6   *Are You in HR? The Union? In Advertising or the Media?*

Women in high-profile positions can use their fame to supreme effect. That's not to pressure them into being role models. No individual woman has to be a standard-bearer for other women. It is her life. She can do what she wants. However, what a terrific opportunity she has to empower women.

Are you a celebrity? A member of royalty or the aristocracy (the real or the Hollywood kind)? You can speak about the difficulties of attending a function pregnant, or the hour-by-hour challenge of splicing the kids with life on the film set—and do it honestly, not with the glossarama faux-honesty so typical of styled celebrity magazine interviews and 'happy family' Insta-spiels of today. That's not to say family life can't be glossy, glamorous and happy, but let's be open about the whole reality.

Are you a famous author or mama-creative? Talk about the exigencies of churning out masterpieces with kids underfoot. Taking on any artistic endeavor as a mother is never easy.

Are you in advertising? Speak to women's real needs. Yes, most women aspire to smooth legs or the next-gen coffee-maker, but we also aspire to manageability, and to appreciation of our enormous day-to-day struggles and triumphs as workers both inside and outside the economy. Build that into your ad campaigns.

Are you an influencer, a blogger, a member of the media? Hold women at the top to account. Quiz them about what they're doing to make a better world for women in their organization. Have they introduced an after-school kids' club on site? An optional unpaid half an hour daily for all staff, to be allotted to personal e-mails and phone calls, which can be taken in a weekly two-and-a-half-hour block for errands? A 'power-down in school vacations and power-up in term-time' policy for the company's less time-critical operations?

Women in many professional positions, not just those at the 'top', can use their roles to leverage a better world for women. Are you a careers counselor? You can help young women craft a life plan that will fully and frankly incorporate their home-running and the 20- to 30-year marathon of motherhood, not just set them off on a sprint that hits a brick wall with the first baby. Are you an insurance executive? You can introduce policies designed expressly for moms, like nanny hire when mothers are ill. Are you a union rep? You can negotiate a mothers-come-and-go policy so that moms can transition in and out of the workplace through the day to attend to mothering duties. Are you in human resources? You can implement practices in your organization that truly engage with women's reality over the two to three decades of motherhood, not just some starchy maternity leave plan that lasts six months.

7   Back to the Future

We need not so much a backlash against feminism as a 'forward lash'. We need to pick up back where feminism broke women off, back in the '60s. In some ways—and only in *some* ways, it goes without saying—we need to go back into the 1950s and 1960s to retrieve the baby of womanhood that feminism threw out with the bathwater of woman's oppression.

To remember what it was like to be a woman before feminism stomped womanhood out of us, I like to watch old re-runs of pre-feminist TV shows like *I Dream of Jeannie* and *Bewitched*. I watch them not to see the condescension and belittling and pigeon-holing of women that seeps through those programs. A lot of male attitudes to women were disgusting, and it is to feminism's credit that we find those attitudes unacceptable today. However, I watch these shows to see the liberating absence of the equally unacceptable condescension and belittling and pigeon-holing of women by feminism that followed in the decades to come. I watch to see the actresses and the characters they play at complete ease with themselves as women. They feel no *shame* to be at home. They feel no need to justify themselves via a career to cover up the lack of validity that feminism has yet to make them feel. They don't talk their 'achievements' up, because they know that a woman already *is* an achievement. They don't rant with masculinist braggadocio about how 'strong' they are, because they are not weak in the first place. They feel a perfect pride in 'Being' as a woman without recourse to 'Doing' as a man. That's not to say they aren't keen to have a job. It's to say they don't rely on a job for their self-worth as women. Held up against the repellent way that feminism makes at-home women feel like a failure today, Jeannie's and Samantha's lack of shame at their career-less state is nothing short of breathtaking. That total freedom from shame is a form of true woman-power in action, a power that virtually no woman possesses today.

So I'm not joking when I suggest that this is one thing we can do: we can watch old TV shows.

8 *Are You a Man?*

If you are a man, you have a key task—to open your eyes to the work the woman in your life does. You will never fully perceive the immensity of it all. No matter how cuddly-wuddly a dad you are, or how dapper a house-husband, a man is not physiologically capable of perceiving it. While you are working at a pace of one person-load—playing 'aliens attack' with your children, say, or making hamburger faces for dinner—she is ducking and weaving and anticipating and toiling at a pace of two or three person-loads or more, underneath and above and all around you. A sizeable amount of that work escapes your purview, even though it's right in front of you. Being a stay-at-home dad is not the same thing as being a stay-at-home mom. That doesn't mean you should not do your utmost to pull your weight.

Also understand that, especially in a home with children in it, financial necessity aside, you are not entitled to a second income. It is you who needs to do more in the home before you are her 'equal', not she who needs to do more in the workplace before she is your 'equal'.

9   *Dare to Be*

As a woman, you are here to Be, not just Do. You are not a work-horse, and you are not just a man, no matter how much feminism tells you that's all you are. Your Being-power means you are something a man isn't—the center of humanity, a radiator of life, a force for love and meaning, the keeper of humanity's purpose. All human beings work to live, not live to work, and when you do the Being-work you do outside the workplace, you are doing that living on behalf of all men, women and children. He can't do it. Only you can. Being-power is unique to woman.

And last and most importantly of all:

10   *Speak Up*

Your voice is the most powerful tool of all.

Peer group pressure can be our greatest enemy. It can also be our greatest ally. Instead of giving in to the negative pressure to work for validation because every other woman does, let's create a positive counter-pressure that proclaims a woman as a valid human being without a career.

It is within the power of all of us to build that pressure, just by speaking up.

We can say things to one another like, "I am not going back to work until the children are off my hands. I already work as a mother." Or maybe, "I don't want to work more than two days a week. I feel more in charge when I spend a day volunteering at the women's shelter, and I absolutely love and need my Monday mornings off, which are my me-time." Or, if you're a full-time housewife without kids: "Work? Why would I do that? I already work as a housewife, and we live a better, more empowered, more comfortable and satisfying life when I don't work. I'm not giving that up. We are both richer without the income, poorer when we give up so much for me to earn it."

Or in your last year of college you might say, "We're getting married next year and planning to start a family. I'm not planning on working for longer than it takes to pay off my student loan. After that, I might use my double degree in international relations and psychology to team up with other at-home moms to start a support group to empower mothers in the Middle East to bring up peace-loving, respectful young men."

You can make it clear to everyone that you think it is a higher-status thing to cook a twice-weekly casserole for your cousin whose husband was recently made quadriplegic, than to write a corporate sales plan. You can let people see your pride in your power at having time to make the bed, or for sing-alongs with your kids. You can let them see that respect for your own free time, health, pleasure and sanity takes precedence over obliterating these things to scrabble after a career.

When you speak up for yourself, and speak out about yourself, you give courage to other women. You validate them. You give them permission to dare to be a woman. There is no greater gift.

Bring on the Woman

Fifty years ago we burned our bras, figuratively speaking. It's time to burn our CVs. Symbolically, that is. Only burn them literally if you want to and can afford to. I don't mean that we throw in our jobs, necessarily. Not that we set fire to the passion, purpose and income work may give us. Not that we give up one inch of our right to be in the workplace. What I mean is that it's time to incinerate that sick fake nexus between our womanhood and our careers. A woman is a valiant, dynamic, wholly worthy human being, with or without a career, and we need to start believing it.

And when we do, it won't just be feminism's masculinist subservience to career that goes up in smoke. The half-century-long prohibition on recognizing the entire womanly dimension will lift. We will revel in *all* the contributions we women make. Women who create homes and raise the next generation will stride through the world as distinguished and intelligent people in their own right, commanding respect. Beyond that, the manifold living, loving, and feeling ways in which we women bring the world into being will be honored. We will reinstate our radiant female energy of *Being* to its exhilarating place as humankind's ultimate power. For too long, woman's sheer Being-force has been relegated to second place behind the restrictive, dehumanizing role of *Doing* man-identical paid work in the narrow world of business and government. And when we restore that Being-power to the world, the power that only a woman fully possesses, we will restore purpose to the lives of all, men, women and kids, young and old. We will re-ignite the flame of humanity's soul.

That vision is not the distant future. It is next to now. It happens as soon as we women step out of the dark of the masculinist shame that feminism has made us feel for being women, and forward into the light of respect for our own womanhood. That's all it takes.

And for the first time in history, women will know freedom and power.

ABOUT THE AUTHOR

NATALIE RITCHIE is a mother of two school-age sons. She is
a former media relations consultant and travel writer, and
is features editor for Australia's biggest parenting magazine.
She lives in Sydney, Australia.

She would love to hear from you at roar@roarlikeawoman.com